Towards an International Law of the Commons

Developments in International Law

VOLUME 84

The titles published in this series are listed at *brill.com/diil*

Towards an International Law of the Commons

By

Konstantinos Tsitselikis

BRILL | NIJHOFF

This work was based on the book originally published by Nēsos in 2023 under the title, *O monodromos tēs utopias kai ta oria tu adynatu.*

ISSN 0924-5332
ISBN 978-90-04-75092-0
ISBN 978-90-04-76411-8 (PDF)
DOI https://doi.org/10.1163/9789004764118

Library of Congress Control Number: 2026936616

Brill Nijhoff and Koninklijke Brill BV are part of De Gruyter Brill.
www.degruyterbrill.com

Questions about General Product Safety Regulation: productsafety@degruyterbrill.com

To Dora
To those who care about the commons

Contents

Preface

My initial interest in the commons was sparked by my participation in the Research Group for the Commons, established at the Aristotle University of Thessaloniki in late 2014. Thanks to this initiative, I was motivated to conduct research on the commons and their significance for two years. While researching common goods, resources, and spaces in an international context, I observed a substantial gap in the literature addressing these topics from an international law perspective through the lens of commons theory. The consolidation of what I term 'universal commons' has far-reaching implications for multiple facets of human existence, prompting complex questions concerning the design of new regulatory frameworks and the redefinition of justice in relation to the equitable distribution of goods, resources, and spatial access among individuals, communities, and generations.

One of the most rewarding outcomes of this research was the cross-fertilisation of different ideas drawn from diverse areas. Bridging different branches of law, as well as other sciences, drawing on examples as varied as the internet, the subsoil, seeds, radio waves, the human genome, satellites, science, and knowledge itself, proved to be a great challenge: to understand or at least explore the essentials of the many different elements that constitute the diversity of the commons on a global scale.

I am greatly indebted to friends and colleagues with whom I have had invaluable discussions, which helped me avoid unproductive lines of inquiry. Their contributions have been crucial, both in correcting my errors and in illuminating areas where I faced uncertainty and difficulty. Each of them, in their own way, pointed me towards new directions of research and helped me to deepen and expand the scope of my conclusions. At this point, I cannot know how successful my synthesis has been. Inevitably, the internationalist approach was a rather solitary path to follow.

Be that as it may, the least I can do is to express my gratitude by name to those who have given me such generous assistance: Alexandros Kioupkiolis, Angelos Kornilakis, Vassilis Kostakis, Theodora Kotsaka, Giorgos Papanikolaou, Dimitris Papathanasiou, Andreas Takis, and Polymeris Voglis. I am grateful to David Bollier, whose wholehearted encouragement prompted me to deepen my reflections on the commons through the lens of international law and human rights, at a time when the subject still appeared quite opaque to me.

I also wish to thank the staff of the Library of the University of Macedonia for their help in locating the materials I needed within the vast ocean of bibliographical sources. My thanks are likewise due to Andrew Watson for preparing the first draft of the translation from the original Greek, and all those who edited the initial manuscript with patience. Since then, the study has been reshaped repeatedly through further research and reflection, ultimately taking the form of the present publication. I'm more than indebted to Dimitris Akrivoulis who edited with passion, dedication, and accuracy the final draft.

Finally, I'm thankful to Brill for their support and flawless cooperation.

Figures and Tables

Figures

Tables

Abbreviations

AI	Artificial Intelligence
CBD	Convention on Biological Diversity
COP	Conference of the Parties
EEZ	Exclusive Economic Zone
ECHR	European Convention of Human Rights
ECtHR	European Court of Human Rights
EU	European Union
FAO	UN Food and Agriculture Organization
HUGO	Human Genome Organisation
HGP	Human Genome Project
IACtHR	Inter-American Court of Human Rights
ICJ	International Court of Justice
ICAO	International Civil Aviation Organization
ILO	International Labour Organization
ISDS	Investor-State Dispute Settlement
ITU	International Telecommunication Union
ITLOS	International Tribunal for the Law of the Sea
OCDE	Organisation for Economic Co-operation and Development
NATO	North Atlantic Treaty Organization
PACE	Parliamentary Assembly of the Council of Europe
SSE	Social and Solidarity Economy
TRIPS	Agreement on Trade-Related Aspects of Intellectual Property Rights
UK	United Kingdom
UN	United Nations
UNCLOS	United Nations Convention on the Law of the Sea
UNDP	United Nations Development Programme
UNESCO	United Nations Educational, Scientific and Cultural Organization
UNFCCC	UN Framework Convention on Climate Change
US	United States
WIPO	World Intellectual Property Organization
WHO	World Health Organization
WTO	World Trade Organization

Glossary

The following terms are subject to differentiated assessment and consideration through different narratives. Therefore, the definitions provided here should be read in relation to the content of this study.

Commons Tangible or intangible things, i.e., goods, resources, and spaces, that are functionally connected with communities of commoners at local, regional, or global level, which co-produce the formal or informal rules of governance and allocate responsibilities and rights.

Public goods A commodity or service provided by a state or local authority that every member of a society can use.

Common things Shared goods, resources and spaces, tangible or intangible, exhaustible or non-exhaustible, found in nature or products of the human civilisation.

Commoning The practice of collaboratively creating and managing shared resources by a community.

Global common resources (goods and spaces) Common things that lay beyond or through interstate jurisdiction.

Commoners Members of communities which are formed in relation to a common resource, and share concern and responsibility in favour of the commons.

Digital Commons Digital Commons are defined by: a digital resource; a community that produces and maintains the resource; a governance system with established rules for access and sharing of the resource.

Digital Public Goods Digital goods that are technically and legally designed as non-rivalrous and non-exclusive digital resources.

Peer-to-peer production A form of creating common goods through the direct, open, and participatory cooperation of equals.

Res/terra nullius Goods, resources, or spaces that do not belong to anyone.

Res/terra communis Goods, resources, or spaces that potentially belong to all, are shared by all or can be accessed by anyone.

Universal commons *Universal commons* are the global common goods, resources, and spaces that exist beyond – or extend across – interstate jurisdictions. They are governed by policies and rules established by (actual or potential) communities of commoners, who are subjects of both rights and obligations.

Commoners of universal commons Members of differentiated communities of states, individual human beings, groups of people, indigenous peoples, or international organisations who actually or potentially share concern and are attributed at different levels rights and duties in favour of a shared global common resource.

Enclosures Individual, state, or corporate appropriation of a common resource or restrictions applied to resources to become commons.

CHAPTER 1

Introduction: On Commons

Since the earliest formation of human societies as political entities, the goods, spaces, and resources essential to collective survival have been central concerns of all peoples across time. Political, economic, and normative considerations have shaped, defined, advanced, or abolished relations of management, exploitation, access, and appropriation of vital common goods. Historically, natural resources have been the primary objects of attraction for those in power, often giving rise to conflicts both within and between states. Later, space itself and the products of human creativity became new domains of contestation.

Today, common goods, resources, and spaces remain a central point of reference for communities at every scale, from the local to the global. They continue to exist at the fraught intersection of the interests of states, corporations, and people – both individually and collectively. Tensions, as by-products of globalisation, intensify as numerous localities converge and form overlapping realities. All of this directly affects the people and communities who manage common resources. From this perspective, the commons acquire particular importance, offering alternative proposals for sustainability distinct from those of market structures, which are driven primarily by individual profit.

At the beginning of the twenty-first century, civil society organisations, states, and international organisations face critical challenges that must be addressed if life and well-being are to be safeguarded. Global crises demand new orientations in politics, economics, and international cooperation, as well as how people relate to shared spaces and resources, such as the atmosphere, the oceans, seeds, and scientific knowledge. Conversely, policies that favour extraction and neoliberal greed prioritise private profit over the common good, reinforcing aggressive patterns of enclosure. These tendencies increasingly dominate the global landscape, while international law struggles to keep pace with the transformations underway.

In this evolving environment, the global significance of the commons highlights the need to understand community through the roles and claims of its members – that is, the *commoners* of the commons. At the international level, communities are composed not only of individuals but also of states and international organisations, which play crucial roles in protecting life and collective well-being. International law can contribute to this process in several ways. First, by its very nature, it regulates relations at the supranational level

HTTPS://DOI.ORG/10.1163/9789004764118-002

and can thus provide a regulatory framework – though not necessarily a uniform one – at the global level, where commons are often 'inaccessible'. Second, it can structure and mediate relations among heterogeneous commoners. Finally, it can recognise and affirm the rights of people and communities over the commons. In other words, international law has the potential to translate moral and political claims into normative entitlements, establishing rights and obligations at multiple levels: between members of a community of commoners, involuntary users and potential commoners; between commoners and states; between states themselves; between commoners, states, and corporations; and between all of these and international institutions. Law offers the tools to define the legal relations among commoners, to enshrine rights, and to enforce the principles that protect common resources on a global scale. As new commons and new spheres of protection emerge, a new legal framework must be developed that transcends the traditional national-international divide.

The legal demarcation of rights and obligations regarding natural resources and human creations remains a continuous process of inquiry – a central economic, political, and even existential issue for humanity's present and future. It is, at its core, a search for what is or ought to be fair and just. This is particularly true when common resources lie beyond state sovereignty, are unregulated, or fall under forms of international governance. The absence of rules for the management of a commons inevitably leads to its dismantling or to the erection of enclosures around it – that is, to the restriction or appropriation of access.

Before discussing the delimitation of rights and obligations in relation to the commons and their legal recognition, we must first address several preliminary questions: Which resources, spaces, and goods are subject to appropriation or exploitation at the international level, and which are not? What are the rules under which commoners operate, and what are their rights and obligations? Which common resources can – or should – belong to all, and which to none?

Following the Roman law distinction between things that belong to all (*res communis*) and things that belong to no one (*res nullius*), international law continues to oscillate between these two categories, thus perpetuating conceptual ambiguities.

Under international law, common goods, resources, and areas have once again become central concerns, as states and international organisations undertake duties of care to protect them. This trend contrasts sharply with the rapid appropriation of shared resources by states, private actors, and multinational corporations – often with the tacit or explicit support of governments. The interconnection of state and non-state levels produces complex jurisdictional entanglements that obscure where authority and responsibility lie. The central question, therefore, concerns peoples' claim to the protection of rights over the commons – the rights of access, use, exploitation, and participation in their governance.

Can we discern the emergence of a body of law, or at least a normative tendency, that guarantees the collective governance of common resources on a global scale? Could such a law attribute rights and duties through democratic procedures serving the common good and the collective interests of a universal *demos*?

The climate crisis and the Covid-19 pandemic (2020–2022) have brought the question of the commons back to the centre of global attention. Both have underscored the defence of rights against forms of power that exploit gaps in the rule of law – gaps often produced by structural exceptions and states of emergency. Yet crises can also open possibilities: to construct an economy grounded in the commons and a political culture of sharing – one that generates surpluses for the benefit of humanity while ensuring democratic participation and care for the vulnerable. The establishment of such a legal culture could foster a new legal literacy and, with it, a consolidated grammar of the commons.

Before proceeding to an analysis of the exceptionally complex issues that arise, some clarifications are necessary – though none can be entirely watertight. Indeed, one of the defining features of the debate is its very vagueness, a difficulty immediately apparent to anyone who seeks to reframe it.

[*The Triadic Character of the Commons*]

Common goods, resources, or spaces are defined by an interrelated trinity consisting of:[1]

1 **The shared resource, good, or space**;
2 **The community of commoners**, i.e., the subjects who have a relationship with the shared resource, good, or space; and

---

1 Ostrom 1990; Benkler 2006; Bollier 2014; Bauwens, Kostakis & Pazaitis 2019. Commons may acquire other features depending on the analytical perspective adopted. According to Bollier & Helfrich (2019), the framework of the *Triad of Commoning* 'is based on the premise that commoning is primarily about creating and maintaining *relationships* – among people in small and big communities and networks, between humans and the nonhuman world, and between us and past and future generations. This *relational* understanding of the world will necessarily bring about new ways of thinking about *value*.'

3 **The institutional dimension**, determined by regulatory and political factors.

1 The Shared Resources

The first manifestation of this trio of essential elements, which form the commons, is linked to the concept of a resource, good, or space – i.e., a natural or artificial 'raw material' that can be of benefit to all humanity. Resources are ideally – or actually – shared among people. Examples include air, water, minerals, fisheries, the internet, the atmosphere, the radio spectrum, culture, open-source software, information, and scientific knowledge. From another perspective, a common good can be defined as anything that meets the material or intellectual needs of the user or producer, who acts as a member of a community responsible for exploiting, maintaining, and protecting the resource.[2]

A good, resource, or space can also be shared, within or beyond the territory of a state, between the public and the private, in a permeable world of open or controlled interaction. In particular, common places create 'circuits of encounter' for commoners, individuals and communities, states, companies, associations, or international organisations. A space may be used for transportation, facilitating the movement of people or their machines (sea passages, space orbits, roads, or airstrips), or for the disposal of objects and waste (the sea, the subsoil, or the atmosphere).

Common resources, spaces, and goods can be divided into two categories depending on their origin and intrinsic nature: those that are natural and those created by humans, i.e., constructions or products of technology or intellectual labour.

In terms of their exhaustibility, resources such as hydrocarbons may be finite and depleted through use (rival goods), subject to competition and exclusion. Some of these resources, such as water, seeds, fish, wildlife, and forests, may be replenished or reproduced naturally. Others, such as the surface of the sea, light, the radio spectrum, scientific knowledge, or culture, are inexhaustible and can therefore be used without major restrictions. Exhaustibility refers to the practical ability to access and use the commons simultaneously. Even the air and the sea surface are finite spaces, but they cannot be entirely occupied by human means of transportation. The smaller the scale of the space, the more likely it is to be saturated.

2 Buck 1998: 3.

A concept related to the commons is that of 'public goods', which constitute a special category of goods, values, or goals in human societies. Public goods include, among many others, environmental protection, energy management, administration of justice, information, public health, and education. A central feature of public goods in contemporary welfare-state models is that their enjoyment is not solely dependent on monetary exchange. In many cases, commons and public goods arise more from the activity of institutions – organisational structures that are political, social, and economic – than from the structures themselves. Like common goods, public goods constitute a key element of a commons, alongside their commoners, at local or international levels. Public goods, like commons, may be fenced off according to the logic of profit and individual utilitarianism. Both categories are crucial conditions for the existence and coexistence of human societies.

The commons may be located within or beyond the territory of the state. However, they cannot be separated, as they form a single ecosystem, whether literally or figuratively. The existence of a common resource (*res communis*) does not automatically imply the existence of a commons, since the latter presupposes two additional aspects: the community of commoners and the normative framework. Terminological confusion is usual, so care should be taken when distinguishing *res communis* from commons.

2 The Community

A commons also constitutes a field in which social relations are shaped among the subjects that make up communities, i.e., the commoners. Commoners are primarily human beings acting individually or collectively. At the international level, they may include states, non-governmental organisations, social movements, or international organisations. Commoners are subjects of rights and obligations related to the commons. Communities of commoners are formed according to the interests, benefits, or needs that mobilise them in relation to a commons. Moreover, the commons – mediated or unmediated – are dynamic fields for multiple communities. As Alexandros Kioupkiolis observes, communities do not have a pre-modern character; rather they are produced and reproduced through variable patterns of cooperative relations at the limits of modernity.[3] Consequently, new terms of coexistence and interactivity develop between commoners and their respective commons.

3 Kioupkiolis 2014: 222.

Common goods, spaces, and resources can only be understood in an inseparable relationship with their commoners and actively engaged users, the community of people who have an interest in and benefit from preserving them. Commons are not 'homeless' things; rather, they form a whole with the communities that manage and exploit them under a specific normative framework. Common resources on the global level presuppose interconnection with their user-commoners, who may be located anywhere on the planet. In this sense, the universal community of people consists of all potential user-commoners of these commons.

Thus, the term 'commons' refers not only to the shared good, resource, or space but also to the community of commoners that sustains and reproduces it. Commoners – actual or potential – are subjects of rights and obligations, both among themselves and towards the common resource, good, or space. They are the agents who create legal relations with, around, and for the commons. At last, the community of commoners is shaped and determined by the features and the nature of the common resource. The 'community' thus constitutes the second dimension of the triadic character of the commons.

3 The Institutional Framework

The third dimension of the commons includes the normative and political aspects of the institutional element, bound together by production, governance, and management relations between commoners and over the commons (*commoning*). Commoning is a sine qua non condition of the commons.[4] Yochai Benkler observes that the commons is an institutional field in which one can exercise a particular form of freedom, different from what is typically available in market conditions.[5]

The institutional organisation, formal or informal, is determined by the rules governing the relations between users, communities, and guarantors of the commons. Establishing a commons requires a founding act – a political decision or statutory collaboration, from which the commons is created.[6] This is often renewed and reproduced, and its origins may become obscured over time by fluctuations of rupture and legitimacy.

Commons, therefore, cannot be understood outside their socio-political environment, which shapes their institutional dimension. Giorgos Papaniko-

4 Bollier 2014.

5 Benkler 2003.

6 Dardot & Laval 2014: 369–401.

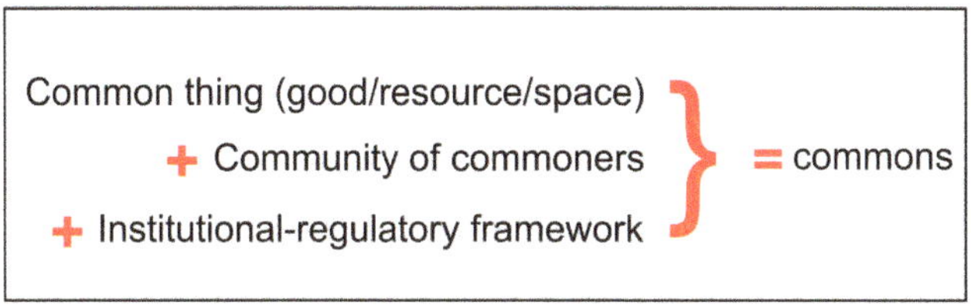

FIGURE 1. The constituent elements of the commons

laou notes: 'in the realm of the commons, production, reproduction and sharing of resources are carried out according to the terms of a social contract that incorporates the traditions, ethics and culture of the community. It presupposes everyone's contribution and respect for rules that are morally legitimised'.[7] The processes of establishing the commons constitute a common good. Consequently, a central issue is the role and function of the entity exercising power and responsibilities over the commons, including a guarantor function.

Regulation of relations among subjects and their rights and obligations regarding a resource, space, or good occurs through formal or informal legal rules, subject to material limitations that depend on the nature of the resource and the characteristics of the community of commoners. Democracy, redistributive justice, and human rights should underlie the existence and functioning of the commons as living forms of social and economic organisation. However, the commons do not necessarily imply a progressive or democratic governance paradigm.[8]

Numerous examples exist of natural and artificial resources functioning as commons under state or international jurisdiction, or under regulatory frameworks established by commoners. These institutions may operate on positive or customary law and may be limited or disappear due to enclosures, which occur when resources shift from the commons (for the benefit of the community) to appropriation (for private or state interests through privatisation or patenting).

The commons will henceforth be understood as tangible or intangible things – resources, spaces, and goods – functionally connected with communities of commoners who co-produce the formal or informal rules of governance and allocate duties and rights. These rules entail distinct yet interrelated social, economic, and political responsibilities at local, regional, and global levels.

7 Papanikolaou 2017.
8 Gallaway & Thacker 2007: 13.

[*Commons in Theory*]

Since antiquity, philosophers have engaged in critical debates over the concept of the *common good* v. *enclosures* – the latter securing private or state interests of a hegemonic nature while neglecting the interests of the many. The notion of the common good inevitably triggers a host of ambiguities. Whose interests define it? Do the interests of the public coincide with those of the state, the majority of citizens, or the commoners of a commons? Who holds the authority to interpret and implement policies in its name?

The discussion suggests that the 'common good' reflects the fundamental interest of the majority in achieving a decent subsistence, supported by the democratic management of the commons in both the intensity and quality of participatory governance.[9] The universal characteristics of the commons – their shared attributes and interests – transform the collective of commoners into a community. The status of the commoner is primarily linked to individuals and, secondarily, to communities authorised to participate in the exploitation, decision-making, management, and governance of the commons. Ultimately, the commons themselves shape the conditions of coexistence and cooperation among subjects at each level in the pursuit of their own 'common good'.

Over recent decades, three approaches have emerged regarding the most effective governance of the commons: polycentric governance,[10] federal governance,[11] and commons-based peer production.[12] All three imply the organisation of communities of commoners – producers and managers of resources of all kinds, both material and immaterial, exhaustible and inexhaustible – within a polyhedral framework in which each subject-commoner contributes to the creation and maintenance of a common resource for both personal and collective benefit.

One of the most comprehensive theories of the commons was developed by Elinor Ostrom,[13] whose work exerted significant influence on subsequent scholarship. Ostrom's research highlights the importance of participation in the commons when designing and implementing property rights.[14] When par-

9 On the contribution to the debate made by Cicero, Aristotle, Augustine, Rousseau and Hegel, see: Dardot & Laval: 28–33. The 'common good' is defined by Rawls as 'certain general conditions that are equally to everyone's advantage' as referred to in Boer 2014: 291.

10 Cf. the work of Ostrom and many others.

11 Dardot & Laval 2014.

12 Bauwens, Kostakis & Pazaitis 2019.

13 Ostrom 1990. For the impact of her work on legal thought, see: Rose 2011: 28–49.

14 Ostrom 2000: 351 where related bibliography.

ticipants do not perceive such rules as legitimate, effective, or fair, they are likely to devise strategies to circumvent them. Following a comparative study of numerous cases, Ostrom identified key similarities among self-organising institutions managing common resources that endure over time and formulated the principles of governance that guide them.[15]

The depletion, depreciation, and obsolescence of common resources at the global level are all linked to the value attributed to private property as a form and process of appropriation. Individual ownership is often regarded as a *superior* mode of appropriation compared to common ownership. The dominant ideological and academic view holds that collective ownership is obsolete and that individual ownership constitutes the very essence – and the driving force – of continuous progress and prosperity. Through the hegemonic institutionalisation of private property, enclosures were imposed, and common goods, shared spaces, and communal resources were rendered 'relics of the past', deemed ineffective in an economic order defined by the free market. The conflict between the commons and private property has thus arisen from deliberate and unintentional misunderstandings.

These theories of the commons stand in contrast to the doctrine of the 'tragedy of the commons' proposed by Garrett Hardin,[16] which has been used to argue against the self-management of resources by commoners, advocating appropriation as the only way to save them. Hardin's argument, grounded in the 'logic of the individual', posits that a pasture – an archetypal common space and resource – is doomed to destruction when each farmer adds more cattle than the land can sustain. The 'individual', presumed to act solely out of self-interest, has since been uncritically reproduced in political thought, reinforcing an ideology of unrestricted appropriation. This view assumes that resources exist in a homogeneous, unregulated space and that people act exclusively through competitive individualism, which can only be restrained through privatisation.[17]

This reasoning conceals a history of violence and the usurpation of global resources by those with the power to appropriate them. It also propagates an untruth: it presupposes, without evidence, that pre-modern rangelands were open and overexploited by greedy users indifferent to others, resulting in their destruction.

15 Ostrom 2000: 142.

16 Hardin 1977: 16–30.

17 Hardin later added 'socialism', but he meant 'state appropriation', Ranganathan 2016: 699.

Historically, however, the commons presupposed coordinated and regulated access to, and use of, the resource for the benefit of the community and the preservation of sustainability.[18] In medieval England – the classic example of the pre-modern commons – access to forest commons was neither free nor unregulated. Local customary law governed the rights and obligations of community members and the use of resources. Management was mixed, subject to governance and boundaries, rather than homogeneous or ungoverned, as depicted in the tragedy-of-the-commons theory.

Hardin's argument was later challenged by the idea of the 'common heritage of (hu)mankind', advanced by Maltese ambassador Arvid Pardo during the period of decolonisation (see Chapter 3.1).[19] These debates form the foundational theoretical propositions of the *universal commons*, to which we shall return.

[*Management and Ownership of the Commons*]

As noted, the debate about the commons is underpinned by the concept of ownership, rooted in the enduring dichotomy between state or public property, private property, and communal or collective property – or even the absence of property. Notions of ownership are themselves grounded in religious beliefs, moral values, and historical practices that have, over centuries, reflected political-economic systems such as feudalism, capitalism, socialism, and communism. The ideas of common ownership and the communal distribution of resources also trace their origins to Roman law and to regulations governing religious foundations and charitable institutions.

Authority over the commons can take many forms, often overlapping: acquisition of ownership, management control, rights of access and use, conditions of exclusion, extraction of benefits, and transfer of ownership. Common goods, spaces, and resources may be owned or managed by individuals, companies, private associations, communities, municipalities, states, or international organisations. The attribution and enjoyment of rights over the commons depend on decision-making capacity, while their management relies on principles such as equality, justice, efficiency, and sustainability.[20]

Yet the content of these principles is contested. Who defines 'sustainability', for whom, and by what means? The widespread use of the term *sustainable development* is often linked to the legitimised commodification and appropri-

---

18 Wolcher 2009.

19 For a comparative evaluation of the arguments of the two personalities, see: Ranganathan 2016.

20 Hess & Ostrom 2007: 6.

ation of the environment through mechanisms such as 'pollutant trading' and the 'economic valuation' of natural resources – tools premised on perpetual market expansion.[21] At the same time, however, the term can be redefined by states, organisations, and advocacy networks to denote the sustainability of life and society through moderate and responsible use of natural and human-made commons.

Conceptual confusion is a recurrent challenge in public debate. As Ostrom observed, misunderstandings have been exacerbated by the ambiguity surrounding concepts such as property, the commons, common-property regimes, common-pool resources (i.e., commons permitting open access with risk of depletion), and open access.[22] Common-property regimes encompass a broad range of ownership modalities, including transitional forms between common ownership and ownership in common.[23]

Commons are not necessarily open to all. Many are 'mixed' or 'semi-commons',[24] combining elements of individual ownership, state control, and communal management. Power relations within these systems are equally mixed. For example, in England's New Forest, the rights of the Crown, the commoners (e.g., grazing rights), and private landowners coexist legally[25] alongside obligations to protect biodiversity. Ownership thus appears as a plural condition, not standardised under neoliberalism's dominant value system, which promotes the unbridled accumulation of private profit.

Nonetheless, commons can simultaneously function as systems of resource management by communities and as recipients of effective policy within a market economy – albeit not a neoliberal one.

Certain common resources, however, are so vital to human existence that they cannot be treated as products, nor subjected to ownership or transfer.[26] Who, and by what criteria, can determine which commons are exempt from private property?

---

21 For example, Article 191 of the EU Treaty and the 15th Principle of the Rio Declaration (1992) refer to the much-debated notion of 'sustainable development', as well as to the principles of protection and precaution. According to Article 21 par. 2.6 of the EU Treaty: 'The Union defines and implements common policies and actions [...] with the aim of contributing to the development of international measures to preserve and improve the quality of the environment and sustainable management of the world's natural resources, with the aim of ensuring sustainable development [...].'

22 Ostrom 2000: 332–379. For the conceptual confusion regarding the commons, see also: Caffentzis 2010.

23 Kornilakis 2024: 58.

24 'Semi-commons', as described in Fennel 2011: 27.

25 Edwards & Steins 1998: 357.

26 Mattei 2011.

TABLE 1. Accessibility and law

	Approach favouring the commons		Approach favouring appropriation / profit	
	With rules	**Without rules**	**With rules**	**Without rules**
Exhaustible commons	Yes	–	Yes, clearly in favour of appropriation	Yes, in favour of the first one that can be appropriated
Inexhaustible commons	Possibly of a limited procedural nature	–	Possibly in favour of appropriation	Yes, in favour of the first one that can be appropriated

In regimes of common ownership, the right to exclude others depends on the nature of the commons and the applicable legal framework. Members of a defined group may exclude third parties from using a resource. Where resources fall under state jurisdiction, local rules may grant exclusive access – for example, fishing rights reserved to members of a local union – while still imposing restrictions to ensure sustainability. Open-access regimes, by contrast, tend to exclude outsiders only ineffectively, and resources that are de facto common may become de jure public, i.e., state-owned.

Common-pool resources exhibit high exclusion costs, whether practical or legal, and the use of the resource by one member diminishes its benefits to others. As with public goods, it is difficult to set clear criteria for exclusion or to manage overuse. When commoners exceed a certain number, resources may deteriorate or even collapse.

[*Accessibility and Enclosures*]

In practice, common-pool resources may fall under the authority of states, international organisations, local governments, corporations, or communities, or may be subject to open access by anyone with the capacity to exploit them. Understanding the diversity of commons requires classifying their sustainability according to accessibility and governing rules.

As shown in Table 1., free access to exhaustible commons by free riders, without regulation, endangers both the resource and its value. If rules exist, the key question is whether they serve the shared benefit derived from the commons or purely individual profit. For inexhaustible commons, the absence of rules benefits those with the power to impose their own, making procedural safeguards essential. Regulatory protection – whether implemented by states, international organisations, or individuals – ultimately serves communities' interests by safeguarding the commons' sustainability.

The goal is not to impose an idealised notion of user-communities as a universal solution to privatisation and corporate exploitation. The crucial test is how governance rules – on management, participation, exclusion, and benefit-sharing – serve human wellbeing and, above all, safeguard life itself.

We can distinguish between open-access commons, such as the air and the high seas, and limited-access commons, such as Antarctica, which are governed by a specific legal framework. In the latter case, access and rights are restricted to an 'Antarctic aristocracy', creating 'club goods', while 'common pool goods' remain theoretically open to all, though in practice accessible only to those with the requisite technological, economic, and political power.

'Access' denotes both the opportunity and ability to use or share goods, resources, or spaces, as well as to participate in the community managing them. One can navigate the open sea without owning it and freely fish its waters. Yet access often presupposes scarcity and the establishment of regulatory frameworks, particularly against those who enclose resources for exclusive use – the 'free riders' and 'parasites' of the commons.

The use and exploitation of the commons always entail power relations: the access of some implies the exclusion of others. Benefits vary across social, political, and economic contexts, as the significance of common resources differs across societies and histories.

Technology plays a crucial role: it enables access, reproduction, and even the conceptualisation of the commons. New technologies expand accessibility – ships for the sea, planes for the air, rockets for space, transmitters for the radio spectrum, and computers for cyberspace.

Accessibility can also have a darker side. In the case of digital commons, the absence of protective legal frameworks and institutional oversight means that the more open and accessible the data – whether public or private – the more it ultimately benefits powerful market actors. These actors exploit openness to consolidate their control and extract profit from what was intended as a shared resource.

Technology itself is deeply entwined with capital, irrespective of the way that capital is accumulated or the structure it assumes. A recurring sequence can thus be observed: capital generates technological advancement, which in turn facilitates access to and the exploitation of common goods, resources, and spaces. Depending on the nature of this relationship – whether one of private appropriation aimed at financial gain or of stewardship by commoners for collective benefit – the outcomes diverge. Both economic and social value may arise, but when benefits are capitalised, the same cycle of accumulation perpetuates, producing either the abundance or the depletion of the resource itself.

Both literal and figurative enclosures separate what was once accessible to all from the continuum of open spaces, goods, and resources. This separation typically takes the form of exclusive private ownership or state monopolisation. Enclosures, therefore, bring about the dispossession of what had been a commons. Today, such practices are evident even in the open seas, where the continuous expansion of coastal and exclusive economic zones narrows what remains of shared maritime space. As technology-driven global trade advances without adequate safeguards for the commons, market values – consumerism, profit, and unrestrained growth – are imposed upon every domain of social life. What David Bollier has aptly termed the 'silent theft' unfolds through the commodification of all goods, resources, and spaces, including those that are public or common: from public space itself to culture and education.[27]

Enclosures of the commons typically involve the plundering of resources – both their current and potential future yields – through their appropriation by free riders. Exclusive and preferential regimes, such as sovereign rights, private property rights, exclusive licences, and pollution rights, are among the mechanisms that institutionalise enclosure, thereby dispossessing commoners of their shared resources.[28] The long-term consequence of such appropriation has been the dissolution of the communities of commoners who once depended on common goods for their livelihood, rendering them subordinate to the market as producers, workers, and consumers.

In reaction to neoliberalism's inherent hostility towards the commons, 'both the ideology of official socialism/communism and nationalism created the imaginary impression of a sharing and co-management of social wealth by the citizens'.[29] In practice, access to the commons continued to be restricted, and their use monopolised by ruling elites. In the current political and economic climate, it is therefore of paramount importance to safeguard the global common resources from enclosure, as they are essential to human survival.

27 Bollier 2003.

28 Taylor 2016: 122.

29 As Caffentzis put it (2010: 24).

This task is especially urgent in an age of accelerated economic and political transformation, characterised by intensified extraction, consumption, and systemic inequality.

*

This study seeks to examine the normative framework governing common goods, resources, and spaces at the global level and identifies the principal challenges they face. The emerging crisis in their governance highlights the urgency of a paradigm shift spanning the legal, economic, and political domains. Can the scope of international law be expanded to include the protection and management of the commons? Can the duty of care for global resources be clearly defined? What happens when such resources fall within state jurisdiction? Could international law adopt a commons-based perspective, reorganising rights and norms to ensure the sustainability of universal commons–those goods, spaces, and resources essential to life and human well-being? These questions defy easy answers. Any transformation of the legal paradigm would necessarily intersect with the realms of economics and politics, which are addressed only briefly here.

This work advances a methodological approach to common goods, resources, and spaces on a global scale, grounded in the theory of the commons. It seeks to move beyond the narrow interpretation of 'global commons' found in international law and to develop a more comprehensive concept of 'universal commons'. In this framework, commons are not merely things or resources; they presuppose an active community of commoners operating within variable institutional and legal structures particular to each commons. The study thus offers a new perspective within the literature on 'global commons', which has traditionally focused on earth governance and environmental law. By contrast, it does not aim to provide an exhaustive analysis of specific resources – such as the ocean, cyberspace, or outer space – but rather uses them as examples to link commons theory to human rights and international law. A detailed exploration of these domains would be, quite literally, a Herculean task.

The chapters that follow explore common goods, resources, and spaces situated both within and beyond state jurisdiction, including those located in international areas subject to potential oversight by international authorities. The analysis examines how legal norms emerge, evolve, and function, particularly in the relationship between universal commons and their commoners. Yet commons occupy an indeterminate position between national and international law – both within and beyond their reach. Given the conceptual and institutional asymmetries, tracing the origins of these ideas becomes essential. The current framework, based on the imperfect and fragmented notion of 'international stewardship', has already proven inadequate in preventing the enclosure of global common resources. Terms such as the 'common heritage of mankind' – applied to the seabed, outer space, and biodiversity – and 'common concern' – used in relation to climate, fisheries, and Antarctica – remain basic yet unstable tools for navigating the uncertain terrain of the universal commons.

A fundamental ambiguity continues to obscure the global treatment of common resources. Are common goods, resources, and spaces *res nullius* or *res communis*? Do they belong to no one, or to everyone? Is there, in fact, a genuine community of commoners engaged in their stewardship? And do the fragmented norms governing them constitute an emergent international law of the commons? Such ambiguities generate uncertainty and unrealistic expectations across legal, political, and economic domains. To understand this indeterminacy, the study considers a range of examples – the invisible radio spectrum, expanding knowledge and information networks, deep space, oceanic whales, oceanic deep seabed, cyberspace, and even the human genome as an existential commons. The tensions and conflicts surrounding these domains lead to a central question: To whom do these commons belong, and how can they be used for the 'common good'?

If governance, access, management, and use of the commons are indeed connected to the human rights recognised today, it becomes imperative to determine which resources merit protection and to clarify the rights and obligations of those who use them. Establishing such a framework will require new governance rules, protection mechanisms, and institutional procedures – developments that will inevitably challenge the balance between state sovereignty and the organisation of global society. Amid the legal, political, and economic struggles over control of the commons – between commoners and enclosures alike – how will these rights function? How might we envisage a methodological transition from common resources to commons on a global scale, ensuring democratic participation in their governance? Finally, is a paradigm shift already underway – marked by the emergence of shared principles and a growing recognition of 'community interests' – that could lay the foundations of the international law of the commons?

The answers to these questions hinge on acknowledging the critical importance of the commons to humanity as a whole. Only through such recognition can we begin to pave the way towards a realistic utopia of collective prosperity.

CHAPTER 2

From Common Resources to Commons: From Local to Global

> The commons (…) constitute a paradigm that incorporates its own logic and its own models of behavior, and that acts as a different kind of operating system for society.[1] (David Bollier and Silke Helfrich)

Common goods, resources, and spaces often extend beyond the jurisdiction of any single state, are locally interdependent, and are subject to conflicting legal rules and policies regarding access, management, and sharing. The evolution of legal norms in this field is frequently dictated by local or regional interests, with little regard for the global dimensions of the relationships they are intended to regulate.

Sharing is a key concept at both the national and supranational levels, and it is fundamental to a community of commoners. The debate over sharing global common resources is at once social, economic, political, and normative. International movements calling for new political arrangements around the commons include a diverse range of actors – activists, organisations, international organisations, and states. At the national level, natural resources are often approached from a nature-centred perspective, whereas public goods are viewed from an anthropocentric one.[2] At the international level, however, both commons and public goods assume a universal social dimension. Numerous aspects of the commons can thus be identified at both levels, although the boundaries between them are rarely clear. In other words, global resources often require local protection, just as local common goods, resources, and spaces often require global oversight.

The modes of access, management, and use of a common resource are equally crucial within and beyond state sovereignty. The pursuit of fair, sustainable, and equitable management of common resources on a global scale depends on three factors: first, the identity of the governing body of the community – that is, the collective of potential or actual commoners with decision-making authority; second, the way in which the concepts of accessibility, appropriation, and use are applied; and third, the mechanisms of regener-

1 Bollier & Helfrich 2012: xi.
2 Brando et al. 2019: 11.

 | HTTPS://DOI.ORG/10.1163/9789004764118-003

TABLE 2. Spatiality of the common resources and jurisdiction

Location	Jurisdiction	Commoning
Within state jurisdiction	Under strict state jurisdiction Eventually, under the concern of international organisations	Common-use Public commons *Res/terra communis*
In locations that run through states and non-state locations	Intergovernmental cooperation International organisation	Interstate commoning
Outside state jurisdiction	International organisations States [Corporations]	*Res/terra communis* Often, in practice *res/terra nullius*
Far reached space/resources	International organisations States [Corporations]	Legally considered *res/terra communis* In practice *res/terra nullius*

ation, conservation, and protection of the resource. In the case of common-pool resources at the global level, the regulatory landscape is often characterised by fragmentation, vagueness, and, most notably, the absence of coherent rules (see Table 2).

Conservation of a resource frequently entails preventing overexploitation. Protection and restoration, however, require financial investment and administrative cooperation. Which commoners should be entrusted as guarantors of the commons, and who should bear the associated financial burdens? Who qualifies as an active commoner in relation to a commons located within or beyond state territory? The answers to these questions – particularly concerning the fulfilment of duties to act and to contribute – may differ depending on whether the common goods, resources, and spaces in question lie inside or outside the bounds of state jurisdiction.

1 The Commons within the State

The sustainability of the commons is both a goal in itself and a guarantee of the vital interests of present communities of commoners and potential future users. The appropriation of common goods, resources, and spaces by human communities has a long history. Aristotle famously observed that 'what is common to a large number of people enjoys the least care'.[3] At the same time, the state has always played a central institutional and political role in the management of the commons. Often acting as guarantor and custodian, the state has exercised incomplete stewardship and has, in many cases, facilitated enclosures through private appropriation.

Local customary norms have long regulated legal relations concerning the commons and have sometimes received formal recognition in national law. 'Vernacular law' serves as a broad umbrella term encompassing informal, customary local laws that have evolved through everyday interactions across history.[4]

In Roman law, things were classified into four regimes of ownership: private (*res privatae*), public (*res publicae*), common (*res communes*), and things belonging to no one (*res nullius*). Centuries later, two key legal texts from medieval England marked a turning point in the legal recognition of the commons and their protection against central authority and the risk of appropriation. The Magna Carta (1215) and the Charter of the Forest (1225)[5] – later unified in 1297 – enshrined the granting of rights by the king to his nobles and subjects. These texts confirmed the established practice that the use of forests, meadows, rivers, and other natural resources in a given area (which provided essential raw materials for food and survival) was reserved for members of the local community.[6]

Often, the right to make use of a resource was a reward for services rendered to a lord or the result of a long-standing association with that resource. This relationship is not easily understood through the modern concept of ownership.[7] The evolution of these rights was complex and contentious. Throughout the sixteenth to eighteenth centuries, the rights of the King of England, feudal lords, bishops, and peasants over the forest's natural resources were continually negotiated and disputed. The law governing resources was a central arena of conflict in which the critical boundaries between the arbitrariness of power

3 Aristotle (*The Politics*, 1261b), in Ostrom 1990: 2.

4 For the term, see: <https://bit.ly/4vznejy>.

5 Linebaugh 2008; Bollier 2015a; Dardot & Laval 2014: 278–280.

6 Cf. <https://common-land.com/> (all websites cited were accessed between May 2021 and January 2025). In a distant echo of the Magna Carta, today about 3% of land in England 'belongs' to dispersed commons that are under legal protection.

7 Buck-Cox 1985.

and the rights of the community were drawn – an early struggle for what we now call the 'rule of law'.[8]

Similarly, the traditional Japanese law of *iriai-ken* was revived in the twentieth century, granting groups of village residents the right to exploit a common good – namely, the valuable wild *matsutake* mushrooms of Kyoto Prefecture – through an auction system. This arrangement protected both the forests and the broader ecosystem from degradation. Crucially, the right to collect mushrooms pertained to a specific area of land that was partly public and partly privately owned. Thus, the common good (the mushrooms) depended on the community, rather than the state or individual landowners. A portion of the revenue from mushroom farming was returned to residents, who contributed one day of work each year to cultivation. Since the early 2000s, however, landowners have claimed and won exclusive rights to their own mushrooms. As a result, the collective system has lost momentum, community income has declined, and the broader ecosystem has begun to degrade, leading to reduced mushroom yields.

The *iriai-ken* example demonstrates how a common resource can be sustainably managed outside the rigid dichotomy of private and public ownership. When the relationship between commoners and the commons is effectively secured, both the shared benefits and the resource's sustainability are maximised.[9] Once the rules balancing access in favour of the commons are disrupted and enclosures are erected, the common resource contracts, and with it, the collective benefit. The doctrine of 'first possession' ('the first to possess the resource secures it for themselves') still prevails in many contexts. In Iceland, for instance, only a few companies have acquired fishing rights through quotas, while in the US mining rights are granted to the first discoverer, without any obligation to redistribute the benefits for the public good.[10]

Commons are distinct from things belonging to the state (*res publicae*). In the case of commons, the state ensures that access, use, and exploitation remain open to all. Over public things, however, it exercises direct authority. The concept of ownership, though, is complex. A shared resource constitutes aspecial category of commons, encompassing natural or human-made resources such as a lake or an irrigation canal. In many jurisdictions, public goods – understood as spaces for common use, including shores, roads, squares, forests, wild fauna, fisheries, and minerals – are protected under law. Not all public or state-owned properties, however, are for common-use. Mili-

8 Dardot & Laval 2014: 287.

9 Bollier & Helfrich 2019: 265–267.

10 Armstrong 2017: 157.

tary installations and government buildings, for example, are public but not accessible to the public.

Many parallels can be drawn between commons and analogous concepts in civil law. Things that are common to all, common-use goods, and those intended for public, municipal, or religious purposes are associated with the collective body of would-be commoners – the people who constitute the civic community. These things are *inexchangeable*. In most national legal systems, things common to all (*res communes omnium*) include the air, the sea, and wild fauna. These are not 'things' in the strict civil-law sense but remain subject to control, particularly under public law, as in the case of airspace or coastal zones.

The notion of something 'common to all' conveys the principle of free access for everyone. Obstruction of such access constitutes a legal infringement of personal rights. Examples of common-use places include waterways with continuous flow, riverbanks and lakeshores, roads, squares, bays, seashores, forests, and ports. The state – or local municipality – possesses the authority to enact laws and make decisions regarding these resources and spaces in its capacity as custodian of the commons, exercising stewardship on behalf of the commoners. In any conflict of rights, the 'common good' must prevail in favour of the commons.

In several cases, constitutional law imposes stewardship duties regarding common goods in the form of a public interest that the state must serve. This is not necessarily based on the concept of the commons. Consequently, the role, rights, and obligations of commoners remain undefined. Similarly, resources designated as 'exploitable' and constituting 'national wealth', such as the atmosphere or underground and underwater deposits, are protected without the relevant conditions being clearly specified. What is lacking is a balanced, holistic consideration of the various common resources, as well as mechanisms of social control in favour of their users. Indeed, any economic exploitation should demonstrably benefit the public and contribute to the development of the commons.

Gradually – though far less frequently – laws or constitutional provisions make explicit reference to the commons. The Italian Constitution (art. 118, para. 4) provides a noteworthy example: In addition to its role as guarantor, the state undertakes to maintain or encourage municipal support of any non-profit initiative pursued by individuals or legal entities that promotes activities of general interest, based on the principle of reciprocity. Numerous examples can be found of the emergence of urban commons, with or without the support of municipal authorities, in which residents share food, shelter, or energy.[11] Of these, Bologna has become a flagship example.[12]

Since 2008, a clear global trend has emerged of municipalities reclaiming control over water and energy management. Many local authorities have resumed control of water and sewage networks following the expiration of contracts with private companies. As Theodora Kotsaka observes, 'in some cases, as in Berlin, the municipalities have decided that it is in their interest to pay very large sums in compensation for the termination of these contracts, in response to the false promises of private companies and their failure to put the needs of communities above profit'.[13]

Water is recognised as a protected common good in various national legislations. In Quebec, for instance, water is defined as a 'collective resource forming part of the common heritage of the nation'.[14] while, under the law of the state of Maine (USA), 'oceans, lakes, and rivers are public property. The waters of the ocean are under the stewardship of the state for the benefit of the citizens. All the shores around the ocean to the extreme high-water mark belong to the state, and all citizens have access to them'.[15] Similar regulations are set out in numerous national laws, ensuring access to water bodies within the state territory.

A particularly fascinating example concerns the treatment of animal resources as commons under national law, recognising the rights of the commoners while placing stewardship under the state's authority. Since the early twentieth century, industrial exploitation of lobster has flourished in US territorial waters and the open sea. As early as the mid-1930s, intensive fishing – using trawls and other methods without restriction – had drastically reduced catches. In 1949, faced with the prospect of lobster extinction in the Gulf of Maine, coastal communities and the government adopted rules for the public management of a commons, whereby local communities set regulations within the framework of state law. More effective rules and community organisation were introduced in the mid-1990s. Since then, lobster fishing has been subject to restrictions such as time limits, permitted methods, and minimum catch sizes. Moreover, decisions on all day-to-day matters are made by local fisher-commoner councils operating within legally designated protection zones. In this way, state law and community law coexist to form a commons,

11 For urban commons see: Sharable 2017.

12 Bologna Lab, at <https://bit.ly/2JRipzB>. Also: Bauwens, Kostakis & Pazaitis 2019: 61–62.

13 Kotsaka 2016: 183.

14 National Parliament, Quebec, Act 27 of 2009, at: <http://bit.ly/40Z9Y7C>.

15 Kelly 2012.

founded on respect for the sustainability of the resource and the viability of the community.[16] In another example, Greek law provides regulatory protection for an intangible resource such as scientific knowledge: universities are mandated to 'develop common, open resources in education, research, technology, and culture'.[17]

In several of these cases, the state assumes the management of the commons as guarantor and guardian of the 'common good' or the 'public interest'. Yet, the terms associated with the 'public' – that is, the sphere in which state authority operates through government management – sometimes lose their meaning as originally understood in the context of the social contract. Through unfair practices that privilege unrestrained private profit at the expense of the common good, 'the public sector came no longer to refer to citizens with shared meanings and norms for the use of their mutual resources, but to the government that promises to improve their individual wellbeing through privatised goods disguised as public goods'.[18]

As James Quilligan observes, a 'concept drift' has taken place, allowing common goods, spaces, and resources to be managed – and public services to be delivered – in ways that fall short of serving the needs of either the commons or the public interest:

> In a mystifying sleight of hand, the resources we use in common are identified as public goods and then deregulated and turned over to the private sphere for production and distribution. As in the shell game of the magician, common goods disappear through the adept switching of categories: forget where you saw it before, which legal container now holds the good? In this way, goods that were once managed as commons or public goods – water, food, forests, energy, health services, schools, culture, indigenous artefacts, parks, community zoning, knowledge, means of communication, currency, and ecological and genetic resources – have either been privatised outright or remain public or common goods in name only.[19]

At the national level, several key principles have been identified as prerequisites for the sustainable governance of the commons: The boundaries between the users (commoners) and the common resource itself should be clearly defined; rules governing the exercise of rights to the commons should align

16 Caffentzis 2008. See also: <https://wiki.p2pfoundation.net/Maine_Lobster_Commons>.
17 Law 4185/2017, Article 4.1.g (Official Gazette A 114).
18 Kotsaka 2016: 189.
19 Quilligan 2012.

with the local or regional culture of commons managing; the commoners or their representatives should undertake supervision; those who violate the rules should face a graduated scale of sanctions; for common-pool resources that belong to broader systems of commons, management initiatives should involve institutions at both local and national levels.[20] At the international level, analogous principles could be formulated to reflect the sui generis nature of common resources and the diversity of commoner communities.

When we move from the local-national to the universal level, a new dimension emerges in the protection of common-use and public goods. Many common goods, resources, and spaces are located within the state's territory and thus fall under domestic legal regimes. Yet, by their nature, they also extend beyond state jurisdiction or form part of a universal network. How, then, are these governed – and by whom? Most importantly, can we verify the existence of commons in accordance with the theoretical model that requires three constituent elements: the resource, the community, and the norm?

2 Common Resources Inside and Outside State Jurisdictions: The Evolution of Ideas

According to Thucydides, common resources and spaces referred to territories that did not belong to any nation – the 'undefined', without borders.[21] Many centuries later, Hugo Grotius described the ancient commons as boundaryless, heterogeneous, universal, and uncircumscribed. Do these statements still hold today? And if they do, could the commons, at the global scale, be attributed to the broader human community? If these questions seem pertinent, reference to ancient considerations detached from their modern context risks lapsing into ahistorical reductionism.[22]

For the Romans and the Byzantines, some things could be used in common by all people, even if they were not their own, but they belonged to nature. According to this understanding, things that belonged to no one – such as the sea, the sand, and the shore–were considered sacred. The Roman legal con-

20 Buck 1998: 32.

21 Thucydides (*Book I*, 141), in Grotius 1916: 27.

22 In antiquity, the concepts of the commons and the 'tragedy of the commons' were already discussed in the work of the Spanish Jesuit theologian Luis de Molina (1535–1651). See Akrivoulis 2018: 194.

cepts of *res nullius* (the open sea),[23] *res publicae* (navigable rivers and territorial waters),[24] and *res communis* (the catch of fish),[25] as codified in the Justinian Code, have shaped legal development up to the present day. The sixth-century legislation, which consolidated earlier Roman law, protected the commons and even made explicit reference to humankind as a subject of law:

> Under natural law, the following things are common to humankind – the air, running water, the sea and therefore the seashore. [...] Also all rivers and harbours are public, so the right of access to a harbour or a river is common to all. Under the law of nations, the use of the coast is also common and so is the sea itself. The right to fish in the sea from the shore belongs to all people.[26]

The decline of the ancient commons and the emergence of the modern public space – subject to enclosure and appropriation – resulted from the violent transformation of the rights of local 'commoners' in favour of new administrators and owners across the world. According to Immanuel Kant,[27] one can possess any object one desires. Translated into legal terms, this axiom implies that the object of desire must be in a state of non-possession, without an owner. This condition, however, conflicts with Law and Justice; thus, the will of humankind replaces the earlier notion of sacred objects dedicated to the gods. In this way, Kant introduces the concept of *res nullius* to the modern age by making nature subject to Reason,[28] since human Reason becomes the measure of all things.

According to the colonial logic that accompanied modernity, *res nullius* belongs to no one until ownership is established. It is a thing in a temporary legal state of non-appropriation, destined to be acquired by whoever has the legal, political, or military capacity to seize it (*occupatio*). From a wild, 'uncivilised' state, everything can be brought to a higher, 'civilised' one, entailing

---

23 As a legal term, 'commons' first appeared in the English language in 1259. It was used primarily in the nineteenth and twentieth centuries. Wild animals, for instance, are considered *res nullius*, as they enjoy a natural freedom.

24 The term has been used since the Roman era with two meanings: common things and the state itself, thus serving as a synonym for statehood and commonwealth. Gradually, the *res publica* of the Middle Ages was transformed into *the republica* in the modern sense of a democratic state.

25 As a legal term, it first appeared in English in 1259 and reappeared during the eighteenth and especially the nineteenth century.

26 Codex Justinianus, Book II, Article 1, at: <https://bit.ly/32ZWwEY>.

27 Kant 1996.

28 Milun 2011: 76–77.

relations of appropriation.[29] Land, people, and resources thus become 'objects' over which a 'subject' has rights. The subject of appropriation becomes real precisely because he possesses the capacity to appropriate – activated when the suitable *res nullius* is found. The Industrial Revolution further accelerated the spread of enclosures, giving decisive impetus to the appropriation of common goods, resources, and spaces – a process that continues to this day.

During the first era of globalisation, driven by international shipping from the fifteenth century onwards, it became necessary to establish universal legal rules governing control of the high seas. Spain and Portugal concluded two treaties – Tordesillas (1494) and Zaragoza (1526) – that divided the oceans along meridian lines, pre-securing sovereignty rights over newly discovered lands. Similarly, England and France drew 'friendship lines' separating their spheres of dominion in the New World (Cordial arrangements, 1904). In this system of demarcation, the Tropic of Cancer and the Meridian of the Azores divided the realm of law from that of lawlessness, where anything was permitted. Beyond these lines – to the west and south – Christian European powers claimed the freedom to appropriate open space.

A crucial distinction thus arose between the freedom of the extra-legal state of nature and that of the legal order of civilisation. As Carl Schmitt put it, 'global linear thinking' was consolidated with the discovery of the 'New World' and developed alongside a new global consciousness. The global replicated the planetary, following a superficial logic that equated land and sea.[30]

European colonialism demarcated maritime zones of sovereignty, defined rights of exploitation, and recognised the interests of third powers. 'International law' was, in essence, European law, and 'culture' was European culture – both legitimising expansion and the occupation of free space. Yet these zones were alternately treated as *res nullius* or *res publicae*, while modernity, undermining the ancient commons, introduced new forms of authority. Beyond the sovereignty of the state, the guild, and the feudal lord, individual property – and soon corporate property – became consolidated.

Thus, in the seventeenth century, the foundations were laid for the modern law of the sea and other areas beyond state sovereignty: territorial zones open and accessible to all, drawing conceptually on the earlier regime of *res communis*. In 1609, Grotius advanced the theory that, in the case of the oceans, the ancient commons had bequeathed to modern times the *res communis* – a remnant of a mythical Earth without states or property. According to Grotius, there are two forms of tenure in the commons. The first derives from the ancient,

29 Hendlin 2014: 142.

30 Schmitt 2006: 87, 95.

heterogeneous commons that predate property – for instance, the catch of fish from territorial seas. The second emerges from the modern, homogenous commons, grounded in Reason and the needs of states under natural law:[31] commons that cannot be made exclusive, such as free navigation on the open and free sea (*mare liberum*), which Grotius defended against British claims to a territorial, closed sea.

In 1636, John Shelden defended English interests by advocating the concept of a closed sea (*mare clausum*), extending state sovereignty from land to sea across both sides of the Atlantic.[32] At the time, it was widely assumed that fish in the sea were an unlimited, ever-renewable resource and could thus be appropriated as *res nullius*. Only when whale populations declined towards the end of the nineteenth century did awareness of the finite nature of marine resources emerge.

Grotius already noted a fundamental tension: The acceleration of state and private activity in common spaces pushes the exclusivity of the commons to its limit, revealing its saturation. This occurs when there are so many ships that the sea can scarcely hold them, so many aircraft in the sky, or so many satellites orbiting the Earth. It became increasingly accepted that state sovereignty must be moderated – either by the economic interests of other states or by the common good of the international community.

A few decades after Grotius, John Locke argued in favour of private property and its benefits to society, since human well-being depended on individual initiative and improvement through labour. Yet, for Locke, the oceans and their resources were not susceptible to 'improvement' by private enterprise, as they were self-generating by nature.[33] Hence, the rationale for private property gives way here to free access – even to a 'commons of humanity' – beyond claims of state sovereignty.

As mentioned earlier, the debate on common goods, resources, and spaces emerged during colonialism and resurfaced during decolonisation with two opposing narratives: the threatened destruction of common resources due to the absence of private interest ('tragedy of the commons') and their protection through collective management ('common heritage of mankind'). For centuries, international law was shaped by the dynamics of colonialism, which gave legal expression to the notion that some parts of the Earth belonged to no one (*terra nullius*), while others belonged to everyone (*terra communis*). Colonial expansion, however, resulted in the loss of indigenous rights to land and nat-

31 Grotius 1916.
32 References to the work of Locke and Shelden in Armstrong 2018: 3.
33 Locke 1988.

ural resources.[34] The enclosures imposed by conquerors were regarded as 'progress' within a legitimised paradigm.

The idea of *res nullius* has reappeared in certain areas of the universal commons, partly through Giorgio Agamben's concept of the *state of exception*. According to this view, globalisation must be examined in light of exclusionary and exceptionalist policies. This principle continuously shapes how people are defined, politically organised, and subjected to regulation, extending Michel Foucault's analysis of biopower and biopolitics exercised by each state within its territory.[35] Ultimately, the legally free and 'empty' space lies beyond the line where state power and national law end – where the state of exception applies to the regularity of law and politics, as Carl Schmitt argued.[36] John Locke and Thomas Hobbes had earlier described this zone as a 'state of nature', existing 'outside law'. In such exceptional conditions, anything may occur as long as the occupying sovereign wills it and the actual or political conditions permit it. Today, this ambiguity fuels neo-colonial incentives and legitimising arguments for states, individuals, and corporations seeking to appropriate global resources.

The space is interwoven with the hard borders of state sovereignty that delineate what lies within or beyond their monopoly of authority – and thus determine the legal status and governance of the commons. To conceptualise authority over the commons, Gilles Deleuze and Felix Guattari propose a metaphor: the objects of authority correspond to 'smooth' (or 'soft') and 'striated spaces', which, owing to their surface characteristics, respond differently to authority. Historically, one could say that, since the 1440 dispute between Spain and Portugal over ocean navigation, a soft, malleable, and thus non-homogeneous space was gradually transformed into a strictly striated one – homogenised and subject to uniform measurement. A global system of latitude and longitude emerged, receptive to uniform sovereignty and authority and subject to a homogeneous legal framework: the international law of the sea.

The lines of demarcation drawn across the sea's surface and extended vertically to the seabed and its subsoil evolved in tandem with technological advances in movement, warfare, and the exploitation of living and inert resources. The most recent evolutionary stage of this law is embodied in the UN Convention on the Law of the Sea, adopted in Montego Bay, Jamaica, in 1982 (UNCLOS, in force since 1994). Consistent with principles of sovereignty,

34 Shiva 2013.

35 Biopolitics as a 'technology of power' has been exercised through the history of 'governmentality' through the trinity of sovereignty, discipline, and security (Foucault 2004).

36 Agamben 1998: 37.

international law now regards the oceans – the primary global commons – as homogeneous rather than heterogeneous spaces lying between states.

Moreover, as Deleuze and Guattari argue, movement itself constitutes space. The mover is the 'subject' and the 'sovereign force' that, through motion, generates spatial dimensions. Within the paradigm of global common spaces, subjects-commoners exercise both economic activity and political authority. Typically, however, the acting subject is not the individual but the state or corporation endowed with the technological, economic, or political capacity to operate in these spaces. Yet the human being remains the ultimate recipient of the consequences of this dominant movement-activity.[37] The more the subject moves, the 'denser' the space becomes; the less it moves, the 'sparser'. New spaces emerge by extending or expanding adjacent ones. These concepts provide international law (see Chapter 6.5) with valuable analytical tools, particularly when it is called upon to regulate relations involving space, its extensions, and movable things.

Consequently, the *res communis*, as part of a universal commons, is associated with rights of use over areas belonging to all, but where the law is not effectively applied. This association occurs through the expansion of state sovereignty, which creates 'lines of homogeneity' under international law, while also revealing the inherent pathology of the law's non-enforcement. Every *res nullius* holds the potential to become a site of intense 'striation': initially a neutral, non-state condition, but gradually subject to exploitation according to each state actor's leverage. States thus move dynamically, as nomadic units, generating tension and motion. These movements and tensions are also triggered by other agents – associations, corporations, international organisations – as well as non-human actors in perpetual motion: sea currents, air, climate, fauna, culture, the internet, seeds, science, and genomes. Such agents can animate communities of commoners by producing tangible changes in the material world.

3 Defining the Commons at the Global Level: Why *Universal Commons*?

[*The Commons on a Scale*]

The commons differ from one another according to the scope of the community and the extent of the shared resource, space, or thing. Distinct character-

37 Deleuze & Guattari 1980.

istics emerge at the local, national, regional, and global levels. The number of commoners is more limited at the local level, much larger at the national and regional levels, and potentially encompasses the whole of humanity at the global level. This change in scale directly affects many areas, including management, decision-making, and rule-making. As the community expands, the principles of equality and democracy inevitably lose their immediacy.

Size also influences the character of governance concerning the commons. This can increase or decrease exclusion, affect the substance of managerial powers and decision-making processes, and shape the delegation process. For instance, this may result in the minimisation of the will of people and communities in favour of larger entities (e.g., states or international organisations). As we move upward – from the local to the international level – governance and decision-making processes tend to be more hierarchical. The closer a public is to the local level, the more cooperative and democratic its relations tend to be, relying on direct democratic processes.[38] Yet, can the democratic management practices of local commons be translated into effective policies and laws at the highest scales?

Changing the scale significantly alters how we can perceive and understand the commons. Tools suitable for addressing problems at one scale may be wholly inappropriate for similar issues at another. A management model effective for a local common resource may fail entirely in the case of a global one.[39] Synthesising different theoretical approaches can therefore provide insights into the nature of large-scale commons.

The uniqueness of the universal level lies in its inclusivity which may involve all people as commoners. Global challenges – pandemics, climate change, pollution – inevitably affect everyone's lives. Yet, humanity cannot form a single, undifferentiated political subject, as vast portions of it remain excluded from political and economic participation.

This complexity highlights the need for multilevel and trans-scalar models of governance[40] that combine top-down and bottom-up approaches to decision-making. A defining feature of universal commons is their composition of heterogeneous communities of commoners – groups of individuals, states, international organisations, transnational actors, and corporations. The hybrid character of both the commons and their potential stewards is an intrinsic feature of the universal commons, one that demands a specific analytical methodology.

38 Kioupkiolis 2020: 25.
39 Harvey 2011: 102.
40 Brando et al. 2019: 566.

Having commons at a high scale does not necessarily mean 'better commons', nor does it justify approaches that prioritise 'scale-at-all-costs'. The interconnection of common resources and commoners across local, regional, and global levels creates constellations of commons, often resulting in interdependencies. 'Cosmolocal scalability' enables local communities to recognise their global significance and to form cooperative networks. By cultivating dynamic relationships between scales and blending global connectivity with localised practices, cosmolocal commoning advances decentralised projects that aim to 'scale wide' rather than 'scale up'.[41]

The objectification of the benefits of common goods, resources, and spaces at the global level counterbalances or prevents harm caused by a 'global evil' – such as the depletion of, or exclusion from, common resources – and establishes *erga omnes* obligations in favour of resource sustainability. These obligations apply to all states within the international community without requiring specific individual commitments. Each state's freedom of action is therefore limited by an 'obligation to cooperate'.[42] Such obligations serve to protect a common, collective, or community interest that concerns all states equally.[43] The *common interest* implies *common care* and a duty of *stewardship* towards a benevolent nature (discussed below in Chapters 3 and 6), arising from the tension between safeguarding state sovereignty and fulfilling the duty of common care.

One of the most significant domains of large-scale commons concerns the challenges facing the natural environment, which have given rise to new considerations, legal norms, and international mobility. The idea of *Earth Trusteeship*,[44] which has emerged over the past decades in response to the environmental crisis, has strengthened the development of international environmental law. The concept of trusteeship, together with the need for Earth Governance, underscores that states and international organisations bear a responsibility to both humanity and the environment to safeguard the planet's resources. It is closely tied to the notions of sustainable development and environmental justice, which can serve as foundational normative principles for all global common resources – both *res communis* and *res nullius*. We will return to this discussion in subsequent chapters.

41 Lowenhaupt Tsing 2012; Kostakis, Lemos & Kouvara 2024.

42 Shelton 2009: 39.

43 ICJ: *Barcelona Traction, Light and Power Company Limited (Belgium v. Spain)*, 5.7.1970, and *East Timor (Portugal v. Australia)*, 30.6.1995; International Law Commission 2001: 126, and International Law Commission 2022, conclusions 10, 11 and 19; Simma 1994.

44 Bosselman 2015; Burdon 2015; Cullinan 2011.

[Applying Commons Theory at the Global Level]

If common goods, resources, and spaces can be discerned at the global scale, then, according to triadic theory, commons must combine a legal framework with a community of commoners. Defining commons that exist simultaneously outside and within state sovereignty, while also possessing universal scope and significance, is no easy task. Yet such characteristics are vital to the lives of user-commoners, both locally and globally. Resources such as land, water, forests, the atmosphere, the internet, and knowledge extend across numerous state jurisdictions and into the international realm.

As the commons move beyond the sphere of state sovereignty, the terminology surrounding them becomes increasingly blurred and ambiguous. The most important ambiguity in international law stems from a methodological confusion between 'common resources, goods or spaces' and 'commons'. The prevailing terminology conflates common resources and commons. The most commonly used terms, referring to shared resources, are the following:

- 'Global commons': resources, goods, and spaces to which all states have access.[45] According to mainstream international law theory, there are four recognised 'global commons': the oceans, the atmosphere, outer space, and Antarctica.[46]
- 'International commons': resources, goods, and spaces shared by two or more states, but shared in different ways. For example, the polar regions and the Mediterranean are areas where particular groups of states exercise responsibilities of varying legal scope.[47]

According to Young, who proposed a distinct approach, common resources in the international sphere can be divided into three categories: (1) international commons, encompassing natural resources outside state jurisdiction but of shared interest to two or more states, such as fishing in international waters; (2) shared natural resources, located within the territories of two or more states, such as transboundary rivers; and (3) commons of the natural environment, situated entirely within one state but exerting transboundary effects on others, such as tropical rainforests.[48] Another approach, articulated in the *World Conservation Strategy* report, aligns more closely with a sovereignty-centred view: 'the global commons includes those parts of the Earth's surface beyond national jurisdictions (notably the open ocean

45 Buck 1998: 3, 6.
46 Vogler 2000; Buck 1998.
47 Among others: Stern 2011.
48 Young 1997: 5.

and the living resources found there) or held in common (notably the atmosphere). The only landmass which may be regarded as part of the global commons is Antarctica […]'.[49]

However, there exist many more common goods, spaces, and resources[50] at the global scale – such as the atmosphere, culture and science, biodiversity, cyberspace, water, or the human genome – that affect all humanity, or large parts of it, and constitute preconditions for prosperity, if not for life itself.[51]

Nevertheless, the terminology still reflects approaches that focus exclusively on common resources, goods, and spaces rather than on commons as relational systems requiring active interdependence among resources, communities, and regulatory frameworks. Can we meaningfully conceptualise such commons at the global scale?

[*Why Universal Commons?*]

To answer this question, we must revisit the definition of the commons, as discussed in the introduction, and apply it to common goods, resources, and spaces at the global scale. Inevitably, the transposition from the local to the global modifies the rigidity of the criteria that define the commons. Yet, if we accept that commons are active at the local scale, it would be difficult to deny their presence and vitality at the global scale. Hence, a new methodology is required to qualify them as commons.[52]

The methodological tools of international law, insofar as they address *global commons*, concern only resources, goods, and spaces, and therefore fail to capture the triadic nature of the commons. I therefore propose the term *universal commons* (see Table 3), defined through a methodology that cumulatively encompasses the three requirements of the triadic model: the shared resource, good, or space (i), the community of commoners (ii), and the normative framework (iii):

49 Report on the protection of the environment (International Union for Conservation of Nature and Natural Resources 1980), Chapter 18.1.

50 Hess 2008: 31. It includes a bibliography on the New Commons up to 2008.

51 A 2013 United Nations Working Group report explicitly refers to the emergence of new commons at the global scale: 'Resources of interest or value to the welfare of the community of nations—such as tropical rain forests and biodiversity—have lately been included among the traditional set of global commons, while some define the global commons even more broadly, to include science, education, information and peace', which may be regarded as global common resources of a new generation. UN System Task Team on the UN post 2015 UN Development Agenda, 2013, 5–6.

52 See also: Sinou 2022.

i. We have already enumerated a range of *common resources, goods, and spaces* that exist at the global scale. These extend beyond or overlap with state jurisdictions. They are essential to human existence – such as clean water, air, food, and the genome (*commons of life*) – or vital to human well-being, such as the radio spectrum, the internet, science, and culture (*commons of prosperity*). The boundaries between these categories are often indistinct.

Common resources, goods, and spaces at a global scale may be limited by nature yet remain accessible to all (common-pool resources) and are therefore vulnerable to overuse. Others may be non-competitive but exclusive – such as internet access – or non-exclusive but competitive, such as satellite orbits. Certain state jurisdictions may also share some of these as club commons. One example is fisheries within the European Union: a common good located within the member states' EEZ, open to all EU members but not to third-party states.[53] At the extreme end of the global scale, the natural environment – and the Earth itself – constitute the supreme common good: a super-commons, the *sine qua non* of humankind's existence.

These resources relate to humanity as an abstract whole, and to each human being – present and future – as an indivisible part of the universal ecosystem. Whether finite or inexhaustible (see Table 4), natural or human-made, they cannot be confined within one-dimensional conceptual categories or subjected to simplistic regimes of access and exploitation. Despite their conceptual ambiguities, common resources, goods, and spaces satisfy the first condition of the definition of the commons.

ii. The *normative framework* is determined by international law, which in recent decades has produced a growing corpus of norms concerning common resources, goods, and spaces at the global scale. These norms are dispersed across multiple legal instruments; they are heterogeneous and vary in enforceability. They remain sporadic and do not yet constitute a distinct branch of international law.

Nevertheless, we can discern the emergence of an international law of the commons – a body of law 'under construction'. Its norms constitute a dynamic and evolving regulatory landscape extending from outer space to biodiversity, and from the oceans to the internet. These fragments – comprising elements of soft law, positive law, law under negotiation, and relevant jurisprudence – are discussed more fully in Chapter 4.

States remain the primary lawmakers, yet international organisations, activist NGOs, and social movements play crucial roles in the law-making process.

53 Soroos 2005: 37.

This evolving international law of the commons also establishes a framework of rights and obligations for commoner-users and managers. To a considerable extent, the rights of commoners are intertwined with human rights. As Ostrom has shown[54] with respect to intra-state commons, cooperative forms of governance over vital resources often emerge in the absence of a strong authority capable of enforcing its decisions. Effective monitoring, conflict-resolution mechanisms, and sanctions can be achieved through collaborative arrangements. Even in cases where a centralised authority appears best suited to address issues of universal concern – such as the climate crisis – polycentric governance structures tend to produce more effective outcomes.

The internal and external functions of the commons, and the rights and bligations of commoners, are regulated by scattered international law norms rooted in fundamental principles such as effectiveness, solidarity, distributive justice, community interests, *erga omnes* obligations, and *jus cogens*, among others (see Chapter 6.5). These principles channel the established rules on shared goods, resources, and spaces towards the crystallisation of the law of the commons. For some topics, such as the law of the sea, norms have evolved towards a consolidated branch of international law. In contrast, others, such as the law governing the internet, suffer from serious loopholes. Thus, the third requirement of the triadic commons definition is fulfilled.

iii. The most complex issue in developing a methodological approach to commons at global scale lies in identifying *the community of commoners*. The subjects of law associated with common resources do not form a homogeneous group of legal entities: they include individuals, collectives, states, and international organisations. Yet all have vital interests in common resources, even at a global scale. Depending on the circumstances, they form communities of active subjects-commoners.

The intrinsic nature of each resource shapes and defines its community. These communities are therefore mixed, fluid, and variable – and, above all, potential. Commoners gather around shared interests and concerns, according to their wishes, needs, and the socio-economic context. One might argue that the absence of a clearly defined community corresponding to each resource, good, or space precludes the application of commons theory. On the contrary, the fluidity and potentiality of such communities do not disqualify them as commoners; rather, they are members of multiple global communities, each possessing different capacities for participation and action. The global scale

54 Ostrom 2010.

TABLE 3. Understanding universal commons

- *Universal commons* can be defined as the global common goods, resources, and spaces that exist beyond – or extend across – interstate jurisdictions. They are governed by policies and rules established by (actual or potential) communities of commoners, who are subjects of both rights and obligations.
- The commoners of the universal commons can be diverse entities: individual human beings and collective groups (such as communities or peoples), states, non-governmental organisations, international intergovernmental organisations, and potentially also commercial actors.
- Universal commons are of fundamental importance to human life and wellbeing. They are at the centre of major political and economic interests and often serve as a means to mitigate tensions between competing interests.
- Universal commons vary according to their degree of *exclusiveness, subtractability*, and *accessibility*.
- Universal commons are subject to stewardship exercised by a centralised authority or through complex, decentralised forms of governance.
- The greater the cooperation among commoners – ranging from individuals to states – under collectively established rules, the more effectively the universal commons can fulfil their purpose.

requires precisely such an approach and mandates a redefined understanding of the commons.

The composition of the community of commoners – and of those subjects responsible for managing commons at the global level, within and beyond state jurisdiction – is highly complex, particularly because certain actors, especially the states, may play dual roles, both as commoners and as overseers.

Individual commoners are likewise potential subjects of rights related to the access, use, and management of common resources, goods, and spaces. This connection rests on the foundation of human rights – on respect for human dignity and life. Active and conscious membership in the community of commoners gives rise to communal rights, insofar as these rights relate to the sustainability of life and well-being. For states, these rights are regulated by international law governing global common resources; for individuals and groups, the right to commoning is already recognised in several human rights instruments. Therefore, multiple and variable communities of commoners fulfil the third requirement of the definition of universal commons.

[*Universal Commons and Global Public Goods*]
As stated in the introduction, *global public goods* can be directly or indirectly linked to common goods, resources, and spaces at the global scale, since they encompass values and goals shared by all states, societies, and the international community as a whole. Global public goods include, among others, environmental protection, the administration of international justice, coordination of public health services, and the development of international policies to combat hunger. These are functions typically assumed by the public sector within national jurisdictions. However, at the global level, analogies become blurred. The 'public domain' is neither fixed nor clearly defined, lacking both stable legal qualifications and established political modalities. Although the discourses on global public goods and the commons share many challenges, their solutions diverge.[55]

In the late 1990s, the United Nations Development Programme (UNDP) underscored the importance of global public goods by adopting an economic perspective that tended to depoliticise the issue, leaving conflicts among social groups and economic interests at the margins of analysis.[56] Yet, according to another interpretation of the UNDP's approach, public goods inevitably acquire social dimensions that require their production and distribution for socio-political reasons, particularly to promote equity among states and individuals worldwide: 'The UNDP thus calls attention to the necessary participation of all actors in the decision-making process and the distribution of the benefits of public goods'.[57]

Inge Kaul identifies key global public goods that represent major international political challenges: 'global climate stability, international financial stability, communicable disease control, peace and security, the institutional architecture of international trade and finance, global communication and transportation systems, and global norms such as basic human rights'.[58] In addition, the failure to ensure access to public goods decisively affects living conditions across the globe. States and international organisations must therefore guarantee such access through cooperation and the strengthening of distributive mechanisms. Both universal commons and global public goods depend on governance arrangements in which states and international organ-

55 Brando et al. 2019: 570.
56 Dardot & Laval 2014: 486.
57 Bance 2018: 9.
58 Kaul 2013: 7. Cf. the contribution of the United Nations (mainly UNDP) to the debate on global public goods, as well as the initiative of states (International Task Force on Global Public Goods 2006).

isations play central roles. Stewardship bodies must prevent both the overuse of the former and the under-provision of the latter.

As secondary resources, global public goods may be linked to the governance of universal commons. Henceforth, the discussion of global common goods, spaces, and resources will also encompass global public goods, as they form an indivisible unity with the commons. For instance, the natural environment exists as both a tangible common good and a normative and moral imperative; knowledge exists as an intangible yet concrete common good, while education represents both the process and the services provided by the state, as well as the right of access to that knowledge.[59]

The commons, however, are not equivalent to public goods. Criticism of the economic theory underlying public goods should focus not on rejecting[60] or rigidly separating the two concepts,[61] but on the conditions and purposes of these goods – terms of access, extent and recipients of benefits, guarantees of provision, and the role of the community of commoners in their management. The concept of global public goods has dominated international debate, legitimising significant institutional and financial expansion within international organisations in the early twenty-first century.[62] Yet, these discussions often proceed from a narrow perspective, lacking the holistic approach that the complexity and universality of the commons demand.

That institutions such as the UN or the World Bank approach public goods within a capitalist framework does not diminish their fundamental importance to the global community of commoners. Rather, the discourse on public goods must evolve toward a coherent political and legal perspective that connects them – at least tentatively – with the universal commons, given their critical importance to the community of commoners.

The Covid-19 pandemic underscored this interrelation. It demonstrated not only the significance of health as a global public good requiring collaborative action by all states, but also the vaccine as a concrete, material common good of global importance. Nevertheless, vaccines were often referred to as a 'global public good',[63] thereby deepening terminological confusion. Henceforth, universal commons and global public goods will be treated as distinct conceptual categories, differentiated yet interrelated by shared characteristics.

---

59 Especially about education 'as a public and common good', see: Locatelli 2018.

60 As, for example, Dardot & Laval (2014: 485–486) choose to do.

61 See among others: Cogolati 2020: 30–40.

62 Bodansky 2012: 655.

63 For the use of the term, see inter alia: Council of Europe 2021, in Chapter 5.6.

TABLE 4. Exhaustibility of global common resources and global public goods

	Material	**Non-material**	**Spaces**
Exhaustible	Water, soil, ores, industrial raw materials	Knowledge and patented devices	Enclosed spaces (satellite orbits, analogue frequencies), energy from combustion
With inherent or artificial renewability or extension	Oxygen, water, biodiversity (animals, plants, seeds)	Knowledge, culture	Space, radio spectrum
Inexhaustible	Renewable forms of energy, radio spectrum, cyberspace, open knowledge and technology, and culture		Open natural spaces (air, space, ocean)
Inexhaustible Non-competitive	Public goods as derivatives of governance: Governance of international society, global public health, international justice, international law, international economy, people's prosperity, equality, freedom		

CHAPTER 3

Restricting Enclosures

> The noble and well-to-do [...] are no longer content to live lazily and comfortably, which brings no good to society, they must actually do it harm by all the land that passes through their hands in the pastures and leaving nothing for cultivation.[1] (Thomas More)

Throughout history, the common good, resources, and spaces have been consistently constrained by legal, economic, and political enclosures that favour state or private appropriation. Conversely, the importance of common resources is constantly growing. They acquire increasing gravity for the global human community and the global ecosystem as a unified commons, in direct interaction with scattered local commoners and recipients of the benefits of these resources. With the emergence of ownership, as shaped by the modern state, the commons have been rebranded and their heterogeneities homogenised and universalised. However, as Kathryn Milun observes:

> With the emergence of states, commons oscillate between a form of commons that states can use (universal, unlimited, and homogeneous) and a form of commons that resist state capture, as they still retain their original heterogeneity under the protection of the original authority of the ancient mythical image of the Golden Age, an authority which Grotius incorporates into the new category of Natural Law.[2]

Goods, resources, and spaces that are common to all concern rights and expectations regarding access and use – the rights of commoners who, under specific preconditions, can exercise rights of exploitation. Yet pressing questions remain: how can the common good be protected from the enclosures of private profit at the global scale, including those imposed by non-steward states and communities? How can resources that belong to no one be transformed into a universal commons?

Enclosures – real or potential – of universal goods, resources, and spaces, as well as acts of resistance to them, move through vague approximations of the 'common good' and 'community interests', abstract references to contradict-

1 More 1984: 32.
2 Milun 2011: 82.

HTTPS://DOI.ORG/10.1163/9789004764118-004

ory subjects such as 'humanity', and obligations with ambiguous content, such as the 'duty of care'. 'Humanity', though a legal fiction, gradually assumes the profile of a quasi-community of commoners. As Bruno Simma noted, community interests express a consensus that respect for certain fundamental values should not be left to the free disposition of states – either individually or jointly – but should instead be organised and sanctioned by international law as a matter of concern to all.[3]

States increasingly develop joint intervention practices within their own jurisdictions to 'protect' common resources at the global scale. Yet, the meaning of 'protection' itself is open to conceptual confusion and may even invert its intended purpose.[4] For instance, as explored below, the 1982 UN Convention on the Law of the Sea explicitly links the creation of a just and equitable international economic order to the interests and needs of 'humanity' as a whole, particularly those of developing nations. However, it does so by promoting policies of 'resource extraction' rather than schemes aimed at 'resource regeneration'.

The 'common heritage of mankind' and the 'common concern' based on 'community interests' shared by humanity form fluid and uncertain bonds that connect all international subjects and actors. These bonds arise from pressing and potential issues that affect everyone's lives and prospects for wellbeing – ecological emergencies and the aggressive enclosure of global goods, resources, and spaces.

1 The 'Common Heritage of Humankind': Everywhere and Too Little, in the Open Sea and on the International Seabed

The idea of protecting common resources in modern international law against enclosures originates in the concept of the 'common heritage of mankind'.[5] This concept sought to transcend the legal fictions of *res nullius* and *terra nullius*. It stems from a universal moral intuition implying collective responsibility towards nature. As a legal notion, however, it remains vague as long as the content of 'mankind' is so ill-defined that its anonymity simultaneously misleads and generates contradictions.

---

3 Simma 1994: 233.

4 Jasper 2012.

5 Kiss 1985; Başlar 1998; Pinto 2012.

If the term is meant to secure the interests of all people, it also risks opening the way for political and economic elites to advance their own agendas in the name of an unspecified subject invested with ethical surplus value. Thus, it can perpetuate exclusion and discrimination. The concept of 'heritage' implies property transmitted across generations, yet without a specific beneficiary. Despite numerous attempts to give it normative substance, the notion of 'mankind' as the collective heir to this 'property' remains fluid, spanning space and time. It includes both present and future generations (see Chapter 6.1). This inclusive understanding is gaining traction, even if it has not yet been codified in legal texts. Humanity remains a fragmented set of individuals divided by contrasts and exclusions that defy monolithic legal formulations. Yet, despite its ambiguity and misuse, the 'common heritage of mankind' may serve as a cornerstone of a universal conception of the commons grounded in social equity and sustainability.

In 1926, José León Suárez, a member of the League of Nations commission for the codification of international law, argued that international law of the sea aimed primarily at securing trade rather than protecting marine life – linking the sea's resources to economic interests and the common good. He warned that without common rules of exploitation, marine species would disappear, since the sea constitutes a single ecological realm. Thus, he declared, 'the riches of the oceans and especially of Antarctica are the heritage of the entire human race', urging joint international exploitation of the sea's resources to secure food for all.[6] Decades later, at the 1958 Conference on the Law of the Sea, Prince Wan Waithayakon of Thailand revived this idea, describing the sea as the 'common heritage of mankind' to be held under common protection for the benefit of all.[7] In the 1960s, the principle was enshrined in the normative framework of the international law of outer space (see Chapter 4.6).

In principle, the 'common heritage of mankind' refers to resources belonging to 'all people' – mediated by 'all states', and, in practice, by those with the power or authority to speak in the name of humanity. Its implementation presupposes equal access, though this ideal is rarely met. In the 1970s, the Group of 77 (developing nations) advanced the concept within the framework of the proposed New International Economic Order, crystallising in two UN General Assembly declarations on the right to development.[8] In these texts, 'equity' occupies a central place: the redistribution of global wealth and equal access to (potentially) shared wealth-producing resources.

6 In Schrijver 2016: 1255.
7 In Schrijver 2016: 1257.
8 Cf. UNGA, A/RES/3201 S-IV, 1st May 1974 and UNGA, A/RES/41/128, 4 Dec. 1986, respectively.

The North-South divide became evident in these negotiations and in the resulting texts, which sought to balance conflicting state interests. Since then, the commons have been understood – often controlled by powerful states – and as a rhetorical instrument invoked by developing states to promote redistributive justice.

The partial retreat of state sovereignty before the collective interest in protecting universal commons is evident in certain treaty texts. One of the earliest examples concerns cultural and natural monuments protected by the 1972 UNESCO World Heritage Convention.[9] It declares that 'parts of the cultural and natural heritage that are of outstanding interest must be protected as part of the world heritage of humanity as a whole' (para. 6), though the meaning of this 'humanity' remains opaque. In practice, a cultural asset under the exclusive jurisdiction of one state also becomes *world cultural heritage* – the imagined property of global civilisation – subject to the loose supervision of UNESCO's World Heritage Committee.[10]

Here, states collectively undertake, through an international body, to protect (or assist in protecting) monuments that form part of humanity's shared cultural capital, even when located within national boundaries. Though the Convention's legal force is limited, its symbolic significance is profound: it transcends national sovereignty, placing certain goods under international oversight as part of the universal commons 'inherited' from previous generations. Yet, cultural heritage assessment often relies on abstract scales that ignore local communities' rights of access.[11] The Council of Europe Convention on the Value of Cultural Heritage for Society (Faro Convention, 2005) went further, linking the cultural environment to the ongoing evolution of human civilisation, the risks of economic change, and the need for protection through democratic participation and shared accountability.

Numerous other international treaties reference the commons through terms such as 'humankind' or 'common heritage'. The Moon and outer space are 'regions of all humanity';[12] waterfowl constitute an 'international resource';[13] natural and cultural heritage is 'part of world heritage as a whole';[14] and the wild fauna are to be protected 'for the good of humankind'.[15] The

9 Ringbeck 2018; Jokilehto 2008.
10 On the Committee, see: <https://bit.ly/38Dz6sW>.
11 Fairclough 2020: viii.
12 Outer Space and the Moon Treaty 1967.
13 Convention on Wetlands of International Importance 1971.
14 Hague Convention for the Protection of Cultural Property 1954.
15 Convention for the Protection of Migratory Wild Animals 1979.

Moon, the ocean floor, and subsoil resources are described as the 'common heritage of mankind',[16] while the human genome[17] and plant genetic resources are similarly designated as the 'heritage of humankind',[18] while Antarctica is deemed an area of 'interest for humanity'.[19]

The concept of the 'common heritage of humankind' is guided by five principles:[20]

1. It belongs to no one.
2. It is subject to common management, prioritising global over national interests.
3. The benefits from its exploitation must be equitably distributed.
4. Military activity is prohibited.
5. The results of scientific research must be shared with all.

In practice, these principles have rarely been fully implemented, allowing new enclosures to arise. The field where the concept has found its most concrete application is the Law of the Sea. The ocean, as the archetype of open space, shaped the very evolution of international law. Because it cannot be possessed or enclosed by individual actors, nor can states easily exclude others, the open sea stands as the paradigmatic commons at the global scale – a good, a resource, and a space simultaneously.[21]

The open sea was the first universal commons recognised in modern international law, initially enabling exploitation under colonial conditions. Colonial powers invoked 'freedom of navigation and fishing' to protect their economic interests against rivals asserting exclusive claims. In the twentieth century, states again turned to the sea – this time to redefine their relations in exploiting the seabed, its subsoil, and the surrounding waters.

The 1982 Montego Bay Convention (UNCLOS) delineated areas belonging to all – zones of the sea, seabed, and subsoil – and established specific rights of exploration and exploitation alongside obligations to prevent pollution. Yet, it stopped short of providing an unambiguous framework for protecting marine resources from intensive state and corporate activity.

16 Moon Agreement, 1979 (Section 4.d); Convention on the Law of the Sea 1982.
17 UNESCO, Universal Declaration on the Human Genome and Human Rights.
18 UN FAO, 37th Sess., U.N. Doc. C/83/Rep. (1983). Cf. Buttigieg 2012.
19 Antarctic Treaty 1959.
20 Frakes 2003.
21 Milun 2011: 76.

[*The Sea as an Exploitable Body of Water*]
With the adoption of the new Law of the Sea, states gradually extended their exploitation rights to international straits (114 in total) and, more significantly, to a volume of seawater extending up to 200 nautical miles from their coasts. This development led to the progressive shrinking of the open sea.[22] The surface of areas beyond national jurisdiction decreased by roughly 40%, giving way to zones under national control – a trend that continues today. For instance, the recent expansion of France's EEZ has notably altered the global map of fishing rights.[23] Before 1980, most fish were caught on the high seas; today, the overwhelming majority are caught within EEZ, subject to national jurisdiction.[24] Only 12% of the global marine catch now comes from the high seas (taken mainly by fleets from ten states), while 88% is taken within national EEZ. Strikingly, just 4% of the world's fishing fleets account for 65% of the total ocean catch.[25]

The purpose of the EEZ was to allow states to manage their own catches as their 'property', on the rationale that regulated management of living resources would be more sustainable than open, unregulated access. The EEZ was thus intended to ensure the maintenance of fish populations sufficient to meet both local and global nutritional needs.

As early as 1974, the ICJ ruled that *laissez-faire* exploitation of international fisheries had given way to a regime of regulation, recognising states' obligations to exercise due diligence in protecting the rights of others and to safeguard the collective interests of all in an era of intensified fishing.[26] Yet the cosmopolitan diplomat Arvid Pardo, Malta's ambassador to the UN, and his supporters foresaw that the EEZ would erect new enclosures within the oceans. They lamented the Convention's adoption, which – despite contrary proposals – reserved a 200-mile maritime zone for the economic benefit of states, effectively reducing the universal commons of the high seas to 'a few fish and seaweed'.[27]

22 For maritime areas beyond state sovereignty zones, see: Freestone 2018.
23 For the mapping of EEZs and the open sea, see: <https://bit.ly/2K2RZuY>.
24 Thara Srinivasan et al. 2012: 544.
25 Global Ocean Commission 2014, at <https://bit.ly/35nlEXS>.
26 ICJ, *Fisheries Jurisdiction Case* (*UK v. Iceland*), ICJ Rep., 25.7.1974, para. 72: 'It is one of the advances in maritime international law, resulting from the intensification of fishing, that the former laissez-faire treatment of the living resources of the sea in the high seas has been replaced by a recognition of a duty to have due regard to the rights of other States and the needs of conservation for the benefit of all.'
27 See: <http://wcl.american.libguides.com/c.php?g=563260&p=3877818>.

The results of this experiment have been disappointing: global fish stocks have continued to decline dramatically.[28] Why? Because regulatory regimes are uneven. Some states have established sustainable fishing regulations; others do not enforce them, while many have none at all. Fish, of course, are oblivious to national borders – many are migratory species traversing multiple EEZs and the open sea.

Traditional coastal fishers, with limited equipment, pose little threat to marine biodiversity. The real damage stems from large industrial fleets equipped with factory ships capable of sweeping entire stocks from the sea, often operating in the EEZs of other states or in unregulated high-seas areas. Frequently subsidised by their governments, these companies pressure authorities to raise quotas even as catches dwindle. The result is not only the depletion of marine life but also the collapse of local economies dependent on artisanal fishing. A notorious case is the Somali coast, where industrial overfishing has devastated the local fisheries economy. Isolated by civil conflict and deprived of livelihood, some coastal inhabitants turned to piracy – a direct consequence of ecological and economic dispossession, and one of the most striking disruptions to the freedom of navigation in modern times.[29]

The Montego Bay Convention does not regulate catches on the high seas, nor does it impose rules or management standards within national EEZs (art. 116). Nevertheless, a number of international treaties have attempted to fill this gap. The 1995 UN Fish Stocks Agreement (in force since 2001) complements the 1982 Convention, but it lacks specific enforcement mechanisms or self-monitoring obligations for major fishing states. Nor does it provide effective guarantees of sustainability for small-scale fishing communities in developing countries.[30]

A more promising development was the 1993 FAO Agreement to Promote Compliance with International Conservation and Management Measures by Fishing Vessels on the High Seas (in force since 2003). This was the first legal instrument to impose concrete obligations on states to monitor and control their vessels, aiming to prevent reflagging and ensure compliance with international measures. Building upon it, the 2009 Agreement on Port State Measures to Prevent, Deter and Eliminate Illegal, Unreported, and Unregulated

---

28 Armstrong 2017: 207; FAO 2018, *The state of world fisheries and aquaculture*, Brief, at <https://bit.ly/36rCl3K>.

29 There is another aspect of illegal fishing, apart from exceeding catch quotas or the methods used, namely that of slavery. More than half of fishermen on Asian-Pacific fishing vessels are in forced labour, World Economic Forum 2019, at <https://bit.ly/2UnzVh3>.

30 Gullett & Hanich 2018.

Fishing (in force since 2016) became the first binding international treaty explicitly targeting illegal fishing.

Bilateral and regional arrangements have also played a role. A 1997 China-Japan fisheries agreement (effective from 2000) was based on mutual recognition of EEZs and fishing rights, though it contained no provisions to address the impacts of climate change.[31] Regional cooperation bodies – such as the Commission for Indian Ocean Tuna, the North-East Atlantic Fisheries Commission, the Permanent Commission for the South Pacific, and the Sub-Regional Fisheries Commission for West Africa – have been established to combat illegal fishing. The EU has also promoted the Agreement to Prevent Unregulated High-Seas Fisheries in the Central Arctic Ocean, introducing precautionary conservation and management measures.[32]

Particular attention should be given to the Antarctic EEZ. The 1972 Seal Convention and the 1980 Convention on the Conservation of Antarctic Marine Living Resources established protection regimes over the open sea in the region. Yet the creation of EEZs around the Antarctic perimeter has permitted – or, more accurately, failed to prevent – overfishing, especially of krill, a keystone species vital to the region's fragile ecosystem.[33]

A delicate balance is therefore required between food security and biodiversity conservation. According to the 2024 FAO report on Fisheries and Aquaculture, global capture fisheries production has remained broadly stable since the late 1980s. In 2022, total capture amounted to 92.3 million tonnes (11.3 million from inland and 81 million from marine sources). Despite the rise of aquaculture, capture fisheries continue to supply the bulk of aquatic animal production. However, the share of marine stocks fished at biologically sustainable levels fell to 62.3% in 2021. Meeting the nutritional needs of a growing world population will require an additional 36 million tonnes of aquatic food – an increase of 22%.[34] This will put even greater pressure on already stressed aquatic ecosystems.

A biodiversity-oriented analysis reveals the shortcomings of current management regimes. Maximising the simultaneous goals of biodiversity conservation, carbon sequestration, and food security could yield far greater collective benefits.[35] Following long negotiations, the 2023 High Seas Biodiversity Treaty explicitly states that 'Parties shall be guided by the principle of the

31 Zou 2022.

32 See Decision (EU) 2019/407, Conclusion of the Agreement to Prevent Unregulated High Seas Fisheries in the Central Arctic Ocean.

33 Vogler 2016: 60–62.

34 FAO, Report, The State of World Fisheries and Aquaculture, at <https://bit.ly/44LFlb2>.

35 Sala, Mayorga, Bradley et al. 2021.

common heritage of humankind', recognising 'the importance of contributing to the realisation of a just and equitable international economic order which takes into account the interests and needs of humankind as a whole and, in particular, the special interests and needs of developing States' (preamble).

Despite such advances, the tragedy of the global common resources persists – both within national EEZs and across the open sea. No universally applied norms govern catch limits, redistributive mechanisms, subsidy control, or the protection of small coastal fishing communities. Nor is there an effective global monitoring mechanism for biodiversity conservation and marine ecosystem integrity.

The ICJ has underscored these tensions, ruling that the United Kingdom's establishment of a Marine Park in the Chagos Archipelago in the Indian Ocean (covering 0.5 million km^2) was inconsistent with its rights and obligations under the Marine Park's founding convention and the Law of the Sea, particularly regarding Mauritius' fishing rights.[36]

Intergovernmental cooperation thus remains the key to preserving shared marine resources. The management of oceanic resources through collective international institutions endowed with meaningful authority is of paramount importance.[37] The International Tribunal for the Law of the Sea (ITLOS) reaffirmed that cooperation among states in the conservation and management of shared fisheries resources is a well-established principle of the Convention. It also promoted the optimal utilisation of these resources and defined norms against illegal, unreported, and unregulated fishing.[38]

Although closely linked, the rights to exploit marine resources (nature as a commodity) and the duty to protect marine life (nature as the ecosystem containing human beings) remain difficult to reconcile. 4.1 and 4.2 further examine the protection of marine ecosystems and biodiversity, respectively.

---

36 Permanent Court of Arbitration, Advisory Opinion, *The Chagos Marine Protected Area* (*Mauritius v. the UK*), 25.2.2019. In 2025, the UK decided to hand over the Chagos Archipelago to Mauritius, while retaining the Diego Garcia airbase.

37 The idea was promoted by Elisabeth Mann Borgese, who founded the Canada-based International Ocean Institute. The Institute has contributed in many ways to defending the oceans as a global common resource, at <http://internationaloceaninstitute.dal.ca/index.html>.

38 ITLOS, *Request for Advisory Opinion submitted by the Sub-Regional Fisheries Commission*, Advisory Opinion, 2.4.2015, p. 4.

[*The Ocean Seabed*]
In 1945, US President Harry Truman declared that the United States owned the international seabed and the continental shelf of the open sea adjacent to its shores, paving the way for the modern enclosure of the oceans.[39] A decisive intervention followed in November 1967, when Arvid Pardo proposed before the United Nations that exploitation of the international seabed should remain outside national jurisdictions and that its resources should be declared the 'common heritage of humankind':

> The dark oceans were the womb of life: from the protecting oceans, life emerged. We still bear in our bodies – in our blood, in the salty bitterness of our tears – the marks of this remote past. Retracing the past, man, the present dominator of the emerged earth, is now returning to the ocean depths. His penetration of the deep could mark the beginning of the end for man – and indeed for life as we know it on this earth. It could also be a unique opportunity to lay solid foundations for a peaceful and increasingly prosperous future for all peoples.[40]

Pardo insisted that the waters above the seabed should remain outside state jurisdiction, even if parts of the seabed itself were subject to state exploitation rights. He further argued for the establishment of a universal fund to redistribute profits from ocean resource exploitation in favour of economically weaker states. A few years later, the Group of 77 vigorously promoted the idea that the ocean floor and subsoil should constitute the common heritage of humankind, and that an international agency should establish rules ensuring the state receiving the products of any mining would contribute proportionally to others.[41] Over time, however, many states championed the extension of their sovereign rights at the expense of the common good.[42]

Article 136 of the UNCLOS explicitly states that 'the Area (e.g. the sea bed and ocean floor, and the subsoil thereof) and its resources are the common heritage of mankind', yet without providing clear regulatory protection for the legal interests behind this concept – even as technology enables increasingly intense exploitation. After years of negotiation, an additional agreement was concluded in 1994 to implement Part XI of the Convention. It aimed to address economic inequalities among states regarding seabed exploitation and pro-

39 Truman Proclamation 2667/1945, at <http://bit.ly/3Xra9Yu>.
40 Pardo 1967: 2.
41 Adede 1979.
42 Ranganathan 2016: 709.

tection. Adopted by the UN General Assembly, the Agreement entered into force in 1996.[43]

The preamble reaffirms the belief that the Area constitutes the 'common heritage of mankind' and cannot be appropriated. The exploitation of the ocean bed and subsoil (open sea) is therefore managed 'on behalf of humankind' through a specialised international body – the International Seabed Authority.[44] Yet the global resource is still governed within an 'extractive imaginary':[45] the regulatory focus lies on ores and hydrocarbons located on or beneath the seabed, without imposing concrete obligations concerning sustainability or environmental protection. States also retain exploitation rights over their continental shelf and the seabed of their EEZs, with varying intensity and environmental impact depending on the resource.

State exploration and exploitation rights extend to the underlying subsoil, which, depending on the seabed's composition, may reach 350 nautical miles from the coastal baselines or 100 miles from the 2.5 km depth line (art. 76). The legal status of the open sea is thus inconsistent, varying between the seabed and subsoil, and between zones under state jurisdiction and those beyond it. The result is an irregular legal landscape that begins in the state's territorial sea, extends to the continental shelf, and ends at the international seabed.

[*Exploitation Rights under Stewardship*]

The shift towards seabed exploitation marks a radical change in how the principle of 'the common heritage of mankind' is understood.[46] The International Seabed Authority, as noted above, coordinates, licences, and supervises exploration and exploitation undertaken in the Area by companies and states under contract. It exercises both legislative and executive powers over all activities within the Area, with the stated aim of protecting human life and the marine environment. The Enterprise – an organ of the Authority – was conceived to advance the collective interests of mankind in the exploitation of marine resources.

Originally, revenue from licences was intended to fund the Enterprise's scientific research and ecological oversight in sensitive areas. The Group of 77 envisioned the Enterprise as a coordinating and decision-making body

43 The UN General Assembly Resolution 48/263 of July 28, 1994, was adopted by a very large majority: 121 in favour and seven abstentions, at <https://bit.ly/2JUybty>.

44 Franckx 2010: 544.

45 The term is coined by Ranganathan (2019: 580).

46 Feichtner 2019.

that would ensure both the sustainable exploitation and the redistribution of the ocean's subsoil wealth to economically weaker nations. This vision, however, was challenged and eventually diluted by industrialised nations.[47]

The 1994 Agreement substantially weakened the redistributive aspects of the Convention: developed nations are no longer required to transfer technology or finance the Enterprise's activities. Any redistribution of economic resources now depends on their express consent, undermining the original intent of applied redistributive justice. Consequently, the international seabed and its subsoil receive limited protection with respect to exploitation, which remains primarily mining-oriented. Other uses – such as cable and pipeline installation, scientific exploration, and artificial island construction – are also foreseen, but remain secondary, of the ocean floor are also envisaged, such as the installation of cables and pipelines, exploration and the settlement of artificial islands.

In this way, the shared complex resource is transformed into an economic good, valued according to market logic. Even environmental rules adopted by the Authority often serve to facilitate rather than limit resource extraction.[48] The fate of the seabed stands at a historic turning point as exploitation has already begun. In 2025, the Authority issued 22 exploration and exploitation licenses to multinational corporations.[49] Each contract area is precisely delineated by geographic coordinates, and contractors must progressively relinquish portions of their zones as they identify promising sites. The Authority has designated nine Areas of Particular Environmental Interest, covering 2 million km^2 in the Clarion-Clipperton Zone, where mining is prohibited to protect marine biodiversity and ecosystem functions.

The Convention requires that exploitation be equitable and that economic benefits be redistributed in ways that reflect the interests of developing states and the rights of all states to use surface waters (arts. 140, 145, 147). In principle, this framework establishes the foundations of redistributive justice, reflected in differential financial support for poorer countries. In practice, however, the Authority must balance conflicting economic interests in light of the geographical representativeness and developmental status of member states. Since its establishment in 1994, the Authority has evolved from an

47 International Seabed Authority 2002.
48 Ranganathan 2019: 596.
49 International Seabed Authority 2024.

administrative body into an industrial and financial actor in its own right – an arena of opposed visions rather than a neutral steward.[50]

If redistribution were effectively implemented, it could partially offset economic disparities between developed and developing countries and secure access to global common resources for those otherwise excluded. Yet, although the Area itself is non-appropriable, the ores and hydrocarbons it contains become the property of whichever state or company extracts them. Regulatory safeguards are, therefore, crucial to prevent the de facto appropriation of common resources.

The Enterprise's responsibilities include monitoring underwater mining technologies, assessing scientific findings, and supervising exploitation. However, following the 1994 Agreement, the Enterprise was effectively dismantled and has never been operational. As Elisabeth Mann Borgese aptly observed, the Enterprise 'was put on ice *sine die*'.[51] The Convention on the Law of the Sea was thus weakened in two crucial respects: the redistributive mechanism for seabed exploitation and the ecological protection of the seabed itself. As with other global common resources the absence of effective governance of the oceans benefits powerful states and multinational corporations, as if the shared marine resources were *res nullius*.

Tensions continue to grow between industrialised nations eager to commence exploitation and those advocating stronger environmental protections or moratoria on deep-sea mining. The United States' non-participation in the Authority has produced a dual system of seabed governance: one based on international regulation and cooperation, and another favouring unilateral, profit-driven initiatives. In 2025, US President Donald Trump authorised the issuance of 'seabed mineral exploration licences and commercial recovery permits in areas beyond national jurisdiction', claiming to ensure 'efficiency, predictability and competitiveness for American companies'.[52] Conversely, Norway suspended the granting of deep-sea mining licences within its Arctic EEZ in late 2024 following intense domestic and international opposition.[53]

The expansion of unregulated, 'free-rider' activities will test the coherence of emerging international law on seabed exploitation and the viability of cooperative governance. What would happen if a licence issued by the United States overlapped with an area protected by the Authority in the Clarion-

50 Bräuninger & König 2000.

51 Mann Borgese 1998: 112.

52 President of the USA, Executive Order of 24 April 2025, 'Unleashing America's offshore critical minerals and resources'.

53 Deep Sea Conservation Coalition, 3 December 2024 <https://bit.ly/4lS7cvP>.

Clipperton Zone? Could international institutions and courts intervene to uphold universal commons-oriented norms and governance?

[*Can an Advisory Opinion Open the Door to the Future?*]
The demarcation between state jurisdiction and the shrinking domain of common resources remains an open question, continually adjusted in accordance with technological advances and the politico-economic ambitions of states and corporations. Even before the emergence of the modern law of the sea, the ICJ ruled that the 'physical extension of the seabed' forms the basis for establishing states' claims to the continental shelf and beyond.[54] This principle was subsequently incorporated into the 1982 Convention (art. 76, para. 1).

In February 2011, ITLOS delivered an Advisory Opinion concerning the responsibilities and obligations of states sponsoring activities in the Area. The case involved Nauru, which lacked the financial capacity to undertake research and exploitation of polymetallic nodules and sulphides on the seabed and subsoil of the Pacific Ocean. The Tribunal addressed three key questions to clarify the legal position of states and the international community regarding the exploitation of the Area:[55]

1. What are the legal responsibilities and obligations of States Parties with respect to the sponsorship of activities in the Area under the Convention, in particular Part XI, and the 1994 Agreement?
2. What is the extent of a State Party's liability for failure to comply with those provisions?
3. What measures must a State adopt to fulfil its obligations under the Convention, especially Article 139 and Annexe III, and the 1994 Agreement?

According to the Advisory Opinion, any State undertaking activities in the Area through a sponsored entity is obliged to contribute to the common interest of all States by ensuring 'the proper implementation of the principle of the common heritage of humankind by assisting the Authority and by acting on its own with a view to ensuring that entities under its jurisdiction conform to the rules relating to mining on the international seabed' (para. 226). The responsibilities and obligations of the state and the sponsoring company are governed by principles already established in international law. These create duties for states under the *precautionary approach* and the *precautionary prin-*

54 ICJ, *North Sea Continental Shelf (Federal Republic of Germany v. Netherlands)*, 20.2.1969, para. 19.

55 ITLOS, Seabed Disputes Chamber, *Responsibilities and Obligations of States Sponsoring Persons and Entities with Respect to Activities in the Area*, Advisory Opinion, 1.2.2011.

ciple, requiring them to avoid the risk *of serious or irreversible damage* by adopting measures to prevent *environmental degradation*. These principles underpin the *duty of due diligence* and the sustainability of the resources.

All states – developed and developing alike – as well as companies, are required to assess the environmental impacts of any proposed activity. However, as the Tribunal noted, developing states must receive assistance to ensure equal access to the exploitation of the Area's resources (para. 163). In effect, sponsoring states act in the service of the 'common interest', in cooperation with the Authority.[56]

States must therefore take all necessary, appropriate, and effective measures, in collaboration with the Authority, to ensure that the exploration and exploitation of the international seabed by the contracting company are carried out lawfully. Questions of liability and consequences involve determining compensation (amount, method of payment, etc.) and identifying those entitled to claim it – states, international bodies, companies, individuals, or organisations. Liability arises *erga omnes partes*: any affected party may seek compensation or restoration of the previous state of affairs. The International Seabed Authority itself may both request and be subject to such claims. The Tribunal held that a state is liable when it fails to take the necessary preventive measures and when a causal link between its acts or omissions and the damage is established. According to the Tribunal, 'the liability of the sponsoring State arises from its own failure to comply with its responsibilities under the Convention and related instruments' (para. 204).

The Advisory Opinion thus serves as a guide to the obligations incumbent upon states in relation to a global common resource – a domain of intense competition in which technological progress enables access to resources previously beyond reach. However, the persistent failure to operationalise the Enterprise most clearly demonstrates how the obligation to ensure equitable participation of developing states in seabed exploitation has been avoided.[57] Likewise, the ongoing conflict of interests and views is reflected in the Authority's longstanding effort to adopt a code of rules for the exploitation of the seabed and its subsoil.[58] While concern for the natural environment is a constant feature of the drafts, references to the 'common heritage of mankind'

---

56 Mickelson 2019: 651.

57 Bourrel et al. 2016.

58 Mickelson 2019: 651. The code will include the regulations adopted by the Authority in 2000 and 2010 for the exploration and exploitation of polymetallic nodules, sulphides, and cobalt-rich crusts.

appears infrequently – more symbolic than substantive – and rarely reflected in the commitments of the companies engaged in exploration and extraction.

The negotiations expose a fundamental clash between two objectives: on the one hand, the protection and equitable use of the resource, and on the other, its exploitation for private profit. What remains unresolved is whether biodiversity, minerals, and hydrocarbons will be treated holistically as components of a single ecosystem and a global common resource under international management, where rights and obligations are balanced. How, indeed, can the commercialisation of a common good be compatible with the notion of sharing its benefits?

Put differently: To what extent can the status of the international seabed as part of the common heritage of mankind be reconciled with policies of industrial exploitation aimed at profit and the so-called 'common good'? The current situation suggests that the ocean floor's wealth is open to appropriation by certain states and corporations operating under national and international legal frameworks – paradoxically, in the name of the 'common heritage of mankind'.[59] What, then, is the benefit to humanity when the mineral wealth of the oceans is extracted without redistribution? To what extent does a project such as Japan's Shimizu Corporation's proposal to build underwater cities for the 'common good' truly serve that end? (Chapter 5.1.5). Can we expect international law – which presently enables the plunder of the ocean floor – to evolve into a mechanism that redistributes the benefits of exploitation to the international community?[60]

Moreover, as many have argued, obligations to protect the commons in favour of commoners must apply *transgenerationally*;[61] otherwise, international commitments lack meaning and effect. These considerations, together with legal developments concerning marine resources, put the 'common heritage of mankind' to the test. The concept remains ambiguous and imprecise, lacking a definition that would translate into concrete and enforceable commitments to protect the commons. It ought to provide the conceptual thread linking environmental protection, sustainable use, benefit-sharing, risk assessment, and technology transfer.[62] Properly defined, the 'common heritage of mankind' could establish inter- and intra-generational equity and, through law, advance the sustainability and viability of the universal commons.

59 Feichtner & Ranganathan 2019.
60 Ranganathan 2019: 600.
61 Frakes 2003: 409.
62 Tladi 2015.

At present, however, the application of the 'common heritage of mankind' reflects the broader pathology of the so-called '*ecological question*', perpetuated through profit-driven logics of exploitation that enable the appropriation of shared resources. Instead of serving the universal community of humankind, the concept has been instrumentalised to promote the profitability of multinational corporations and the interests of powerful states, while undermining collective responsibility and the principle of non-appropriation;[63] put differently: 'when freedom marches alone without equality, unaccountability follows'.[64]

Today, the principle stands as a compromise between the ideal of a just global order and the pragmatic realities of international negotiation. Whether it can fulfil its original vision of fairness and shared stewardship of the global common resources remains uncertain.[65] As Sutabhi Ranganathan has argued, international governance of an open commons may paradoxically generate new forms of enclosure by restricting genuine freedom of access.[66] The challenge, therefore, is to define the conditions for the 'good use' – or 'non-use' – of the common resource. This argument is particularly useful for determining the conditions that should govern the establishment of a commons, rather than for questioning its necessity. In practice, the 'plunder' of the oceans and seabed occurs through the very discourse of the commons itself:[67] under the supervision of international bodies that, by issuing permits, facilitate and legitimise appropriation.

Ultimately, the 'common heritage of mankind' remains a malleable concept, continually reshaped by the aspirations of states and the pressures of global events. Its meaning changed profoundly when the seabed regime was reformulated to incorporate market mechanisms. Future reinterpretations may again move either towards stronger environmental protection and sustainability or towards further commodification and enclosure.[68] Under transformative con-

---

63 Taylor 2016.

64 Akrivoulis 2018: 192, 200.

65 Pinto 2012.

66 Ranganathan 2016: 714. In 2017, Michael Lodge, Secretary-General of the Authority, expressed similar concerns about balancing the results of mining and exploitation with the protection of the marine environment. In Mickelson 2019: 660.

67 Ranganathan 2019. Initially, the United States, like other developed nations, used the term 'plunder' of the seabed to describe the perceived threat of establishing a global governance regime over the seabed that would exclude them from unrestricted access and exploitation. Subsequently, they ceased using the term, having succeeded in preventing such a development.

68 Mickelson 2019: 662.

ditions – and resisting the erosion of reciprocity between states – the 'common heritage of mankind' could yet serve as the normative foundation for a comprehensive model of governance of the universal commons, in the interest of all people and without exclusions.[69]

2 Lost in Translation: Between 'Common Concern' and 'Community Interests'

To the legal construction of the 'common heritage of mankind', a series of other concepts with equally ambiguous, ephemeral, or vague meanings were later added. Among these is the 'common concern',[70] conceived as a prerequisite giving rise to a quasi-obligation of states, which can be linked to 'common interest' or 'community interests' – both themselves grounded in 'common values' that lack concrete content for all members of the international community, or even for a majority of states.

The notion of 'common concern' emerged during debates on the exploitation of 'free' natural resources, long before the discourse on climate change began. For example, the Arctic seal-hunting crisis between the United States and Great Britain led to the 1893 Fur Seals Arbitration, a transnational agreement establishing obligations for the 'common welfare'. Likewise, under the Inter-American Convention on Tropical Tuna of 1949, tuna fishing was considered a matter of 'common concern' among states, which subsequently concluded fisheries treaties to limit unilateral overfishing.

In recent decades, the 'common concern of humankind' has gained prominence within a regulatory environment primarily focused on climate and biodiversity. The Convention on Biological Diversity (1992) declares that 'the conservation of biological diversity is a matter of common concern to humankind'. Ensuring the common good presupposes that the general interest of humanity involves facilitating access to biological resources, accompanied by the equitable sharing of benefits among states, investors, and peoples, including those who grant access to their territories.[71]

It has become apparent that the scope of 'common concern' varies depending on the field of international endeavour in question. It remains a general

---

69 For a universal extension of the idea of the common heritage of mankind, which would overturn the hegemonic hierarchies between the Global North and the Global South, see: Santos 2020.

70 Shelton 2009: 33–40.

71 Francioni 2014: 445.

concept from which no specific rules or obligations can be directly derived and cannot curtail the principle of state sovereignty. According to Shelton's rather optimistic assessment, 'respect for human rights, economic development, and environmental protection have been unified in the concept of sustainable development as a common concern of humanity'.[72]

According to Thomas Cottier et al., findings and proposals concerning climate change may shape an emerging general principle capable of redefining prevailing assumptions about national sovereignty. Although the two terms – 'common heritage', 'common concern' – were initially used differently, they are now employed interchangeably by commentators and legal texts, particularly in relation to tropical rainforests and water resources.[73] Related expressions, such as the 'common interest of mankind', also appear in other legal instruments, as in the Tokyo Convention on Fisheries in the North Pacific Ocean (1952), while the Antarctic Treaty (1959) affirms that 'it is in the interest of humanity that Antarctica be exploited for peaceful purposes'.[74]

UN General Assembly Resolution 43/53 'Protection of the Global Climate for Present and Future Generations of Humankind' (1988), declares that 'climate change is a matter of common concern to humankind, as the climate is an essential condition for sustaining life on Earth'. Similarly, the UN Framework Convention on Climate Change (UNFCC, 1992) states that 'change in the Earth's climate and its effects are a matter of common concern to mankind'. The Convention to Combat Desertification (1994) likewise recognises in its preamble that the growth of desertification is of 'urgent concern to the international community'. Finally, the Paris Agreement (2016), which seeks to limit global warming, reaffirms the 'recognition that climate change is an area of common interest and concern for mankind'.

According to the International Treaty on Plant Genetic Resources for Food and Agriculture (2001), 'these [genetic] resources are a matter of common interest and concern for all countries, especially those that depend, to a large extent, on plant genetic resources obtained from elsewhere for food and agriculture' (Preamble, para. 3). However, the Treaty only placed 64 plants under its protection, avoiding use of the concept of 'common concern' in its regulatory provisions.[75] Likewise, the preamble to the UNESCO Convention for the Safeguarding of the Intangible Cultural Heritage (2003) acknowledges 'the universal will and common concern to safeguard the intangible cultural

72 Shelton 2009: 36–38.
73 Cottier et al. 2014: 299.
74 Boer 2014: 297.
75 Halewood et al. 2013.

heritage of humanity', encompassing all knowledge and practices related to nature (art. 2, para. 2).[76]

The legal instruments invoking 'common concern' did not, however, develop systems of institutional stewardship for the relevant common resources. Ultimately, the principles of 'common heritage' and 'common care' were weakened, as initially radical ideas were put to the service of individual interests – interests that, having harvested resources decades earlier under colonial principles, now claim an oligopoly over universal resources in the name of progress, wielding technological superiority as a weapon.

Nevertheless, numerous issues of common concern fall within the scope of common, community, or general interests, subject to universal oversight. As Gentian Zyberi notes, 'the broader discussion about the emergence and protection of 'community interests' is neither theoretical nor utopian, since community interests are already being enforced at international and regional levels'[77] in various domains such as collective security, shared natural resources, and world heritage.

The promotion of humanity's general interests remains fragmented and dependent on state consent, leaving significant gaps. Community or general interests are under constant pressure from the tension between interference with state sovereignty and the urgent need to ensure the sustainability of global resources and to defend the development of universal commons against new enclosures. These interests carry the promise of transforming international law into a system serving collective rather than purely national purposes – though this promise has yet to translate into universally enforceable norms. To address contemporary global challenges, international law must transcend a purely bilateralist model and develop robust community-oriented structures capable of effectively upholding the general interests.[78]

Community interests are associated with the 'emerged consensus that international law is no longer directed exclusively at the governance of interstate bilateral relations, but protects certain fundamental values of the international community as a whole'.[79] *Jus cogens* norms and *erga omnes* obligations form the backbone of an international community that, to some extent, shares common values and goals. Yet, as Besson argues, states often pursue – and should pursue – both individual and collective interests, whether domestic

76 Cottier et al. 2014.
77 Zyberi (2021: 312) with reference to Simma 1994.
78 Gaja 2012.
79 Hofbauer 2022.

or global. The legitimacy of international law, however, cannot simply be presumed; it must be identified and justified.[80]

Article 1(4) of the UN Charter may hold the key to translating the vague notions of 'common concern' and 'common interests' into concrete legal meaning, as all states have agreed that the United Nations shall serve as 'the centre for harmonising the actions of nations in the attainment of common ends'. These ends, are inherently associated with the management of universal commons, as their just administration requires the cultivation of friendly relations based on the principle of equal rights and the self-determination of peoples, the adoption of measures to strengthen universal peace, and the promotion of international cooperation in addressing global economic, social, cultural, and humanitarian challenges – alongside the encouragement of respect for human rights (art. 1, para. 1–3).

80 Besson 2018.

CHAPTER 4

The Critical Ambiguity: *Res Nullius* or *Res Communis*?

> A century ago it was unimaginable that people would buy water to drink. In a century's time it is quite expectable that people will buy their daily oxygen.

If we are to make sense of the blurred boundaries between goods, resources, and spaces that belong to everyone and those that belong to no one, we must focus on the conceptual content of the terms *res communis* and *res nullius*. Goods, spaces, and resources that exist outside the territorial sovereignty of the state are susceptible to appropriation and exploitation by those who possess the technological, economic, and political capacity and power to act first.

Common spaces – particularly the oceans and outer space – are described as non-state spaces (*terra nullius*), or as spaces outside state sovereignty that belong to everyone (*terra communis*). Thus, they are simultaneously conceived as belonging to all and to no one.[1] According to John Vogler, *res nullius* are 'zones or resources which, by their nature, do not or cannot be subject to sovereign jurisdiction'.[2] The exercise of power and exploitation stems from a sense of legitimisation arising from a collective belief that such action is permissible. As Kathryn Milun astutely observes:

> In international law, *res* and *terra nullius* show how empty space functions as a powerful spatial imaginary behind doctrines that overtly describe domains of public space belonging to all earth's citizens, even as they covertly enable these domains to be treated as if they belonged to no one.[3]

The theoretical paradigm based on Grotius's work influenced the idea of legally empty zones in nature – spaces beyond any societal or political relations. If Grotius heralded a new era for global common spaces through the principle of free ocean navigation, another 'Grotian moment' – a paradigm shift – may be imminent.[4] The postulate that nature is a 'homogeneous and

---

1 For a thorough analysis of the concepts, see Cogolati 2020: 133–153.
2 Vogler 2000: 2.
3 Milun 2011: 9.
4 Falk 1983: 272; Vogler 2016: 174.

 HTTPS://DOI.ORG/10.1163/9789004764118-005

empty region' has proved a powerful foundation for perpetual appropriation, thereby resisting and contradicting the principle of the commons. In fact, it has been the main argument used to legitimise the ongoing appropriation and exploitation by those claiming it as a 'natural right'.

The ambiguity of the terms *terra/res nullius* and *terra/res communis*, and their legal signification, has trapped global common goods, resources, and spaces between two opposing possibilities: on the one hand, they are accessible to all but not subject to appropriation; on the other, they belong to no one yet may be appropriated by the first actor – or whoever possesses the requisite technological capacity. Falling within the category of appropriation may thus lead to exclusive exploitation rights, whereas guarantees of free access may prompt regulations that condition exploitation and promote sustainability. These concepts therefore oscillate between extremes, without offering a stable legal basis for ensuring the sustainability of common resources.

For instance, the bounty of the oceans – a *res communis* – is constantly depleted as it becomes open prey for whoever can seize it.[5] Examining examples of resources placed beyond state sovereignty reveals that while the open sea and its seabed and subsoil are *res communis*, the living and mineral resources they contain (fish, minerals, etc.) are *res nullius,* subject to neo-colonial-style appropriation – either through power and technology or, more r-arely, via licences and regulated exploitation under international supervision. Terrestrial wild fauna and flora are similarly treated as *res nullius*, open to appropriation and commercialisation unless locally protected. Industrial w aste and the harmful consequences of its careless disposal offer a reverse example: they return to the international community as *res communis*, calling upon it to manage these consequences collectively.

Ultimately, both *res nullius* and *res communis* are subject to unrestricted exploitation unless specific legislation creates sustainable protective boundaries. Whereas the concept of unitary empty space once served to extend the sovereignty of colonial powers until the 1930s, a modified version now enables powerful multinational corporations to expand their extractive activities th-rough the apparatus of state authority. Yet, as Alexandre Kiss has argued, some common spaces and resources are not *res nullius* and therefore cannot be subject to any form of state appropriation.[6]

5 Vogler 2000: 4.

6 Kiss 1985: 423. See also: ICJ, *Fisheries Jurisdiction Case* (*UK v. Iceland*), ICJ Rep. 1974, Opinion of Judge de Castro.

In Roman law, *res nullius*, as we have seen, was linked to the projection of the divine onto Earth. Later, with the rise of colonial relations – that is, with the emergence of international law concerning global resources – the unappropriated common resources remained within the archaic realm of proto-property. The history of the commons is, in many ways, a history of resistance to their reduction into the category of *res nullius*.[7]

This oscillation between *res nullius* and *res communis* reflects the persistent inability to restrain economic interests and to achieve universal management of the commons. As noted in Chapter 3, the gradual and sporadic adoption of the concepts of the 'common heritage of mankind' and the 'common concern' of states invigorated international debate and supplied it with legal, political, and moral arguments. Yet, the premise of shared responsibility has always been marked by ambiguity: does it refer to 'common ownership' or to 'joint management' in the 'common interest'? The ambiguity extends to procedures, mechanisms, and sanctions – namely, who decides what, and according to which rules, in the name of 'stewardship'.

The growing complexity of human activity has made it increasingly clear that global resources cannot be entirely separated from state sovereignty.[8] The question, therefore, remains: Which universal commons can be regulated by international law, and what legal relationships exist among the relevant subjects? The following sections examine several resources, spaces, and goods of universal significance that belong to everyone, yet are paradoxically often accessible only to a few.

1 Sharing Nature: Water and Air

If human dignity is intrinsically tied to life in a healthy environment, then human rights extend to the protection of nature,[9] the home of the living biosphere. As the International Court of Justice (ICJ) has affirmed:

> The environment is not an abstraction but represents the living space, the quality of life and the very health of human beings, including generations unborn. The existence of the general obligation of States to ensure that activities within their jurisdiction and control respect the environment of other

7 Milun 2011: 113.
8 Brown Weiss 2014: 1.
9 Daly & May 2016.

> States or of areas beyond national control is now part of the corpus of international law relating to the environment.[10]

Nevertheless, the legal norms governing common resources often fail to account for geographical peculiarities or ecological needs, and thus fall short of ensuring effective regulation and protection.[11] States, for their part, must strive to balance economic development and environmental preservation.[12]

Two diametrically opposed perspectives shape the debate on the exploitation of natural resources. One holds that such resources are inexhaustible and that their exploitation cannot threaten life itself, since human civilisation exists apart from nature and measures its 'success' by taming it (*frontier ethics*). The other contends that resources are largely finite, that humankind is part of nature, and that true 'success' lies in cooperating with nature, which is itself a precondition of life (*sustainable ethics*).[13]

Many states perceive nature as a common good, but interpretations differ depending on development models, legal frameworks, and methods of exploitation – all framed under the ambiguous goal of 'sustainable development'.[14] The term remains undefined and subject to competing interpretations, not only in theory but also in policy and practice. Since the late twentieth century, three pillars of sustainable development have emerged, regulating the global economy, promoting social inclusion, and safeguarding the environment.[15]

The concept was formulated in the Brundtland Commission's report 'Our Common Future' (1987): 'Sustainable development is development that meets the needs of the present without compromising the ability of future generations to meet their own needs'.[16] A few years later, the Commission on Global Governance's report 'Our Global Neighborhood' (1995) identified sustainable development as a global goal intrinsically linked to human rights, justice, and social security.[17] As Mann Borgese notes, sustainable development is a necessary condition for the common heritage of humankind with respect to Earth's total natural wealth. Natural resources as a whole should therefore not be

10 ICJ, *Legality of the Threat or Use of Nuclear Weapons, Advisory Opinion*, 8.7.1996, para. 29.
11 Ranganathan 2019: 591.
12 ICJ, *Gabčíkovo-Nagymaros Dam Case* (*Hungary v. Slovakia*), 25.9.1997, and *Pulp Mills on the River Uruguay Case* (*Argentina v. Uruguay*), 20.4.2010.
13 See: Matthew Fischer, *Environmental ethics*, University of Minnesota, at <http://bit.ly/3G93riD>.
14 Adelman 2017: 188.
15 Khoshnava et al. 2019.
16 For the report's conclusions, see <www.un-documents.net/our-common-future.pdf>.
17 See <https://www.gdrc.org/u-gov/global-neighbourhood/chap1.htm>. See also Bosselmann 2017.

viewed as 'belonging' to humankind, but rather as requiring stewardship by civil society, social movements, and governance institutions at the local, national, regional, and global levels through cooperative relationships.[18]

The way concepts are framed plays a pivotal role in determining their meaning and significance for different stakeholders, shaping their political and legal interpretation and implementation. Equality and development – especially in relation to environmental protection, climate change, and environmental rights – are understood differently within the frameworks of the Global North and the Global South. These frameworks usually crystallise during negotiations involving international organisations or social movements seeking to establish policies and laws. As often, political and economic interests – or ideology – drive their formation.[19]

The development of environmental law has largely proceeded *à la carte*, selecting from among competing possibilities. Although cosmopolitan in aspiration, it has not taken bold steps beyond state sovereignty and private property. Natural resources are not treated as components of a single common resource ultimately shared by all states. Yet the ultimate beneficiaries – the end users, the commoners – are people: an innumerable and ever-changing multitude that constitutes mankind, in the present and across time.

The natural resources comprising the global ecosystem are central to efforts to mitigate climate change, both within and beyond national borders. Despite measures adopted by certain states, scientific studies reveal an alarming trend: key parameters essential for sustaining life are approaching critical thresholds.

In 2010, the UN Secretary-General Ban Ki-moon urged the international community to confront the persistent threats posed by air pollution, stressing the need for decisive measures to reverse the deterioration of natural resources. In a comprehensive assessment of political shortcomings, he emphasised:[20]

> Increasing strains and crises in recent years point to the deterioration of the natural environment. The changing climate is one key manifestation. We are reaching – and increasingly overstepping – planetary boundaries. Efforts to achieve the Millennium Development Goals and other social and economic targets are hampered by the inability to agree on decisive, coordinated action in national and multilateral fora. This inability reveals the weaknesses of our governance structures and our outdated development models. It shows the

18 Mann Borgese 1998: 188.
19 Voss 2020.
20 Folke & Gunderson 2010: 43. On 'global sustainability' see also: Bosselmann 2017.

limits of our current approach, which continues to focus on individual symptoms rather than on the causes and their interrelationships.

The terms 'climate change' or 'climate crisis' encapsulate the urgent predicament confronting our planet.[21] This emergency includes persistent air, soil, and water pollution; deforestation and desertification; and the alarming loss of biodiversity – echoing the 'tragedy of the commons' described by Hardin in 1968. This phenomenon reflects a profound failure of the international capitalist and extractive system, as the global market struggles to internalise the external costs it imposes on society, particularly upon those who depend on shared resources.[22] While cooperation among nations could address this common challenge, it has yet to generate a shared political ethos and a coordinated regulatory framework capable of safeguarding the global ecosystem.

[*Nature in Crisis: The Anthropocene*]
Increasingly, the term *Anthropocene* is used to describe a new epoch in Earth's history, in which for the first time human beings became a determining factor in natural processes. Who can deny that human activity has warmed the atmosphere, polluted water and land, extracted vast quantities of natural resources, and profoundly damaged the atmosphere, oceans, and biosphere?[23] Powerful states and corporations continue to deplete non-human life and natural resources, undermining the regeneration of the global ecosystem. The *planetary emergency*, resulting from the cumulative effects of unsustainable extraction and irreversible pollution, highlights the need for international care and for the formulation of legal, political, and moral arguments that recognise the Earth as a complex system – 'a global ecological commons supporting and shared by all life'.[24] These arguments aim to legitimise the protection of universal natural commons and their commoners, pointing towards a shared legal framework for their preservation. The Anthropocene is thus not only a historical period but, above all, a measure of the density of human interventionism.

In recent decades, international discourse has often tended towards cataclysmic predictions of the world's end, which are not always constructive in

21 As scientific studies are constantly documenting. For example: Ripple et al. 2019; Pörtner, Roberts et al. 2022; World Meteorological Organisation 2026.

22 Pollution, for example, is a by-product of private companies that make a profit, but it is dispersed and causes harm to common goods such as air and water. Within market logic, a company may be required to pay for this damage under the 'polluter pays' principle, yet this does not correspond to the actual cost of repairing the environmental harm.

23 Zalasiewicz et al. 2008.

24 Taylor 2023: 141.

identifying the necessary conditions for protecting nature. Yet certain reliable criteria scientifically define the planetary danger zone. The planetary boundaries – commonly accepted, interdependent indicators essential to the maintenance of life – are as follows:

1. Climate change, i.e., the concentration of CO_2 in the atmosphere,
2. The nitrogen and phosphorus cycles,
3. The reduction of biodiversity,
4. Ocean acidification,
5. The depletion of stratospheric ozone,
6. The overconsumption of freshwater,
7. Land-use change and desertification,
8. Chemical pollution,
9. Atmospheric contamination from aerosols.

Changes in these indicators are characteristic of the *Anthropocene*, and the first three now appear to have exceeded sustainable limits. Consequently, a central question must be answered at the global level: What are the non-negotiable conditions that humankind must respect to avoid the risk of irreparable damage or destruction, regionally or globally?[25]

Human activities influence these preconditions, and their regulation itself constitutes an additional variable determining the threshold of the danger zone – the point at which conditions become highly unfavourable to life. This complexity is heightened by an unprecedented state of uncertainty, which demands solutions that exceed current institutional capacities and challenge 'some of the most fundamental ideas in contemporary law and governance'.[26] A UN-commissioned study projects these indicators across all continents, assuming that human activity continues at current rates of exploitation, consumption, and development. It concludes that within a single generation, many universal resources – such as fisheries, rainforests, freshwater, and arable land – may be locally depleted or destroyed.[27] Crucially, many climatic constants are not reversible. Once melted, the polar ice caps cannot be restored, and the oceans cannot readily regain their capacity to absorb carbon dioxide.[28]

Scientific findings must therefore provide reliable data and expertise on the limits of environmental resilience and inform sound policies for protecting and sustaining the planetary ecosystem. Sustainability requires enhanced collaboration in observation and analysis, adherence to scientific standards, gr-

25 Rockström et al. 2009: 32.
26 Kim & Kotzé 2020.
27 Fischer et al. 2018.
28 See: IPPC 2022 detailed report, at Pörtner, Roberts et al. 2022.

eater public awareness, and, ultimately, cooperative approaches to comprehensive crisis management.

Changes in the atmosphere, land, the water cycle and oceans will displace large segments of the human population, compelling many to seek new habitats beyond their national borders.[29] Can the international community's existing legal arsenal for environmental protection meet the challenges of our time? According to Edith Brown Weiss, humankind faces two unprecedented situations:

> The first is that we are entering a new geological epoch of the *Anthropocene*, in which we humans are a significant force of change. The second is the emergence of a kaleidoscopic world, with millions, if not several billion, participants creating initiatives and dynamism from the bottom up. Our Earth has become a global commons. In conjunction, actions taken worldwide are affecting its resilience and integrity. Increasingly, we are facing problems with profound long-term implications for the wellbeing of future generations. The changes can be rapid. Bottom-up actions can collide with top-down efforts to control them. In this complex, dynamic setting, shared values and generally accepted legal principles will be central to the stability of the international system.[30]

The current state of the environmental crisis indicates that measures to reverse global warming and pollution remain exceptional rather than central, given the prevailing priorities of free trade, perpetual economic growth, and market hegemony. This hierarchy is explicit in Principle 12 of the Rio Declaration (1992), which stipulates that measures to address climate change should not serve as a covert barrier to international trade. Similarly, during the 1994 World Trade Organization (WTO) negotiations, there was no discussion of a regulatory hierarchy to resolve potential conflicts between environmental protection rules and free trade.[31] Consequently, efforts to mitigate climate destabilisation remain subordinated to market imperatives and the pursuit of profit (see Chapter 6.4).

The *Anthropocene* compels a re-examination of the traditional categories of legal subjectivity, prompting a redefinition of human civilisation's relation with its natural environment. It highlights the need to determine which goods,

---

29 See: Raisson 2010. The author set out concerns and scientific findings on climate, displacement, and environmental disruption, as well as on nutrition, demography, water, energy, and human security.

30 Brown Weiss 2014: 16.

31 Klein 2015.

resources, and spaces belong to everyone. Ultimately, it calls for 'a radical reframing of subjectivity, both human and inhuman'.[32] Anthropocentrism must therefore expand to include and presuppose all living beings and their environments. A dignity-based approach could counterbalance the corporate conception of humanity that obscures individual responsibility and silences perspectives favouring holistic conceptions of human beings, non-human species, and the natural world.[33]

[*The Sea, Lakes, and Rivers*]

The UN Convention on the Law of the Sea establishes rules for the protection of the planet's largest integrated ecosystem: the sea, the seabed, and the associated subsoil. Regarding the protection of the marine environment, the Treaty establishes an obligation to prevent, reduce, and control pollution (arts. 192–234).

Despite the adoption of environmental protection regulations by bodies such as the International Maritime Organization (IMO), the uncontrolled use of the open seas as dumping grounds has not been effectively curbed in practice.[34] While all states possess a conditional right to dispose of waste in the open sea, more developed, industrialised nations tend to exercise this right disproportionately, resulting in higher levels of pollution than in other regions. The initial restrictions, established under the 1972 Convention for the Prevention of Marine Pollution by Dumping of Wastes and Other Matter, proved inadequate.[35] It was after years of advocacy by Greenpeace and other organisations that prohibitions on dumping nuclear and chemical waste at sea were adopted.[36] The 1996 London Protocol (amended in 2006) substantially revised the Convention by introducing comprehensive bans and permitting only narrowly defined activities. In 1973 IMO adopted the MARPOL Convention that aims at preventing and minimising pollution from ships – both acci-

32 Birrell 2023: 52.

33 Daly & Lupin 2023.

34 IMO, Revised Guidelines for the Identification and Designation of Particularly Sensitive Sea Areas, Res A.982(24), 6.2.2006.

35 See also Goal No. 14 of the United Nations Sustainable Development Goals that underscores the need to reduce and ultimately eliminate marine pollution to repair the significant damage already done.

36 Vogler 2012: 62–64.

dental pollution and that from routine operations.[37] Other regional instruments also aim at combating sea pollution from land or sea.[38]

These instruments set out the legal framework governing sea pollution. Normative weakness allows the continued intensification of marine pollution from toxic waste and other effluents, as well as the accumulation of plastic debris and microfibers across the world's seas.[39] The spread of plastic waste on land and at sea inflicts severe harm on ecosystems, while the energy consumption required for ongoing plastic production contributes to further environmental degradation and the depletion of natural resources.[40] International law, however, still lacks effective norms to prevent or eliminate the harm caused by plastic pollution.

Protecting underground moisture, aquatic ecosystems, drinking water, and irrigation resources is critical to nature and human life. Water surfaces are also vital areas for navigation. Often, lakes, rivers, and underground streams lie within the territories of adjacent states, as they cross or demarcate borders. The transboundary nature of these resources is thus a defining characteristic. Interdependence in their use creates obligations of shared care and management among the commoner-states at the regional or bilateral level.[41] The 1992 Water Convention[42] (in effect since 1996) and the 1997 Convention on the Law of Non-Navigational Uses of International Watercourses (in effect since 2014) outline obligations regarding information exchange, pollution prevention, avoidance of resource depletion, and the promotion of reasonable and equitable utilisation, due diligence, and collaboration across extensive regions – with the notable exception of the United States. Yet, these measures remain

37 The International Convention for the Prevention of Pollution from Ships was adopted by the IMO in 1973, amended by a protocol in 1978, entered into force in 1983, and has been amended thereafter.

38 Among others: the 1992 Convention for the Protection of the Marine Environment of the North-East Atlantic unified and updated two earlier conventions: the 1972 Oslo Convention (on dumping) and the 1974 Paris Convention (on land-based pollution), as well as the 1976 Protocol for the Prevention of Pollution of the Mediterranean Sea by Dumping, one of several protocols under the broader 1976 Barcelona Convention for the Protection of the Marine Environment and Coastal Areas of the Mediterranean.

39 *When the mermaids cry: The great plastic tide*, September 2019, at <http://plastic-pollution.org/>.

40 Heinrich Böll Stiftung 2021.

41 For instance, see the Great Lakes Water Quality Agreement signed in 1972 between the United States and Canada, or the Indus Waters Treaty signed between India and Pakistan in 1962.

42 Convention on the Protection and Use of Transboundary Watercourses and International Lakes.

partial solutions, as state collaboration in managing international rivers and lakes continues to be inadequate.

[*Air Space and Atmosphere*]

The atmosphere – the layer of gases surrounding Earth's surface – sustains all forms of life and thus constitutes a global space that contains vital substances for humankind and wildlife alike. Since the early twentieth century, technological advances have enabled the operation of flying machines in this domain, prompting states to regulate the use of their airspace as a vertical extension of sovereignty. At the First International Conference on Aeronautics (Paris, 1910), the concept of 'innocent passage' for overflights was adopted.

In the years that followed, the theory of freedom of the air gave way to the principle of sovereignty. The Chicago Convention of 1944 established the definitive framework for international air traffic: 'The contracting States recognise that every State has complete and exclusive sovereignty over the airspace above its territory' (art. 1). It also created the International Civil Aviation Organization (ICAO), which three years later became a UN agency. ICAO, in coordination with its 193 member states, develops international rules governing all aspects of civil aviation – from safety and navigation to environmental protection. It also regulates airspace zones and international air traffic through Flight Information Regions, each managed by a state responsible for its operational control. This arrangement represents one of the few examples of a functional universal commons under a centralised administrative regime.

In 1957, when the Soviet Union launched the first satellite, outer space became legally linked to the atmosphere. It is reasonable to anticipate that, in the future, both the upper and lower space will increasingly serve as zones for transportation and public activity – the former through satellite operations, the latter through commercial drones and, potentially, flying vehicles. Such developments will inevitably challenge the legal understanding of national airspace, reinforcing notions of 'technological inevitability' and obscuring questions of commoning.[43]

The atmosphere is also a repository for pollutants that alter the climate – the system regulating temperature, precipitation, and frost, with direct effects on ecosystems and human productivity. Together, these elements form a global common resource and space, essential to the functioning of other commons dependent on atmospheric stability.[44] The quality of the atmosphere and seas, as well as the stability of the climate, is thus vital to sustaining life.

---

43 Zenz & Powles 2024.

44 Soroos 1997; Edenhofer, Flachsland & Lorentz 2012.

Given that pollution readily crosses borders, the world has witnessed extreme and irreversible events, such as the Chernobyl disaster in 1986 and Fukushima in 2011.

The 1979 Convention on Long-Range Transboundary Air Pollution (following the 1972 Stockholm Conference) entered into force in 1983 and was later supplemented by eight protocols. It was the first international text to set binding commitments to limit gaseous emissions – initially a response to acid rain.

Among the most successful legal instruments for atmospheric protection was the 1987 Montreal Protocol to the 1985 Vienna Convention for the Protection of the Ozone Layer (effective in 1992). Despite early shortcomings in enforceability,[45] the Protocol achieved remarkable success only because nearly all states joined it, fostering behavioural change and global awareness of ozone depletion.[46] Coordinated by the Ozone Secretariat, its implementation is supported by the Multilateral Fund and by a system of expert bodies that assesse scientific and financial needs.[47]

With global warming and air pollution now a central concern, international efforts under the UN culminated in the 1992 Framework Convention on Climate Change (UNFCCC, effective in 1994). This framework, though groundbreaking, has been marked by limited progress and persistent failures to align legal norms and enforcement with the core principle that 'without ecological sustainability, in the long run there can be no economic sustainability'.[48]

Further developments include the 1997 Kyoto Protocol (effective in 2005, amended in Doha in 2012), which set limits on six major greenhouse gases, and the 2015 Paris Agreement, a non-binding but ambitious accord aiming to keep global temperature rise below 2°C – ideally below 1.5°C. It rests on the principle of 'common but differentiated responsibilities' (Arts. 2.2, 4.3, 4.14) and depends heavily on stable financial contributions,[49] though it lacks a global enforcement mechanism capable of imposing policies and sanctions. Despite its promise, the framework has thus far failed to reverse the upward trajectory of global temperatures.[50]

Compliance with UNFCCC commitments remains an ongoing issue. Initiatives such as the UN-REDD Programme and REDD+ seek to combat deforestation and support carbon-reduction efforts, for example, through the Amazon Fund, revitalised under President Lula da Silva's renewed environmental a-

45 Soroos 2005: 44.
46 Scherhorn 2012.
47 Cf. <https://ozone.unep.org/institutions>.
48 Montini 2014: 282.
49 Art. 5, with reference to art. 4.1.d of the UNFCCC.
50 World Meteorological Organization 2022.

genda in Brazil. Regarding air pollution, which kills at least 5.7 million people each year, the 2025 World Bank report states that 'China's *war on pollution* proves that change is possible'.[51]

The International Law Commission has explored the legal dimensions of atmospheric protection and inter-state relations in this dynamic domain. The Special Rapporteur Shinya Murase identified three main challenges: transboundary air pollution in the troposphere, ozone depletion in the stratosphere, and climate change. His guidelines addressed:

- The atmosphere as both a physical entity and a medium for transportation and flight;
- Policy objectives for combating atmospheric degradation, acknowledging the interdependence of the atmosphere, the sea, and biodiversity;
- The legal status of the atmosphere as a natural resource distinct from 'airspace' and tied to states' sovereign rights.

Murase proposed recognising the atmosphere as a *shared concern of humankind* – vital for life and wellbeing, as well as for marine and terrestrial ecosystems. He concluded that it is 'the protection of the atmosphere, which is a common concern of humankind, and not the atmosphere itself', and, for reasons of effectiveness, that it should be linked to *erga omnes* state obligations, rather than treated as *res communis* or part of the 'common heritage of humankind'.[52]

To mitigate the greenhouse effect, special attention has been placed in recent decades not only on lowering production but also on CO_2 storage. While carbon capture and storage (CCS) technologies now make it possible to sequester CO_2 underground, this solution raises further concerns about using the subsoil – another global resource – as a shared repository for vast quantities of potentially hazardous material.[53] The pressing question, therefore, is how the international community might develop common practices and standardised controls to minimise damage to the natural environment and biodiversity – both indispensable to human life and wellbeing.

---

51 Damania et al. 2025: xviii, 109.

52 Report of the International Law Commission, Sixty-Sixth Session 2014, paras. 77–121, Protection of the Atmosphere (Shinya Murase), para. 83, at <https://bit.ly/3kqBTHO>.

53 For more on this technology, see <https://www.globalccsinstitute.com/about/>.

2 Seeds, Plants, and Animals: The Unique and Precious Biodiversity

Seeds are essential for cultivating the next crops in the continuous chain of food production. Access to seeds and their management at the global, regional, and local levels are therefore critical to the economy and the food chain. As early as 1905, the Polish-American farmer David Lubin, reacting to the seed cartels of his time, founded the International Institute for Agriculture in Rome. He played a pioneering role in defending growers' rights to the seeds they produce, countering the patent rights of powerful corporations and leaving an important legacy for subsequent generations of growers.[54]

Today, multinational corporations claim ownership of new species derived from genetically modified seeds, legitimising the idea of nature as empty space and severing these life forms from the complex social, cultural, and ecological relations to which they were historically bound. Seed biotechnology, as a profit-driven tool, has created a robust enclosure around these resources, dictating the evolution of crops according to market imperatives rather than the requirements of a healthy and resilient food system. Some courts have begun to assert that such practices are incompatible with the overarching legal objective of fostering biodiversity for humanity.[55]

One of the most blatant examples of the appropriation of seed commons concerns the actions of multinational giants such as BASF, DuPont, Dow Chemical Company, Bayer-Monsanto, and Syngenta,[56] which in practice promote the sale of mutated, non-reproducing seeds. Many farmers have been forced to pay royalties to multinationals after discovering that their fields were contaminated by a neighbour's genetically modified crops. Genetically modified seeds are also economically unviable for small-scale or poor growers, who must purchase them each year, whereas traditional cultivation allows the production and reuse of one's own seeds.[57] Consequently, in many parts of the world, agricultural productivity is being stifled by seed monopolies. The aggressive corporate monopolisation of seed markets in favour of intensive industrial agriculture has placed severe pressure on food access, leading to the economic ruin of thousands of small farmers.

The commercialisation of genetically modified seeds has resulted in their widespread dissemination without corresponding certification, ensuring the

54 Mooney 2011.

55 Stephenson 2010; International Monsanto Tribunal 2017.

56 'Big 6 Pesticide and GMO Corporations', at <https://bit.ly/3lowkLC>.

57 Regarding Monsanto's practices, see the conclusions of the quasi-court in Chapter 5a.

absence of health risks. Although it has not been definitively proven that the use of such seeds is harmful, the challenge lies in the absence of conclusive and independent scientific evidence – an absence often attributed to the systematic obstruction of research under corporate influence.[58]

Another manifestation of this usurpation of biodiversity is the corporate appropriation of rights to substances derived from the flora of developing countries. Numerous cases of 'biopiracy' – the commercial exploitation of naturally occurring biochemicals or genetic materials through patents – limit their future use and deny fair compensation to the communities of origin. These biological resources are typically found in developing countries and constitute the raw materials for traditional knowledge, managed and refined by local communities.

As observed by Boaventura de Sousa Santos, 'the interface between the traditional and modern scientific knowledge of biodiversity is a social field of bitter political and legal disputes'.[59] For example, brazzein, a fruit native to West Africa, contains a natural sweetener that could revolutionise the food industry. US companies are already preparing for large-scale production of brazzein without securing rights from its countries of origin.[60] Similar legal controversies surround turmeric, basmati rice, and the neem tree in India, where Western corporations have commercialised traditional resources without attributing rights to their original custodians.[61] Common knowledge is thus freely appropriated, transformed into commercial products, and divorced from its community of origin. A comparable case concerns quinoa, a crop indigenous to Peru and Bolivia. In 2011, the Bolivian government declared all intellectual property rights to quinoa to be the exclusive property of the Bolivian people,[62] while India established a national database of all forms of traditional knowledge (see Chapter 4.8.2).

The 1990 Agreement on Trade-Related Aspects of Intellectual Property Rights (TRIPS) obliges WTO member states to guarantee intellectual property rights over plant protection. It conceptualises nature as an 'empty space' and treats biodiversity and biotechnology as the subjects of private ownership. This framework reveals an inherently colonial relationship with nature's genetic resources, conceived as *terra vacantis*.[63] Consequently, the productive

58 See, for example, the 'Monsanto papers': <https://usrtk.org/monsanto-papers/>.
59 Santos 2020: 566.
60 Cf. <https://bit.ly/30iSaC4>.
61 Cf. <https://bit.ly/3dNVU9L>.
62 Cf. <https://bit.ly/34ms74V>.
63 Milun 2011: 33.

elements of the natural environment were excluded from the Agreement's regulatory protection. Over several decades, the global seed supply has shifted steadily from the developing South to the industrialised North.

In response to the threat of seed extinction or appropriation, protective initiatives have emerged. The Svalbard Global Seed Vault in Norway, which stores over one million seed samples under permafrost conditions, was created as part of the International Convention on Plant Genetic Resources network.[64] The largest seed bank, however, is the Millennium Seed Bank in West Sussex, England. Numerous local and regional initiatives have also arisen, such as Navdanya in India, which enables thousands of farmers to access and exchange seeds, fostering a shared genetic commons.[65] Seed banks may serve various purposes: preserving seeds from extinction, ensuring national or individual food security, resupplying farmers, or advancing genetic crop improvement.

The United Nations has been active in the field of biodiversity protection, producing numerous legal instruments. Chief among these is the Convention on Biological Diversity (CBD), adopted at the 1992 Rio Summit. The Convention seeks to conserve biodiversity, promote its sustainable use, and ensure the fair and equitable sharing of benefits arising from genetic resources. It is the first legal instrument to recognise the principle of free access and benefit-sharing of common resources. Each state acts as custodian of the genetic resources within its territory, entering into bilateral agreements with companies for access and use, thus paving the way for the concession of patent rights over biodiversity.[66] The Convention was later supplemented by the 2001 Cartagena Protocol (effective 2003) on genetically modified organisms, addressing human health, transboundary movements, and the precautionary principle, and by the 2010 Nagoya Protocol (effective 2014) on equitable benefit-sharing.

The 2001 International Treaty on Plant Genetic Resources for Food and Agriculture complements the CBD but stops short of establishing an international supervisory authority. It recognises the collective rights of cultivators, rather than private ownership over seeds, viewing farmers as a 'traditional class of overseers supervising the universal genetic commons'.[67] The Treaty created a protective reserve of genetic material from 64 staple crops – includ-

---

64 Cf. <www.croptrust.org/our-work/svalbard-global-seed-vault/>.
65 Cf. <https://www.navdanya.org/>.
66 Filner 1998: 149.
67 Milun 2011: 35.

ing wheat, rice, potato, and maize – essential for global food security. Other states are granted access to this genetic pool, since virtually all countries depend on plants of foreign origin.[68] If economic benefits arise from the use of such seeds, a portion must be contributed to a common fund supporting growers and ensuring equitable access. However, restrictive conditions have rendered this mechanism largely ineffective in practice.

Despite the universal recognition of seeds as the 'common heritage of mankind', the Treaty provides no effective safeguard against multinational corporations that appropriate rights to new seed varieties. When plant genomes travel via pollen and insects, so do corporate claims – translating directly into profit. Thus, the Treaty preserves the biodiversity of the past as *res communis*, while leaving future varieties vulnerable to market appropriation as *res nullius* – the property of whoever claims them first.

The Treaty has been strongly criticised by the 'Genetic Commons Initiative', which argues that the 'common heritage of mankind' paradigm perpetuates inequalities between the Global North and South, particularly in access to and control of genetic resources. In 2002, in Porto Alegre, 250 organisations drafted a declaration asserting that 'the reservoir of genetic material, in all its forms, is a protected universal commons which may not be appropriated in natural or artificial form by governments, companies or individuals'.[69]

In relation to fauna and ecosystems, the Bonn Convention on the Conservation of Migratory Species (1979, in force 1983) has played a significant role in protecting birds, mammals, fish, and invertebrates that regularly cross national borders. It emphasises international cooperation along entire migratory routes. Its preamble recognises that wild animals are an irreplaceable part of the Earth's natural system and must be preserved for the 'good of humankind'. Similarly, the 1973 Washington Convention on International Trade in Endangered Species of Wild Fauna and Flora (in force 1975) restricts trade in endangered species, while the Ramsar Convention on Wetlands of International Importance (1971, in force 1975) currently covers more than 2,300 wetlands, totalling 2.5 million square kilometres.

A nexus of international inter-governmental organisations, such as the UN Food and Agriculture Organization or the International Union for Conservation of Nature, and non-governmental organisations, such as the World Wild-

68 Important seeds, such as soybeans, were excluded from the list of 64 plants which the Treaty ultimately covered. See: Van den Hurk 2011: 165; Food and Agriculture Organization 2022.

69 Rifkin 2017: 168.

life Fund and the World Resources Institute, seeks to promote the sustainable use of terrestrial and marine resources, although their initiatives have not always proved effective. Controversies persist, particularly regarding large-scale extractive development projects (see Chapter 5.4), where tensions arise between nature conservation and the rights and needs of indigenous and local communities.[70]

At the regional level, the EU adopted in 2011 a Biodiversity Strategy[71] designed to protect wild species and habitats, regenerate ecosystems, promote the sustainable exploitation of land and sea resources, and reverse biodiversity loss. Its principal legal instruments are the Birds Directive (1979) and the Habitats Directive (92/43/EEC), which together created the Natura 2000 network and established special protection zones for the conservation of species.[72]

Despite the gradual elaboration of this legal framework, significant gaps and ambiguities remain. Marine biodiversity, in particular, continues to be inadequately protected, as efforts to regulate overfishing and pollution are sporadic and poorly coordinated. The preservation of oceanic ecosystems – both within and beyond national jurisdiction – requires cohesive international cooperation,[73] which at present is largely limited to isolated fishing regulations and anti-pollution measures.

Aspects of exploitation rights of the states within their EEZs have been discussed in Chapter 3.1. Marine Protected Areas, intended to preserve ecosystems through regulated human activity, may be established within territorial waters or EEZs[74] and, in certain cases, even beyond these boundaries. However, complex economic interests frequently undermine their effectiveness. The large-scale, unregulated capture of millions of tropical fish for private aquariums in Hawaii – even within officially protected zones – illustrates these tensions.[75] Since the mid-2000s, the creation of Ecologically or Biologically Significant Areas and Vulnerable Marine Ecosystems under the CBD has led to a network of monitored high-seas regions, sometimes overlapping with

---

70 The 'Yellowstone Model' of conservation called for removing local communities from protected areas. The expulsion of the Maasai people from Serengeti National Park and the Ngorongoro Conservation Area are such examples.

71 Cf. <http://ec.europa.eu/environment/nature/biodiversity/strategy/index_en.htm>.

72 It also adopted legal rules and recommendations regarding the role of zoos in protecting biodiversity and prohibiting wildlife trade, cf. <https://bit.ly/35pHCd2>.

73 Gjerde et al. 2018.

74 According to the Marine Protection Atlas (Marine Conservation Institute), only 2.9% of the ocean area is in a fully or highly protected area; see <https://mpatlas.org/mpaguide/#128.30428,0@0.44>.

75 Cf. <https://bit.ly/3PwDSMP>.

the protection regimes established by other conventions,[76] such as the 1998 Convention for the Protection of the Marine Environment of the North-East Atlantic or the Convention for Cooperation in the Protection, Management and Development of the Marine and Coastal Environment of the Atlantic Coast of the West and Central Africa Region (Abidjan Convention, 1984). Another important instrument, the Convention for the Conservation of Antarctic Marine Living Resources (1980), employees an ecosystem-based approach to achieve balanced fisheries harvesting, although it has not succeeded in establishing a comprehensive global framework for oceanic biodiversity.[77]

After protracted negotiations within the United Nations, the Agreement under the UNCLOS on the Conservation and Sustainable Use of Marine Biological Diversity of Areas Beyond National Jurisdiction (or High Seas Treaty) was opened for signature in 2023, as stated in Chapter 4.1. This is the first cohesive and legally binding international framework for the protection of marine biodiversity beyond national jurisdiction, with the goal of ensuring conservation, sustainable use, and equitable access to marine genetic resources. The Treaty is expected to initiate global coordination of biodiversity policies and promote the fair exchange of scientific knowledge.

In addition to the normative level, several cooperative mechanisms aim to strengthen global biodiversity governance.[78] The Commission on Genetic Resources for Food and Agriculture, established in 1983 and upgraded in 1995, serves as a permanent FAO forum for discussion and legislative initiatives concerning genetic resources.[79] The Common Oceans Programme – a global alliance of stakeholders – promotes the sustainable use of marine resources and their conservation in areas beyond national jurisdiction.[80]

Despite these international efforts, extractive activities remain the primary driver of biodiversity loss. Industries such as mining, oil and gas extraction, forestry, and industrial agriculture are responsible for up to 90% of global biodiversity decline. Although most extraction takes place in the Global South, the principal drivers of degradation often originate in the Global North.[81] Between 1970 and 2018, an estimated 69% of vertebrate populations disappeared. If global temperatures rise by 2°C, 99% of coral reefs are projected to vanish, while more than 10 million hectares of forest are lost each year.[82]

76 Cf. <https://bit.ly/3PvicAK>.
77 Zou 2022; Meredith et al. 2025.
78 Cf. <https://openknowledge.fao.org/items/e2b8d9c0-2eb3-4a01-b2d6-d0a6007a468c>.
79 See <https://bit.ly/35pHrhS>.
80 Cf. <https://openknowledge.fao.org/items/7a2c1f5f-7bc6-4df2-a60f-948a645e0140>.
81 Dempsey et al. 2024.
82 WWF, Report 2022, at <https://livingplanet.panda.org/en-us/>.

In 2010, the parties to the CBD adopted the Aichi Biodiversity Targets, intended to halt biodiversity loss by 2020. None of the 196 signatory states achieved these goals. Following this failure, governments adopted the Kunming – Montreal Global Biodiversity Framework (COP15, 2022), setting new targets to protect and restore biodiversity and to halt human-induced extinction by 2050.[83] Among its key objectives is the '30×30 target', which aims to protect 30% of the planet's land and sea by 2030. The Framework also commits $30 billion annually to biodiversity protection in developing countries.[84] Although not legally binding, it represents a collaborative, consensus-based approach coordinated by international organisations – particularly the United Nations – and shaped by the active engagement of civil society.

Finally, private-sector initiatives to 'de-extinct' species have drawn significant attention. The US company Colossal Biosciences, for example, aims to decode the dodo's genome and restore the species as a contribution to biodiversity.[85] Yet a critical question arises: How can the industrial 're-creation' of extinct life forms be ethically regulated – or restrained – once technological 'de-extinction' becomes scientifically feasible?

3 Whales: Long–Distance Living Commons

Whales serve as wild fauna regarded as a common resource that may be subject to an appropriation regime favouring those who first locate and harvest them. In other words, whoever first has the technological ability to capture them at sea can exploit them as a commercial product. Under Roman law, whales constituted *res nullius*, a concept now legally described as a hybrid *res communis*. As such, states are required, at the regional level, to regulate their relations concerning research and fishing to preserve the ecosystem while safeguarding their economic interests. Accordingly, they established the International Whaling Commission (IWC),[86] which aims to set out rules governing the competitive behaviour of states and individuals in this field. The preamble of the 1946 Convention for the Regulation of Whaling – the founding text of the IWC – recognises 'the interest of the nations of the world in safeguarding

83 Dempsey et al. 2024: 1–2.

84 COP15, Kunming-Montreal, Dec. 2022, at <https://bit.ly/3VqWDlf>.

85 Cf. <https://colossal.com/dodo/>.

86 It was established in 1946 by fifteen states in implementation of the Convention for the Regulation of Whaling (1946). Today, it has 87 member states; <https://iwc.int/home>. The related North Atlantic Marine Mammal Commission was established in 1992 by the Nordic countries; <https://nammco.no/>.

for future generations the great natural resources represented by the whale stocks', and declares its express aim 'to protect all species of whales from further overfishing'.

From 1960 onwards, the agency's interventions can be considered successful, as states began to adhere to the Commission's directives and decisions. However, a marked increase in overhunting during the 1970s led to a decline in whale populations. In 1986, the Commission imposed a moratorium on hunting specific whale subspecies in particular geographic areas using certain fishing methods. Licences were controlled, and an annual record of whales caught was maintained.[87] The imposition of such a measure by a legally binding act constitutes a rare phenomenon of effective stewardship of the global common resource in international practice, particularly at this scale.

The conduct of certain states that have systematically resumed whaling for commercial purposes under the guise of 'scientific research' has provoked strong international reactions. In 2007, for instance, the organisation Sea Shepherd forcibly stopped a Japanese whaler in the Antarctic that was violating the moratorium. The organisation, together with Australia – the ship's flag state – initiated legal proceedings against Japan, while Japan accused Sea Shepherd of eco-piracy.[88] The case was brought before the ICJ, which held that Japan had violated the Whaling Convention and ordered it to review all whaling permits, upholding Australia's argument.[89] The Court also reaffirmed the need to protect the resource, as enshrined in the 1946 Convention, underlining the need 'to allow a period of time for the recovery in population of certain species that have been decimated'. Referring to the Convention's preamble, the Court recalled that 'increasing the number of whales will permit an increase in those that can be caught without jeopardising this natural resource [...]. It is in the common interest for the whale population to reach the optimum number as quickly as possible [...].'

Thus, the purpose of the Convention is to preserve the resource for the benefit of the fishing industries of the contracting parties, so as to 'provide for the proper conservation of whale stocks and thus make possible the orderly development of the whaling industry'.[90] These regulations are designed to maintain whale populations at levels ensuring profitability for industrial exploitation. However, they fail to address issues of equitable access and utilisation by other stakeholders, such as individuals and scientists interested in

87 Cf. <https://iwc.int/total-catches>.

88 Roeschke 2009.

89 ICJ, *Whaling in the Antarctic* (*Australia v. Japan*), 31.3.2014.

90 ICJ, *Whaling* as above, para. 56.

observing and studying whales. Moreover, the Convention overlooks the essential role of whales in the fragile oceanic ecosystem.

The Sea Shepherd incident demonstrates the elasticity of law in a domain where state sovereignty is unevenly enforced, as well as the ambiguity surrounding the competencies of international organisations in the governance of global common resources. As discussed, Japan, acting as a free-rider on the common resource, accused environmental organisations of piracy. The ICJ, acting as the guardian of the institutional framework governing whaling, ruled that international law – intended to protect a living resource – ultimately tended to favour the whaling industry. This episode highlights how the sea, designated as *res communis*, becomes a shared space subject to multiple and conflicting jurisdictions. The oceans and migratory whales form a dynamic ecosystem in which predators and prey move freely. This complex universal commons is still not adequately recognised as such in law.

In 2019, Japan withdrew from the IWC and fully legalised whaling, claiming that doing so supported communities that traditionally depended on whaling for their livelihood. Nevertheless, other countries that once practised commercial whaling, such as Iceland and Norway, have significantly reduced their activities as a result of the Convention.[91]

There is, however, an additional reason why whales represent an invaluable common resource: their capacity to sequester carbon dioxide and their vital contribution, direct and indirect, to oxygen production. They should, therefore, be valued not primarily as a food resource for humans after death, but as living organisms contributing substantially to the regeneration of the planetary ecosystem.[92]

4 An Existential Commons: The Human Genome

The genetic code is synonymous with life itself. Every human being, and their primary biological component – their genome – constitutes a natural and indeed abundant resource, present in every cell of the human body.[93] The genome is also a source of scientific knowledge, accessible only through collaboration and open sharing of research findings.[94] Decoding the human gen-

---

91 Cf. <http://cnn.it/2Wwpzwg>; <http://on.natgeo.com/2Ko48Ln; <http://on.natgeo. com/3h14uDA>.

92 Chami et al. 2019.

93 Mattei 2011.

94 Evans 2017.

ome has radically reopened the debate on the future of humankind along at least two axes: first, the possibility of isolating genes (for example, those responsible for severe diseases) for therapeutic purposes; and second, the potential to intervene in the genetic code to create mental or physical characteristics chosen by their designers.

The management of the human genome as a commons thus carries a dual significance: first, the pursuit of medical goals achievable only through the participation of all relevant research; and second, the use of knowledge for the benefit of humanity through safeguards that prevent the commodification of life itself.

Bioethical issues are of enormous significance, since arguments supporting the decoding of the genome and the use of its findings can serve either the interests of the human carrier or those of the managing decoder. Where, then, should the ethical regulatory boundary be drawn in genomic interventions? Could open self-monitoring processes be institutionalised as humanity advances in this unprecedented endeavour?

The Human Genome Project (HGP), launched in 1990, constituted a landmark global research effort that ultimately succeeded in decoding the genome through unprecedented international collaboration. At the 1996 Bermuda Summit, leading figures of the international scientific community agreed on a set of revolutionary principles for genome research. From that point onward, research results and knowledge produced were to be shared on public databases within 24 hours of generation. The Bermuda Principles overturned the traditional practice of disseminating scientific results solely through publication in academic journals. This example of knowledge sharing broke down barriers among universities, companies, and research institutes, reshaping relationships in knowledge production and scientific development. It established the practice of immediate communication of research results, which could then be utilised without delay by others.

Thanks to this methodology, HGP itself became a universal commons – a universal knowledge resource and a forum where all stakeholders could contribute to the commons, as genome mapping inherently defines it. The resource is divided into separate components working toward a shared objective, even though they operate under distinct rules (those of public interest and those of commercial profit).

Between 1996 and 1997, several organisations adopted similar approaches in their research. The Human Genome Organisation (HUGO), UNESCO, and the Organisation for Economic Co-operation and Development (OECD) promoted frameworks of principles governing genetic research.

In 1997, UNESCO adopted the Universal Declaration on the Human Genome and Human Rights, the first international – albeit non-binding – instrument to establish rights concerning the genome. Based on the principle of human dignity, the Declaration symbolically recognises the human genome as the 'heritage of mankind' (art. 1) and affirms that 'genetic research and its results must be accessible to all' (art. 12). Similarly, the preamble to the Convention on Human Rights and Biomedicine (Oviedo, 1997/1999) of the Council of Europe stresses 'the need for international cooperation so that all humanity may enjoy the benefits of biology and medicine'.

In the same vein, HUGO's Ethics Committee has adopted the normative principle that 'the human genome is part of the common heritage of mankind',[95] and in 2002 stated that databases collecting and mapping the human genome constitute a 'public common good': 'a good whose purpose concerns the whole world without exclusion and when it is used by one person it is not destroyed for the rest'. It has also promoted the free flow of data and the fair and equal distribution of benefits.[96]

The decoding process was carried out through peer-to-peer collaboration, involving specialised university laboratories worldwide. The complete sequence of the human genome was published in 2003, and gene banks were established in several countries.

The gene pool serves as an example of polycentric and multi-stakeholder governance. Prioritising goals, patenting individual inventions, and reaching consensus among states, researchers, and companies require continuous negotiation within an increasingly complex research framework that produces new knowledge. At the same time, research communities must strike a delicate balance between the challenges posed by economic exploitation and the collective benefits derived from it.

The development of genome commons is linked to the asymmetrical goals and policies of diverse communities (companies, scientists, individuals, states, supranational collaborations), which have gradually shaped shared operational rules.[97] A balance of interests has been sought despite the complexity and frequent conflict of aims among the actors involved.

Recommendation 1512 (2001) of the Parliamentary Assembly of the Council of Europe calls on member states to amend patent law and exclude any form of appropriation of the human genome, explicitly referring to the principle of 'the common heritage of humankind'. Yet, once the genome was decoded, the

---

95 HUGO 1996.
96 HUGO 2003.
97 Contreras & Knoppers 2018.

struggle for its appropriation became intense. While the synthetic genome may be used commercially, and many biotech companies claim rights to manage potential applications,[98] the genome sequence itself may not be owned. The limit was definitively established in 2013 by the US Supreme Court (*AMP v. Myriad Genetics*), which ruled that human genes are not subject to patents or commercial use: 'Genes are products of nature and as such not patentable. The mere fact of isolating a gene does not make it eligible for patenting'.[99]

In 2018, however, a cataclysmic event, which violated international regulations, shook the debate and prospects of bioethics. The Chinese researcher He Jiankui announced the birth of genetically mutated twins. This development underscores the significance of the human genome as a multifaceted commons – a foundation on which all future life depends, a form of knowledge essential to life, and a methodology for accumulating knowledge and applying it.

5 Land as Commons

Land is a shared resource with three distinct yet interrelated dimensions, all pertaining to the same 'thing'. First, it is the physical space that constitutes and underpins state sovereignty and political authority. Second, is the soil that contains natural resources such as metal ores, sand, and hydrocarbons, which belong to local states and peoples. Third, land forms the Earth's continuous surface, serving as an essential component of the universal ecosystem – irreplaceable and vital for sustaining life. Consequently, although land retains a unified significance for humanity as a whole, it is governed by fragmented normative frameworks:[100] a commons that deserves a global, consolidated, and effective system of *Earth trusteeship*.[101]

5.1 State and People

Except for Antarctica, land is divided among the national territories of roughly 200 countries. According to early international law concepts such as *res nullius* and *terra nullius*, a state that first 'discovers' new land acquires the right to

98 Regalado 2000; Buttigieg 2012.

99 US Supreme Court, *ruling on Myriad Genetics' patent rights for BRCA1 and BRCA2*, in: <http://bit.ly/3nQo2iq>. Before this ruling, Myriad Genetics had held a monopoly on the genes responsible for breast and ovarian cancer. Cf. Contreras 2021.

100 Adelman 2017.

101 Bosselmann 2016; Burdon 2015.

conquer it – that is, to establish sovereignty over it and its resources. This assumption forms the legal basis of colonialism: the exploitation of natural resources and peoples in other lands. Hegemonic Eurocentrism regarded colonised peoples as having no legitimate claim to their land. In practice, they were deemed to have forfeited any right to authority over or use of their territories. The seizure of their land was legally justified by the *terra nullius* doctrine and carried out through force and violence.

Newly acquired land was appropriated not only by states but also by individuals and corporations. As a result, the areas remaining in the hands of indigenous populations were reduced to isolated zones – legal enclaves surviving from the former status quo and incorporated into modern jurisdictions. With the retreat of colonialism and the rise of independent states, the right of peoples to their territories was gradually recognised.[102] National courts frequently face the question of whether indigenous population maintain legal ties to their land, regardless of the status imposed on them by the state over time.

For example, in 1992, the High Court of Australia held that the island was not *terra nullius* when the British first arrived in 1788. Local Aboriginal peoples, therefore, exercised sovereignty and possessed established property rights over their land. This landmark decision altered the legal regime governing the exploitation of land and subsoil resources in areas where historical management rights were recognised in favour of Aboriginal communities.[103] It led to the adoption of the Native Act (1993). However, the complex system of negotiation between communities and operating companies introduced by this Act, and the management rights developed in other parts of the world (e.g., Canada), have not provided clear answers to the fundamental questions: Who will have the right to access and exploit common resources? On whose behalf, and how, will the benefits be collected and distributed?

Similarly, in 2017, the Brazilian Supreme Court rejected an application filed by the federal state of Mato Grosso seeking the annulment of land titles granted by the federal government to indigenous peoples in the Amazon. The Court held that indigenous land was not *terra nullius* and that authority over it had been established over generations.[104]

---

102 Cf. the identical first article of the two Covenants on Human Rights of the United Nations (1966).

103 High Court, Australia, *Mabo v. Queensland*, 3.6.1992, at <http://bit.ly/3V6ldbM>.

104 Supremo Tribunal Federal, Brazil, ACO 362 / ACO 366, DJe-225 (16.8.2017). See also <http://bit.ly/2Zk1oUT>.

The ICJ, in its advisory opinion on Western Sahara, highlighted the concept of indigenous sovereignty over territory in the pre-modern era, drawing modern law's attention to the genealogy of sovereignty. The opinion legitimised decolonisation and the right to self-determination. The Court found that local nomadic tribes, politically and socially organised, had exercised sovereignty over the territory prior to colonisation, and that the territory was not *terra nullius* when Spanish rule was established in 1884. It even requested that a population census be conducted before any referendum, so that the will of the people regarding their own land could be reliably expressed.[105]

Despite the UN intervention, the referendum was never held due to Morocco's persistent refusal to implement it. The Moroccan military continues to exercise authority across the coastal belt along the Atlantic, confining the Sahrawis within desert enclosures.

Thus, a state (Morocco) occupies a territory between states (Western Sahara), which falls under the jurisdiction of a universal international organisation (the UN) mandated to resolve the dispute, while preventing the holding of a referendum that could establish the right of a people (the Sahrawis) to create a state which would acquire sovereign control over its territory and subsoil. Phosphorus – found there in vast quantities – is an essential raw material for global fertiliser production. Hence, the subjection of a resource of universal importance to an occupation regime reflects yet another form of excluding a people from statehood on their own land and alienating them from the status of potential 'commoners' (both as state and as community) of a resource crucial for the global community.

In the end, Western Sahara has become *terra nullius* for Morocco, which pre-empted the UN resolution and occupied the territory in an almost premodern condition, wherein humanity cannot enforce its collective decisions through the body established to act in its name – the UN. Even when a state's right to manage its own wealth-producing resources is recognised, a further question arises: If a resource is concentrated globally in a particular area, as with phosphorus in Western Sahara, what rights of exploitation and access can other states claim as commoners of global resources? We will return to this question in Chapter 6.

During the renewal of the EU-Morocco fisheries agreement and its extension to the coast of Western Sahara, the question of common goods administered by the Moroccan government and its entitlement to enter into exploit-

---

105 ICJ, Advisory Opinion, *Western Sahara*, 16.10.1975, paras 31, 64, 68.

ation agreements resurfaced.[106] In 2015, the Court of Justice of the European Union, following a petition by the Polisario Front – the Sahrawi liberation movement – annulled an agreement concluded between the EU and Morocco, since it covered resources located in Western Sahara. The decision was justified on the following grounds:[107]

A. Under Article 21(f) of the Treaty of the European Union, the EU seeks to 'help develop international measures to preserve and improve the quality of the environment and the sustainable management of global natural resources, in order to ensure sustainable development'.
B. Under Article 73 of the UN Charter, in territories under trusteeship, the interests of the local population must be taken into account, and the administering state has an obligation to consult and report to the United Nations.
C. The UN Secretariat has stated that 'the practice of States administering non-sovereign territories shows that when the exploitation of productive resources is carried out for the benefit of the local population and in consultation with their representatives, it can be considered to be in compliance with obligations arising from the UN Charter and the principle of "permanent sovereignty over natural resources"'.

Consequently, exploitation of the resources in a territory that is not self-governing or independent must ensure that the resulting benefits are returned to the local population. This judgment is significant for guaranteeing the effective implementation of the principle of self-management for shared resources, which currently imposes constraints on beneficiaries through the exercise of state sovereignty.

The issue of returning land to indigenous populations remains one of the most complex challenges in states that originated from early European settlement. Research shows that land ownership is held primarily by states or private individuals, with a portion legally designated to indigenous communities. China and Canada both work to recognise people's rights to ancestral lands, albeit in different ways and for distinct reasons.[108]

Convention No. 169 of the International Labour Organization (1989) recognises the rights of indigenous peoples to control their institutions, forms of coexistence, and economic development (art. 14, para. 1). A similar provision appears in the UN Declaration on the Rights of Indigenous Peoples (2007).[109]

---

106 Cf. <https://bit.ly/2HwqzMz and www.wsrw.org>.
107 EU, General Court, *Front Polisario v Council*, 10.12.2015, at <http://bit.ly/2NATwde>.
108 Rights and Resources Initiative 2015.
109 UN General Assembly, Declaration 61/295, 2007.

The Convention further emphasises the need to respect and promote the inherent rights of indigenous peoples deriving from their social organisation, culture, spiritual traditions, and worldview – particularly their rights to land and natural resources (art. 26, para. 3).

The UN Food and Agriculture Organization's Guidelines on the Responsible Governance of Tenure of Land, Fisheries and Forests introduce the concept of national food security and the need to ensure continued use of land by customary users. The Organisation calls on states to recognise these relationships and to safeguard the interests of the wider community in land use.[110] The UN 2030 Agenda for Sustainable Development likewise integrates ownership and control of land access as a universal condition for eradicating poverty and hunger. Yet, even the exploitation of subsoil resources by indigenous communities may infringe upon others' rights to protect land and traditional modes of use.[111]

Returning to the concept of territory as a constituent element of the state, Antarctica occupies a unique position as the only continent designated as a global commons. It serves the interests of specific states, primarily those engaged in research within their territories, in accordance with the 1959 Antarctic Treaty and related legislation governing the exploitation of fisheries, biodiversity protection, and environmental preservation. Antarctica thus stands out as a territory shared by a group of states that exercise special rights, mainly for research purposes, without explicitly resolving the question of sovereignty. In practice, therefore, it is not a commons that is open and accessible to all. Moreover, territorial claims by seven states remain unrecognised.[112] Under the Treaty, states operating scientific bases must strictly refrain from extracting subsoil resources, in compliance with the moratorium imposed to protect and conserve natural resources. However, once hydrocarbon and mineral reserves become economically exploitable, this clause of the Treaty will most likely be challenged.

5.2 The Living Skin of the Earth

The land's surface – or its 'skin' – is typically set at a shallow depth of 25–50 cm. This mixture of rock, clay, sand, trace elements, moisture, oxygen, organic and inorganic elements, and living microorganisms is the result of long, gradual processes. It is essential for the creation of life, primarily in the form of plants,

---

110 Food and Agriculture Organization 2012.

111 Owen et al. 2022.

112 See <https://www.visualcapitalist.com/mapping-territorial-claims-in-antactica/>.

and for maintaining the carbon, nitrogen, and phosphorus cycles. Because soil formation and enrichment are extremely slow, soil should be regarded as a quasi-non-renewable common resource. If its capacity to support life, absorb water, and store carbon is degraded, it will ultimately perish. Land can thus be viewed as a biogeochemical resource system that sequesters carbon emissions and is indispensable for global food production and the sustainability of human and non-human life.[113]

Preserving and enriching the outer layer of soil is, therefore, crucial to sustaining life within Earth's ecosystems, at local and global scales. Land thus functions as both a local and a global common resource. While the preservation of forests and the management of rivers and lakes take place within the national territories of specific states, these systems are also interdependent beyond state boundaries. This interdependence requires a form of 'rational governance' based on universally applicable rules. Protection from pollution is a central concern. Exposure to environmental pollutants and hazardous substances widely used in agriculture falls under the scope of the 2001 Stockholm Convention on Persistent Organic Pollutants.

Extensive land cover by human activity – such as the construction of urban surfaces and road networks – seals the soil and nullifies its life-sustaining functions. These processes often coincide with toxic pollution, turning one of the planet's vital organs into a negative factor for biodiversity preservation and the renewal of water and air quality. Furthermore, the detachment and separation of soil components caused by human activity pose significant threats to soil fertility and its capacity to sustain life. The extraction of water resources and the continuous mining of sand, especially for concrete production, also have incalculable ecological consequences.[114] The accelerating processes of desertification, erosion, and soil degradation represent additional manifestations of climate change – both a consequence and a driver of it.

Land is inherently linked to food production, the food economy, and related policies that can lead to land justice – protecting against land grabbing and forced displacement, while ensuring fair measures to combat climate change. The United Nations and other international organisations[115] are working with governments to promote rules and policies for soil protection and the preservation of its constituent elements. The 2018 UN General Assembly Declaration on the Rights of Peasants and Other People Working in Rural Areas (see also Chapter 5.2.1) offers broader recognition of the relationship between

113 On this discussion, see Blomfield 2021.

114 UN, Report of 26.4.2022, at <https://bit.ly/3kzffQ4>.

115 Cf. <http://bit.ly/38ivb2S>.

farmers and land commons and connects land with other common goods, such as water and seeds. According to Article 17.3, 'States shall recognise and protect the natural commons and their related systems of collective use and management'. Similarly, the Committee on the Elimination of Discrimination against Women calls on states, in implementing article 14, to adopt agricultural policies that support women farmers and recognise the natural commons.[116]

The right to food was explicitly linked to the commons in the 2012 Voluntary Guidelines on the Responsible Governance of Tenure of Land, Fisheries and Forests drafted by the Committee on World Food Security. According to Directive 8.3:

> There are publicly owned lands, fisheries and forests that are collectively used and managed (in some national contexts referred to as commons). States should, where applicable, recognise and protect such publicly owned land, fisheries, and forests, and their related systems of collective use and management, including in state allocation processes.[117]

This text emphasises the connection between soil and the nutritional needs of all people, even though it carries limited regulatory force. Soil is also closely tied to the autonomous pursuit of economic development, serving as a precondition for the food chain. The Guidelines on the Responsible Governance of Tenure of Land, Fisheries, and Forests, formulated in 2012 by the United Nations Committee on World Food Security, urge states to develop policies that enable all stakeholders – governments, non-governmental organisations, and individuals – to access technical assistance and knowledge, and to participate actively in land-use planning. Environmental protection, climate change mitigation, and the prevention of armed conflict are identified as key objectives for ensuring the sustainable use of land and preventing the depletion of its productive potential.[118] This dimension is inherently tied to land ownership.

---

116 UN Committee on the Elimination of Discrimination against Women, General Recommendation No. 34, 4 .3.2016, CEDAW/C/GC/34, para. 62.

117 FAO, Voluntary Guidelines on the Responsible Governance of Tenure of Land, Fisheries and Forests in the Context of National Food Security, at <www.fao.org/tenure/voluntary-guidelines/en/>.

118 Committee on World Food Security, UN, 11 May 2012, Voluntary Guidelines on the Responsible Governance of Tenure of Land, Fisheries and Forests <https://bit.ly/3p4kAzh>.

The ongoing transfer of ownership from small farmers to large corporations is dramatically transforming the relationship between individuals and arable land. During the 2008 financial crisis alone, 50 million hectares of farmland were transferred to large multinational corporations or to countries such as China and India. This phenomenon is particularly evident in sub-Saharan Africa and South America. The concentration of large areas of arable land in the hands of states or corporations serves purposes of profit, price control, or nutritional and energy self-sufficiency. In some cases, the sale involves state land, as in Ethiopia.[119] As early as the 1980s, during the debt crisis, the World Bank pressured African governments to privatise community land, triggering profound social upheaval that affected large segments of the population. Similar attempts to impose such policies in Mexico led to the Zapatista rebellion in the province of Chiapas in 1994 and to the consolidation of communal forms of land self-management.[120]

Land also plays a role in human culture as the landscape upon which human habitats have developed. The European Landscape Convention, adopted by the Council of Europe in Florence in 2000, states in its preamble that 'the quality and diversity of European landscapes constitute a common resource' and that landscape is 'an important aspect of the quality of life for people everywhere'. The improvement and protection of the urban, rural, and natural environment are essential for human societies to develop in harmony with nature. Quality of life is thus explicitly linked to the protection of the natural and human environment. The Convention mandates cooperation among European states to formulate landscape protection policies. On a symbolic, rather than a practical level, it gives normative expression to the notion that the terrestrial environment is a common resource worthy of shared management and protection. Similarly, UNESCO's 2011 Declaration on the Conservation of Historic Urban Landscapes highlights pluralism and the democratic management of cultural urban spaces.

6 The Space Odyssey of the Commons

As we have seen, the triumph of Reason during the Enlightenment influenced the division of the sea into zones of state sovereignty and beyond. Where sovereignty is absent, states are quick to assert control. In such areas, both states and other actors are gradually being granted rights of access and exploit-

119 See Dardot & Laval 2014: 94–95, 432.
120 Caffentzis 2010: 27–28.

ation. The concept of 'empty space' gives substance to the governability of enclosed resources. Even when rules exist, they often encourage their own violation. Paradoxically, the principle of equality can contribute to inequality, as only powerful states can access areas where *res communis* transitions into *res nullius*. Through the demarcation of 'inside' and 'outside', outer space – the original intangible universal commons – takes on new significance as it remains in constant motion.

After 1957 and 1961, when the Soviets sent the first satellite into orbit around the Earth and the first human journeyed into outer space, and after 1969, when the Americans first set foot on the Moon, a *corpus juris spatialis*, or body of space law, began to develop. Although not explicitly defined, outer space is generally understood as the region beyond the point where the Earth's atmosphere becomes sufficiently tenuous for combustion to be impossible. In essence, outer space extends outward from the atmosphere and, along with the atmosphere, forms a single realm in which aircraft can fly, and radio waves can be transmitted.

As in other domains of the universal commons, advanced technology plays a decisive role in how outer space is accessed and exploited. Although technological progress has been dramatic since the 1960s, international law remains unable to address the core issues concerning the nature of this common space – a realm through which satellites, space stations, and rocket launchers travel, and where space debris continues to accumulate.

The questions, 'Who does outer space belong to?' and 'Where does state sovereignty end when it is projected upwards from the ground to the sky?' have been debated since technology made possible what once was science fiction – travel beyond the limits of the atmosphere. Analogous questions arise, albeit only remotely, with respect to the oceans, the seabed, biodiversity, the radio spectrum, and the internet. In the case of outer space, we begin with something familiar and subject to state authority – the surface of the Earth – and, by passing through the atmosphere, gradually extend into an external realm that approaches infinity: an existing but largely inaccessible space. 'Inner space' is already subject to an appropriation regime, but 'outer space' is not. As technology advanced and enabled humans to venture beyond the atmosphere, the international community responded by establishing regulations governing state interactions in transatmospheric space. These regulations extended the principles that applied at sea, projecting horizontal spatial lines onto a vertical surface. However, while outer space was originally literally *empty and void space*, it is now increasingly subject to use and activity.

Satellites cannot function without telecommunications; indeed, most are designed primarily to relay telecommunication signals, thereby closely linking their use to the radio spectrum. To operate effectively, satellites must maintain a minimum distance from one another, which makes orbital space a finite resource – even though only a limited number of satellites would suffice to meet global needs.[121] Eight states located in the equatorial zone unsuccessfully claimed a permanent presence in outer space, arguing that, within this zone, orbits remain within the projection of their own airspace into space (Declaration of Bogota, 1976).[122] A few years later, in 1983, the US government announced its intention to use space for military purposes. This grandiose project, known as 'Star Wars', never materialised, but it left open the possibility of the military use of space.

Today, satellites play a crucial role not only in telecommunications but also in collecting and transmitting data on crops, the climate, oceans, and wildfires, among others. The International Telecommunications Satellite Organization (Intelsat) was established in 1964 to own satellites and lease them to nation-states and private companies. States acted as shareholders, expecting direct economic returns from satellite operations. The organisation was privatised in 2001. The privatisation of an intergovernmental organisation created an unprecedented but revealing institutional enclosure within a mechanism that might otherwise have exercised oversight over this particular universal commons. Other international organisations are also active in space,[123] though without authorisation to use satellite orbits. The UN Committee on the Peaceful Uses of Outer Space, created in 1958 after the launch of the Soviet Sputnik-1, is responsible for satellite registration, collision prevention, and addressing pollution issues, while the ITU licenses satellite telecommunications frequencies.[124] Despite these international efforts, individual states still retain authority to license and regulate satellite use. Orbits are increasingly congested and remain unregulated, especially low geostationary orbits, which operate under a *numerus clausus* system and require prompt management solutions.

Space law was developed during the Cold War to address two challenges. First, it sought to prevent the United States and the Soviet Union from using outer space for military purposes. Second, it aimed to avoid a form of 'primi-

121 Vogler 2016: 158.

122 Cf. <https://bogotadeclaration.wordpress.com/declaration-of-1976/>.

123 For instance, INTERSPUTNIK was founded in 1971 on a Soviet initiative; the International Mobile Satellite Organization (INMARSAT) was established in 1979 to provide telecommunications services at sea; ARABSAT, serving the Arab states, is a joint telecommunications organisation; and the European Space Agency (ESA), established in 1980, absorbed earlier structures. Finally, the European Space Programme (EUSPA) has been operating since 2004.

124 See <https://www.itu.int/hub/2022/02/itu-space-interference-free-satellite-orbits-leo/>.

tive accumulation', whereby a resource is exploited by free riders operating beyond any legal limits. However, this new body of law was built upon a purely technological approach that overlooked alternative management strategies.[125]

After five years of negotiations within the UN General Assembly, international law governing relations between states in outer space began to take shape with the 1967 Treaty on Principles Governing the Activities of States in the Exploration and Use of Outer Space, including the Moon and Other Celestial Bodies. In Article 1, the Treaty affirms that 'the exploration and use of outer space, including the moon and other celestial bodies, shall be carried out for the benefit and in the interests of all countries, irrespective of their degree of economic or scientific development, and shall be the province of all mankind'. Therefore, outer space is open to all states, it cannot be claimed as sovereign territory by any state. In the same year, Aldo Armando Cocca, the Argentine ambassador and a pioneer of space law, observed that the international community:

- had recognised the existence of a new subject of international law, namely humankind itself, thereby creating a *jus humanitatis*;
- had entrusted humankind with the greatest shared possession (*res communis humanitatis*) the human mind can conceive – space itself, including the Moon and other heavenly bodies.[126]

In support of the 1967 Treaty, four additional treaties were concluded: the Outer Space Rescue Agreement (1968), the Liability Convention (1972), the Convention on Registration of Objects Launched into Outer Space (1975), and the Agreement Governing the Activities of States on the Moon and Other Celestial Bodies (1979). The principle of the 'common heritage of humankind' thus became a foundational concept in space law,[127] even before it was incorporated into the law of the sea. The 1967 Treaty expressly declares that the exploitation of outer space and the Moon falls within the sphere of activity of humankind as a whole, while the Moon Agreement of 1979 affirms that the Moon 'forms part of the common heritage of mankind' (art. XI) and prohibits its appropriation. Article 4 specifies that the exploitation of the Moon should benefit all countries and promote higher living standards, as well as economic and social progress, for present and future generations. The Treaty also prohibits the use of nuclear weapons or other weapons of mass destruction and holds

---

125 Craven 2019: 568.

126 The statement was made at the Legal Sub-Committee of the Committee on the Peaceful Uses of Outer Space, Sixth Session, 19 June 1967, UN Doc.A/AC.105/C.2/SR.75, pp.7–8. Cf. Cocca 1981: 15.

127 Khatwani 2019.

states accountable for any damage or pollution caused by them or their citizens in outer space.

Yet, because the term 'humankind' remains ambiguous, it becomes a vague subject-recipient of the benefits arising from lunar exploitation – a concept increasingly shaped by states' economic interests rather than collective humanity. The US has adopted a clear policy of not being bound by the 1979 treaty, considering the Moon as *res nullius* rather than *res communis*. At the same pace as the US, technologically advanced states have taken a similar position, leaving the Treaty binding only upon 18 states, none of which are capable of exploiting the Moon directly.

The reluctance of states to accept restrictions – especially regarding the appropriation of wealth-producing resources on the Moon – raises concerns about a new 'tragedy of the commons'. The colonisation of outer space's common resources appears increasingly plausible, given the ambiguity of commitments under international law.[128] As the exploitation of the Moon becomes technically feasible, binding rules that would guarantee a genuinely common approach to this universal commons exist largely on paper, without the universal recognition required for their implementation.

Indeed, several states (the US, Luxembourg, Japan) have enacted domestic legislation allowing their citizens to own space resources, thereby challenging established international norms. The US Commercial Space Launch Competitiveness Act (2015) explicitly grants US citizens the right to 'possess, own, transport, use, and sell' resources extracted from celestial bodies. Executive Order 13914 (April 2020), issued by president Trump, rejects the Moon Agreement and asserts that space resources may be commercially recovered, declaring that 'the US does not view [outer space] as a global commons'. Most significantly, the Artemis Accords,[129] established in 2020 at the initiative of the US, introduced a new dimension to space law by creating a multilateral framework supporting this approach to resource utilisation.

The primary objective of the Accords is to encourage states to cooperate in missions to the Moon, promoting colonisation and sustainable activities. They also seek to divide the Moon into research and exploitation zones. Among the Moon's potentially valuable resources, helium-3 stands out as a particularly promising element, capable of meeting Earth's energy needs once the requisite

128 Noga 2014.

129 The Accords are a non-binding bilateral cooperation arrangement between the National Aeronautics and Space Administration (NASA) and each signatory state (Kaul 2024). More than 50 states have committed themselves, including Australia, Canada, France, Germany, Italy, India, Israel, Japan, South Korea, Spain, the United Arab Emirates, and the United Kingdom. See <https://www.nasa.gov/specials/artemis-accords/index.html>.

technology becomes available. In response to the American initiative, Russia and China have agreed to build a manned station orbiting the Moon, in cooperation with other countries. Meanwhile, private companies such as the French TechTheMoon have pledged to take steps toward establishing a human presence on the lunar surface for commercial purposes.[130] The Finnish company Bluefors, a leading manufacturer of cryogenic cooling systems for quantum technology, has even signed an agreement to purchase up to 10,000 litres of helium-3 annually from Interlune, a US firm developing space-based resource extraction.[131] It appears that the commercialisation of lunar resources has begun even before an extraction team has set foot on the Moon.

Although the Artemis Accords are formally non-binding, they may evolve into customary international law. They establish political principles of cooperation among a select group of states to share the benefits derived from the exploitation of space resources. 'In this sense, it may weaken genuine international cooperation eventually running counter the spirit of Article III of the Outer Space Treaty'.[132]

These developments suggest that future commercial exploitation will be driven more by enclosure and competition than by global, transnational cooperation. There has been a gradual shift from 'freedom to explore' to 'right to exploit', an unregulated trend that recalls the logic of *terra nullius*.

Space law can be compared with the law of the high seas regarding access to and exploitation of resources. Both nomadic elements – involving constant motion – and static components – projecting territorial sovereignty into space – coexist.[133] As Deleuze and Guattari suggest, despite rhetoric about extending state sovereignty into empty space, the rules tend to create a malleable, non-state space that gradually becomes homogenised. This transformation occurs as a unitary space is delineated by the trajectories of missiles and satellites during launch, landing, and remote control. According to Pic, Evoy, and Morin:

> Most space arrangements have refrained from using a global commons framing. There have been a few attempts to draw more apparent contours for space

130 Cf. <https://techthemoon.com/en/>.

131 <https://bit.ly/3VWvGIY>.

132 Deplano 2021: 817–818. Article III reads: 'States Parties to the Treaty shall carry on activities in the exploration and use of outer space, including the moon and other celestial bodies, in accordance with international law, including the Charter of the United Nations, in the interest of maintaining international peace and security and promoting international co-operation and understanding.'

133 Milun 2011: 140.

> governance, chief among them the Moon Agreement, the Bogota Declaration, and the Artemis Accords. However, to date, none has garnered generalized international support. A closer look at the diffusion of normative frames within space arrangements reveals that space governance is perhaps best characterized as a normative stalemate.[134]

Outer space functions as a universal commons in the form of a *heterotopia*: a space devoid of actual life but essential for the operation of machines crucial to life on Earth – a 'place out of place' with no social life of its own. Proclamations that its use should be limited to peaceful purposes faded as early as the First Gulf War in 1991, when the Global Positioning System was used to identify targets in Iraq with precision.[135] Since then, new criteria and clarifications have been needed to distinguish between war and peace. Currently, access to outer space entails enormous economic costs for states, driven by both covert military objectives and overt commercial ambitions.

Outer space is thus becoming a commercial arena for corporations expanding their activities beyond Earth's atmosphere. It is being commodified and commercialised as a neutral extension of Earth's natural environment. In the absence of a comprehensive normative framework, free riders are taking the lead. In 2026, there were approximately 15,000 active satellites, of which Elon Musk's SpaceX owned 10,000. These share orbit with hundreds of thousands of hazardous debris fragments, including more than 16,000 inactive satellites. Jeff Bezos' Amazon also plans to launch more than 2,300 satellites. Through its Starlink programme, SpaceX has effectively been colonising – indeed, monopolising – outer space since 2022. A few years later, Shanghai Telecom (Qianfan project) and Amazon (Project Kuiper) joined the race, each seeking to occupy as many orbital assets as possible. Competition between contemporary powerhouses for spaceflight and satellite orbits is occurring in a largely unregulated environment, as no universally applied Space Traffic Management regime has yet been agreed upon. Any company or state that arrives first can seize orbits without providing guarantees and without any central licensing or international oversight serving the 'community interests'.

State actors are implementing policies and regulations to support private actors whose aims are purely commercial. According to the World Economic Forum, the value of commercial activities is expected to reach $1.8 trillion by 2035. One condition for conducting economic activities in space and on the Moon is the establishment of 'regulatory frameworks that ensure the safety

134 Pic, Evoy & Morin 2023: 298.
135 Craven 2019: 570.

and sustainability of these activities'.[136] However, this discourse never addresses the key features of such frameworks, which inevitably prioritise corporate extraction over commons-based approaches.

Future developments will determine whether the vision of outer space as a commons and a 'province of all humankind', as solemnly declared in the 1967 Outer Space Treaty, will be realised. Concerns about managing outer space and the Moon as a commons are giving way to a race among corporations and states competing to conquer space for their own benefit – a *res nullius*, serving self-interest despite initial declarations to the contrary.

7 The Radio Spectrum: An Invisible Commons

The radio spectrum is a set of frequencies that may be activated and whose utility as a medium for telecommunications became apparent with advances in technology. It is invisible, omnipresent, independent of the atmosphere, and a carrier of signals and energy. In other words, electromagnetic waves, which move or vibrate through space, can be sensed as heat, cold, or light. Microwaves, long and medium radio waves, and television frequencies all belong to the electromagnetic spectrum, which exists in space and cannot be separated from it. Space, moreover, cannot be fabricated or destroyed. However, the radio spectrum is activated at a given place and time to a specific frequency. Since it is omnipresent, it exists both within and beyond state sovereignty; in other words, it is a commonly shared resource and communication medium that extends uniformly in all directions but can only be apprehended as a fragmented medium.

The radio spectrum is a universal medium of communication that allows anyone to transmit or receive a signal anywhere, at any time, and in any way, depending on the available technology, which is subject to regulation. The properties of wireless communication are still largely unknown and continuously evolving.[137] The spectrum can be accessed in two areas: first, on the surface of the Earth, where it is used by transmitters, receivers, individuals, states, and companies and is diffused and subject to state jurisdictions; and second, beyond the atmosphere, in outer space, where it is used by states and companies operating there. Thus, the nature of the commoners varies depending on the circumstances, the use, and the importance the radio spectrum holds for them.

136 World Economic Forum 2024: 25.

137 Werbach 2004: 863–973.

With the development of technology, the spectrum has become subject to regulation at three levels: the state level, the regional level (EU, CEPT – European Conference of Postal and Telecommunications Administrations), and the global level (ITU).[138] Clearly, conditions were completely different before 1886, when Heinrich Hertz discovered the radio spectrum in Karlsruhe.

States began to take an interest in the spectrum as soon as it acquired political and economic significance, after it had become the vehicle for telecommunications. This occurred in 1895, when Guglielmo Marconi, building on Nikola Tesla's inventions, was able to convert frequencies into sound using long-range wireless devices: a transmitter and a receiver.

The exploitation of the radio spectrum is directly related to the devices that permit its use. In the historical process of mastering the resource, patents on the apparatus, the telegraph, and the radio played an important role in the competition between states and companies for dominance and control over frequencies. The UK's support for Marconi's company's monopoly provoked reactions from Germany and the US, both of which supported opening the regime governing wireless transmission. The issue was critical for military communications and intelligence in the years leading up to World War I. Thus, in 1906, the first international treaty governing the use of the radio spectrum was concluded in Berlin, leading to the creation of a global network of radiotelegraph transponders.

The gradual expansion of radio frequencies and the recognition of rights through licences issued within state jurisdictions resulted in two countervailing tendencies: on the one hand, the defence of exclusive rights of use, and on the other, the sharing of the public radio spectrum without authorisation. As the radio spectrum does not exist in a material sense but is an attribute of space that can be exploited through technology, it is difficult to draw analogies to the legal rules governing land ownership or the exploitation of natural resources. Nevertheless, rules governing liability and safety mechanisms can effectively protect users of radio spectrum from interference in the wireless transmission of information and data while resolving disputes over frequency limits.

In addition to concerns about the radio spectrum itself, there are questions about the technological infrastructure supporting signal transmission, decoding, broadcasting, and reception. Consequently, the rights associated with

138 The Geneva-based Organisation is part of the United Nations family. It gathers 193 member states and approximately 800 organisations, companies, and scientific institutions. Cf. <www.itu.int/en/about/Pages/default.aspx>.

patenting and utilising devices evolve in parallel, independently of the use and accessibility of the radio spectrum.

In its traditional form, the medium has a dual character: it is both unlimited and exhaustible, not only in terms of the capacity of a frequency at a given location, but also in terms of interference. The radio spectrum, in its analogue form, is certainly finite since the signal of a transmitter can only occupy a specific frequency. With digital technology, however, the 'capacity' of each frequency has been greatly expanded.

The technological revolution that first produced the telegraph and later radio and television raised the following questions: Who can secure exclusive rights to the medium? Who can regulate relations between states (and companies) regarding the use of frequencies? How far can the limits of supervision and possible appropriation of the radio spectrum as a universal commons extend? If the answer is positive, is it then subject to protection and regulation? Conversely, will we ever need a licence to use a specific colour – that is, a frequency of light, as we do with a particular frequency of the radio spectrum?[139]

Today, there is no comprehensive regulatory regime governing rights in the radio spectrum. For example, while the radio spectrum may be state property, regulation usually concerns exploitation – that is, licensing through a monopoly relationship with the state. A central authority under the auspices of the United Nations, the ITU, issues licences to states for an attribute of empty space. The first centralised authority was established in 1927 at the Washington Conference. According to the Convention on International Telecommunications signed in Montreux in 1965, the members of the frequency licensing authority are 'custodians of an international public good'.[140] After the reform of the ITU operating regime in 1992, other international, scientific, and business organisations also began to play an important role in consultations on frequency allocation. In outer space, where exclusive use of each position is required (only one satellite can occupy a specific location), the electromagnetic spectrum falls within the ITU's sphere of competence, in cooperation with national or regional agencies, such as NASA in the US and the European Space Agency.

Yet, why is it necessary to issue licences to commercialise the use of a global resource that now enjoys unlimited accessibility? The radio spectrum exhibits a wide range of economic value in market terms. Even if regulations aim at ensuring the resource's sustainability, its commoditisation arguably facilitates

139 Horvitz 2008. Cf. *in fine* of the chapter.

140 Vogler 2016: 154.

its appropriation by preventing open access to a critical communications sector. As Yochai Benkler argues, 'we use notions based on the concept of the market to manage resources, and consequently, when the problem is posed in this way, we look for something to which we attribute qualities subject to exclusive proprietary rights and commercial transactions'.[141] In the context of roads, which function as a commons, users (commoners) are free to utilise them with the vehicle of their choice, provided they adhere to traffic rules. By analogy, one could argue that national and international governance of the radio spectrum constitutes an open-to-use commons subject to rules, including specifications for the transmission and reception ranges of devices. This reasoning aligns with the principle of free navigation on the open sea, as established by Grotius.

Regarding ownership of the radio spectrum, it is important to note that although the state oversees this public resource, it typically licenses it to private entities. Frequently, those managing the radio spectrum secure long-term rights that can only be revoked with compensation. Consequently, claims may arise that portray licensees as absolute owners of a specific frequency or group of frequencies.[142] In the contemporary landscape, transnational competitors are less focused on seeking exclusive control over broadcasting frequencies. The proliferation of frequencies through the internet and new technologies, enabling automatic anti-interference adjustments and fostering multiple co-existing compatibilities, has contributed to this shift. Despite these changes, the authority to grant licenses remains under the state's monopoly, reinforcing state power in this domain.

The continuous increase in data traffic and the emergence of new digital technologies are creating a landscape[143] that allows the radio spectrum to be shared as a super-commons.[144] Could the radio spectrum, insofar as it extends beyond national jurisdictions, be considered a global common good and placed under common international management? Could people roam freely in the radio spectrum, receiving and transmitting information?[145] Information is a critical area of human rights in the current complex reality of hegemonic globalisation. Consequently, the exclusions experienced by the Global South raise questions about global equality – not only between states but also between people. After all, the control of telecommunications against people's

141 Benkler 1998: 289.
142 Snider 2002.
143 Mazar 2016: 305.
144 Wehrbach 2004.
145 Noam 1998: 765.

interests not only creates exclusions in terms of access to information but can violate the core of the right to privacy,[146] as the ever-increasing use of telecommunications for spying demonstrates.

Free access to the radio spectrum without licences, with assurance of proper use and without interference or parasites, would not only satisfy the commoner-users (broadcasters and receivers) but also be beneficial to all, as practice shows. Frequencies for operating garage doors, wireless landlines, or microwave ovens are already available free of charge, alongside the unrestricted use of the 2.4 GHz frequency band, which significantly boosted Wi-Fi.[147]

Other frequencies in the radio spectrum are treated as a 'product' or 'space' for rent. The state makes these frequencies available at low prices through auctions but, in practice, is unable to require their return.[148] State control and auctions of radio frequencies have introduced a global resource into local markets, limiting the potential community of commoners who can produce and receive information. On the other hand, the state's monopoly over frequency management can be seen as a form of oversight delegated by the community of citizens to the state as guarantor of the public interest.[149]

Despite the obstacles, this ongoing process includes the European Union's efforts to license radio spectrum use.[150] One proposal, facing resistance, is to share the radio spectrum among multiple users (now technically feasible), thereby facilitating free access to part of the spectrum and ending licence regimes that result in exclusion. Certainly, among the challenges brought about by the explosion of wireless communication and data transmission are public health, telecommunications security, and the prevention of state and corporate monopolies – even in areas of the radio spectrum we have not yet imagined.[151]

According to the Inter-American Court of Human Rights, 'the State must democratize access to media, guarantee diversity and pluralism, and encourage the existence of commercial, public, and community media services'. In this light, the Court concludes that 'states are internationally obliged to estab-

146 Santos 2020: 364–365.

147 Weiser & Hatfield 2005: 664.

148 Snider 2002.

149 Brennan 1998: 791.

150 For the policy drawn up by the European Parliament and the Council in 2012, cf. Delaere & Cullell-March 2014.

151 For example, in 2002, the ITU's administrative competence (Resolution 118) was extended to frequencies of light, i.e., above 3,000 GHz.

lish laws and public policies that democratize access and guarantee pluralism in media in different areas, such as the press, radio, and television'.[152]

Both the locally activated radio spectrum and that which extends into international, transnational, and outer-space areas should be considered a unified common resource. A universal normative approach is required to treat it as such, granting commoners (i.e., individuals, states, and organisations) functional freedom of access to and movement of information, as well as management responsibilities. Furthermore, this approach would ensure the democratic and rational exploitation of the radio spectrum for transmitting critical, accessible, and reliable information – essential for managing other global resources and universal commons, such as the climate, forests, and oceans.

8 Human Knowledge Commons

Humankind's technical and intellectual achievements collectively constitute the material and immaterial dimensions of human culture – distinct from nature and the result of human initiative. As commons are non-competitive resources. Specific manifestations of cultural heritage are difficult to define, as they are open to multiple interpretations,[153] particularly when the discussion concerns a 'common culture' or 'culture as commons'. Knowledge, as a constitutive element of civilisation, can be understood as the totality of intellectual and cultural resources. Knowledge commons, therefore, correspond to the formally or informally institutionalised joint governance of a broad set of cultural resources made available by creators or disseminators of knowledge, without imposing financial or contractual access restrictions on commoners and users.[154]

One of the most prominent expressions of such a commons is found in literature, art, and science. Science, in particular, can be defined as the systematic and rational organisation of knowledge that is accessible to all and open to continuous development from generation to generation. It may be regarded as a global common good because of its diverse and ubiquitous role in human

---

152 IACtHR, *Pueblos Indígenas Maya Kaqchikel de Sumpango v. Guatemala* (6.10.2021), para. 86 and 91 respectively.

153 Lekakis 2020.

154 Madison, Frischmann & Strandburg 2010.

TABLE 5. Classification of knowledge goods

Public goods	Non-excludable, non-rivalrous (open software, open state reports)
Common-pool resources	Non-excludable, rivalrous (crowd-sourced databases [Wikipedia], public library books, folk knowledge)
Club goods	Excludable, non-rivalrous (cable TV, scientific articles in journals with subscription)
Private goods	Excludable, rivalrous (patented knowledge, books sold in bookshops)

society, as well as because the knowledge it produces is openly accessible[155] and its development governed by rules established by its practitioners.

For centuries, academic research has produced and disseminated knowledge. Classic mechanisms for making scientific knowledge available – libraries, including university electronic repositories, open online archives, and the dissemination of research results – operate according to common principles. Notable examples include mapping and database projects on the human genome (see Chapter 4.4), pollen, microbes, and many other fields of research.[156]

Knowledge commons are developing and reproducing rapidly through technology, which offers immense potential for free access while also introducing new mechanisms for enclosing knowledge.[157] They take various forms, including those based on peer production, interconnected with other commons, or as semi-commons – partially open but still subject to market restrictions (see Table 5[158]).

Some knowledge commons, by their inherent nature, resist restriction, as seen in popular traditions, legislation, and jurisprudence, or simply due to the choices of their creators. Crucially, knowledge commons are inexhaustible resources: they are neither depleted nor destroyed by use. Overuse does not threaten knowledge; rather, non-dissemination and underuse act as disincentives for the production and exchange of information, potentially contracting both the commons and the community.

155 Boulton 2021: 5–6.

156 See <https://globalpollenproject.org/>; <https://earthmicrobiome.org/>; Madison, Strandburg & Frischman 2016: 1, 8.

157 Caffentzis 2008.

158 The table transposes the corresponding one of Hess & Ostrom 2007: 9.

The sharing of knowledge and the promotion of collaboration among creators are essential mechanisms in resource generation. Patents and intellectual property rights safeguard the financial and intellectual interests of creators, who seek to generate new value. To ensure the protection of this new value, specific legal frameworks have been established – either by declaration or by priority, depending on each state's system for recognising such rights.

Yet, intellectual property rights function as enclosures of open knowledge in the public domain. Since the late twentieth century, this 'second enclosure movement' has been associated with the commercialisation and securitisation of knowledge.[159] These enclosures have evolved independently of digital telecommunications, which, by their very nature, transcend borders and enable the mass dissemination of information. Moreover, knowledge products are increasingly commodified through the continuous expansion of intellectual property rights, even when publicly funded.[160] However, the universal pool of shared knowledge expands whenever knowledge passes from the private to the public sphere.

Different forms of knowledge commons develop and interact within society, intersecting with other commons at local and global levels. The formation and regeneration of humankind's collective memory is one such mechanism, together with the memory of knowledge, know-how, and culture – the genealogy of ideas and artefacts, whether producing private profit or social benefit. In this dynamic and ever-changing landscape, digital commons and the internet represent a pivotal human invention with profound political implications, as they enable unprecedented access to shared knowledge.

8.1 Collective Memory and Knowledge: Humankind's Shared Past and Present

Collective, or social, memory is the mechanism through which groups, societies, and humanity as a whole remember their past – a process that is continually reshaped. The ways in which this occurs depend on context, actors, and the methods through which the past is perceived and memories are constructed – that is, how knowledge of the past is formed. Ultimately, the ideas and beliefs shared and transmitted among individuals constitute a malleable common good, forming the foundation of human civilisation in its diverse manifestations across time and place.

---

159 The 'first enclosure movement' is considered the one that limited the land commons from the sixteenth century onward. In Boyle 2003; Sand 2005.

160 International Task Force on Global Public Goods 2006: 66.

According to Michel Halbwachs, memory reshapes the past in accordance with society's hegemonic ideas.[161] These ideas are largely determined by political power, which tends either to remain silent about or to transform the knowledge and memory of both recent and distant events. Consequently, the processes through which contemporary realities are reinterpreted or undone profoundly influence the memory inherited by future generations. The present *commons of liquid truth* thus become the raw material for the future *commons of memory*, both locally and globally.

Yet who determines the collective dimension of memory, and what constitutes its content? As this question moves from the local to the regional and global levels, it requires different analytical tools. How can the collective memory of the past – of achievements and failures – be developed and sustained over time? How many of those who have exercised political power can claim to have preserved and transmitted memory without enclosures, omissions, or distortions? What mechanisms control memory, and hence knowledge, by excluding people and communities from it? How does memory fade and vanish into oblivion? As Marc Augé aptly notes, 'memories are made by forgetting, like the outline of the coast from the sea'.[162] Distinguishing the mechanisms that preserve and reshape the various coexisting forms of memory and forgetting, which spread unevenly across the global community, remains a formidable challenge for human societies and, ultimately, for humankind as a whole.

Science, history, technology, politics, and ideology all play crucial roles in solidifying specific aspects of collective memory and reproducing them in new forms. Myth, demystification, falsification, and reinvention are among the mechanisms through which memory is continually reshaped and reinterpreted in response to new needs.[163] The sharing of collective forms of memory, which ensure the preservation and accessibility of knowledge, brings attention to forgotten or suppressed events and ideas, connecting a shared past with the present. This process is of profound political significance, shaping how communities understand themselves and how prior knowledge underpins new cultural forms.

Archives, as repositories of knowledge, preserve documentation about the past. Their accessibility is, therefore, essential for understanding what occurred, what was said, and what was written, while minimising distortions of the source material. Such repositories may be owned by state or private insti-

161 Halbwachs 1992.
162 Augé 2004: 20.
163 Connerton 1989.

tutions, contain printed or broadcast materials, or take the form of databases of social, cultural, political, or scientific nature. Contributors include those who deposit materials, those who classify and maintain them, and those who consult them in search of information.[164] Similarly, museums act as custodians of shared cultural heritage, contributing to another dimension of collective memory. Yet this dimension is shaped by the mediating power of public or private entities deciding which museums to establish and what to exhibit. Thus, even though museums may be accessible to all – often for a fee – they constitute enclosures of the cultural commons within defined and regulated spaces.[165]

Knowledge of the present – that is, understanding one's socio-political environment – is essential for forming opinions and political attitudes, and thus for shaping the future. However, when such knowledge threatens the survival of political power, deliberate manipulation and appropriation of information are likely. Individuals who expose wrongdoing by the powerful have long faced persecution. What is new today is that technology has made previously suppressed truths accessible once they enter the public domain.[166]

8.2 Intellectual Creation, Ownership, and Access

The granting of rights over human creations raises crucial considerations regarding creators' monopoly rights – specifically, their right to exploit their works for personal benefit. These rights must be balanced against the rights of potential users, particularly when the creation is a prerequisite for culture or, as in the case of medicines, essential to life itself. The production of knowledge and innovation is tied to markets and governments, but also to the possibility of sharing knowledge that is open and accessible to all – that is, 'intellectual production without intellectual property'.[167]

In recent decades, vast numbers of knowledge products have been generated, particularly by the private sector and primarily for profit. The opening of borders and the rapid development of the internet and digital technology have further accelerated the circulation of material artefacts, digital products,

164 Anderson & Allen 2009.

165 Kioupkiolis 2014: 218.

166 Julian Assange and Edward Snowden are preeminent examples of whistle-blowers from the beginning of the twenty-first century, at <https://whistleblowingnetwork.org/Home>.

167 The term intellectual property is used here in its traditional legal sense. Creators of a commons also retain intellectual rights, as defined by the terms governing that commons.

and any kind of creation and information. However, the expansion of exclusive rights has created major barriers to free access to the fruits of human ingenuity. This trend has also led to the professionalisation of creative production, rooted in market competition and reflected in the public sphere. As Alan Boyle argues, the true tragedy of the commons in the twenty-first century is the massive, ongoing privatisation of the intellectual public domain.[168]

Intellectual property rights mainly determine access to intellectual products primarily through two mechanisms: patents and copyrights. Other types of creations are protected by special rights, such as trademarks. The protection of intellectual property excludes those who do not pay the required fee from using the goods. These relationships emerge within market contexts but may later extend into the public sphere, where creative works become accessible once exclusivity expires or when creators voluntarily grant open access.[169]

The rules governing the sharing of knowledge and information – and the rights attached to them – are contested for many reasons. How far and for how long should copyright extend? Should the importance of creations be assessed in terms of human well-being? Can the exclusion of those wishing to improve upon a work be justified? National legislation has provided some answers, while international organisations seek to reconcile conflicting interests.

The World Intellectual Property Organization (WIPO) has played a decisive role in regulating relations between creators and the wider community. Established in 1967 to 'encourage creative activity' and 'promote intellectual property internationally', WIPO also administers patent-related agreements such as the Patent Cooperation Treaty (1970/1978).

[*Copyright*]

Copyright ensures that creators receive financial benefits from third-party use of their works. While this legitimate mechanism protects creators' interests, it can also enclose shared resources, restricting common access to widely known knowledge. Popular culture, for instance, is a common good that is, in many cases, enclosed by copyright. As Vasilis Kostakis observes, while market practices in the natural commons 'make what is rare seem abundant, in the cultural commons they make what is abundant rare'. He adds: 'If this policy continues, then the songs of Elvis Presley or the early works of Disney will never

168 Boyle 2008.

169 Copyright lasts 70 years after the death of the creator, and 20 years for patents, i.e., rights over artefacts.

enter the public domain as the works of Mozart and Shakespeare once did'.[170] Could the same apply to languages, antiquities, bodily functions, culinary methods, specific movements in sports or chess?

Globally, academic knowledge constitutes a quintessential public good, yet it is heavily fenced in by publishing rights. It could, however, be managed directly by the academic community,[171] thereby enabling controlled access under certain conditions. Universities and publishers are increasingly making journals and monographs freely available.

The 1994 Agreement on Trade-Related Aspects of Intellectual Property Rights (TRIPS), signed in Marrakesh, commits all members of the WTO to minimum standards for the protection of intellectual property. Its implementation has disadvantaged developing countries.[172] Disparities in economic power have led to intense negotiations, culminating in the 2001 Doha Declaration on TRIPS and Public Health, which permits the suspension of authors' rights in the public interest under conditions of necessity. Yet, as Pascal Lamy, then European Commissioner for Trade, noted in 2010, the Declaration 'solved about 10% of the problem of access to medicines'.[173] Following further negotiations, Article 31bis of the TRIPS Agreement (in force since 2017) allows countries producing generic drugs under compulsory licensing to export them to developing nations lacking domestic production capacity. The potential for such 'compulsory licensing' was highlighted again during the Covid-19 pandemic (see Chapter 5.6), though ultimately without success.

[*Patents*]

Knowledge generated by an individual who first invents something new – together with the results of the research and intellectual effort involved, whether in art or in science – is protected as individual or corporate property through the patent system. While patents are intended to encourage innovation by granting inventors exclusive rights, they also carry potential drawbacks. If a patent is too broadly defined, it may prevent others, whether voluntarily or collectively, from contributing to the further development, improvement, or expansion of the application of that knowledge.

---

170 Kostakis 2012: 34.

171 Beerkens 2018.

172 International Task Force on Global Public Goods 2006; Birkbeck 2009; <www.bilaterals.org/?tripping-up-trips-debates>.

173 Cf. <https://en.wikipedia.org/wiki/>.

As early as 1883, the Paris Convention for the Protection of Industrial Property laid the foundations for securing industrial intellectual property rights globally through an international body based on shared principles. For the first time, international law safeguarded the right of priority for anyone registering intellectual property rights at the international level, subjecting these rights to rules common to all.

The European Patent Office serves as the executive body of the European Patent Organisation,[174] an international organisation that recognises the rights of applicants in any European state. The Office has pursued a policy favouring 'hard' patenting. For example, for many years, it insisted on patenting vegetable varieties developed through natural processes rather than in the laboratory. In a resolution of 19 September 2019, the European Parliament called on the European Commission to ensure that the Office ceased issuing patents to companies that had created new varieties of biological plant materials. According to the debate, 'access to genetic resources must not be restricted, as this could lead to a situation where a few multinational companies have a monopoly on plant breeding material, to the detriment of EU farmers and consumers'.[175]

Among its other objectives, WIPO promotes dialogue on the protection of folk culture and traditional knowledge, which have roots in both recent and distant history and are not subject to the modern copyright system. Since 2000, the Organization has worked towards adopting legal rules to protect traditional knowledge, genetic resources, and traditional cultural expressions effectively. The aim is to draft an international treaty establishing *sui generis* rights in favour of indigenous peoples and communities over cultural resources transmitted from generation to generation and modified through complex genealogical processes, in an open manner where the user 'borrows' the resource.[176]

Following the 2003 Convention for the Safeguarding of Intangible Cultural Heritage, states are already obliged to adopt appropriate measures in favour of traditional knowledge located on their territories. The recognition of traditional forms of production and innovation marks a watershed, as new actors will influence the development and application of international law.[177]

174 The European Patent Organisation, which does not belong to the EU, was created in 1977 according to the 1973 European Patent Convention.

175 Cf. <https://bit.ly/3eUMGsE>.

176 Cf. 2019 interview with Wend Wendland, Director of the WIPO Traditional Knowledge Division, at <https://www.ifla.org/node/92129>.

177 Phillips 2016.

There are numerous examples of companies enclosing practical applications of traditional knowledge, or plants and their derivatives found in another country, without granting the accompanying rights. In a landmark 1980 decision, the US Supreme Court held that a patent is permissible for microorganisms created by humans – such as through mutation – rather than by nature.[178] However, in many cases, litigation has resulted in third parties declaring traditional knowledge unpatentable, thereby precluding commercial exploitation. In addition to the examples given in Chapter 4.2 concerning quinoa or turmeric in the context of biodiversity protection, the legal dispute between India and the United States regarding the patenting of yoga exercises is also noteworthy. Finally, in 2002, after protracted legal battles, India created a database – the Traditional Knowledge Digital Library – containing 34 million pages documenting the uses and applications of natural substances found in India, as well as common or traditional knowledge and practices.[179] The Indian government has thus largely thwarted attempts by European and American companies to claim exclusive rights over traditional knowledge.

As Lawrence Lessig has written, 'patents are not evil per se; they are evil only if they do no social good. They do no social good if they benefit certain companies at the expense of innovation generally. And as many have argued convincingly, that's just what many patents today do'.[180]

[*The Digital Commons*]

The digital commons – all shared digital resources created and maintained by a community for the public good – rely on a network structure that incorporates appropriate technical innovation and a horizontal division of powers that enables autonomous decision-making. These communities engage in peer collaboration and are monitored by peers, ensuring the shared nature of digital peer production.[181] Digital commons typically begin as small community initiatives but have the potential to grow into large-scale infrastructures,[182] attracting a wide range of contributors and enabling global applications. These infrastructures, valued for their economic and social roles, contribute significantly to various activities, though assessing their overall impact can be challenging. Examples of digital commons include open-source software such as

---

178 *Diamond v. Chakrabarty*, 447 US 303 (1980).

179 Cf. <http://bit.ly/2WrM2uB>.

180 Lessig 202b: 259.

181 Kornilakis 2024: 100–103.

182 Krewer & Warso 2024.

Linux and Firefox, collaborative knowledge projects such as Wikipedia, and shared data resources such as OpenStreetMap.

In the name of free access, commercial companies use the digital commons to maximise their profits without giving anything in return. For example, the use of free software by commercial companies is widespread, particularly in mobile phone software (cf. Android). The financial contributions of multinational companies to software communities, after they use the open-source software and turn it into closed source, are disproportionately small compared to the profits they make. Furthermore, both tangible and 'intangible'[183] components of electronic devices produced by companies are often the result of research funded by public funds. Many such companies also relocate their headquarters to tax havens, resulting in significant revenue losses for states and, consequently, reduced funding for public infrastructure due to the decline in tax income from these profits.[184]

Digital commons can be regarded as public goods when they provide services through applications in areas such as education, healthcare, agriculture, transportation, government schemes, and other digital public infrastructure, even when used for profit by companies – as in banking and payments – provided they contribute a fair share to the 'common fund'. India serves as an example of a state that has implemented restrictions in favour of digital commons, designating community and national data as 'sovereign capital' that supports the country's development.[185] The challenge in such cases lies in ensuring that states use data for the benefit of the community, rather than allowing it to be appropriated by national elites, thereby widening the gap between the privileged and the excluded.

Data is the lifeblood of the digital economy. In such a dynamic and multicentred environment, the ability to own and process Big Data provides a decisive advantage in the digital market. Policies related to digital industrialisation must therefore prioritise individual autonomy over the economic profits of multinational corporations, which, owing to their technological dominance, often monopolise the exploitation of Big Data.[186]

---

183 Software, although intangible, also has a material dimension linked to the production of energy required for its use and to the pollutants it emits.

184 Pazaitis & Kostakis 2021.

185 Rizvi 2020. Similarly, the emergence of sovereign rights over a people's data has also been seen in New Zealand (Maori Data Sovereignty Network).

186 Big Data refers to sets of digital data that are so large or complex that they require specialised processing, recording, storage, and analysis techniques. See: James 2020: 83. See also the call by organisations for the democratisation of the 'dataisation' of commoners at: <https://bit.ly/3n8Z8rm>; <https://bit.ly/3n8Z8rm>.

In practice, the digital data generated by our daily online activity is collected by large companies without oversight or public benefit and used to feed their ever-expanding artificial intelligence systems for profit. Thus, digital data – both personal and non-personal – associated with artificial intelligence, instead of constituting a universal commons from which applications could be developed for individuals, communities, and states, is fenced off as the property of specific companies and stored in data centres under a controversial legal regime. Data exploitation thereby becomes a new site of extraction; in other words, it gives rise to a form of *digital colonialism*.[187] Moreover, although the algorithms underpinning artificial intelligence are protected by intellectual property rights, they must also be subject to social control and public accountability, given their dominant role in shaping social and political behaviour, sovereign politics, and the economy – namely, in the public domain.

The control of Big Data by multinational companies (cf. Google, Amazon, Microsoft, Apple) means that states, individuals, groups, and other companies become mere spectators of developments in the global economy and the much-vaunted freedom of e-commerce. Already, SpaceX's Starlink satellite internet service, launched in 2022, could conceivably lead in the near future to non-accountability and monopolistic control over a large portion of communication and data transfer. According to Deborah James, the activities of such companies in the digital domain result in:[188]

- the appropriation of citizens' personal data without cost or consent;
- tax avoidance;
- the undermining of infrastructure development through which states provide public goods for shared wellbeing;
- the violation of rights relating to sensitive personal data; and
- the avoidance of democratic control and accountability.

The claim by companies that only data collectors, rather than producers or the states in which they operate, have the right to create enclosures conflicts with the idea that digital commons have value for communities of commoners – both human and state. Legal gaps facilitate the commercialisation of data. However, as Tommaso Fia notes, 'empirical evidence suggests that the open data approach can work as a default rule governing raw non-personal data'.[189]

Globally, surveillance is becoming increasingly pervasive, serving as a mechanism to influence behaviour, maximise economic profit, and support pol-

187 Vladan Joler, *New Extractivism*, youtube [2022], at <https://bit.ly/4c8tAeU>.

188 James 2020.

189 Fia 2021.

itical forces that favour profit-driven strategies incompatible with democratic participation. The predictability of individuals' behaviour – whether as consumers or voters – has been commodified. One example is Cambridge Analytica, which used Facebook data to influence voters in the 2016 US presidential election and the Brexit referendum.[190] Likewise, individuals' private experiences – an inviolable area of privacy at the core of human rights – are increasingly subject to mechanisms of information commodification.

Although personal data is legally protected against commercial exploitation, it is frequently traded as a product by companies affiliated with social media entities.[191] Data centres collect vast amounts of information from all online communications and transactions without users' direct consent, generating massive profits for companies and creating a vast oligopoly. The consumption of energy and water – resources vital to local communities – adds another critical environmental dimension to the issue.[192] These databases which contain personal information, including metadata, are controlled by entities that cannot be regarded as 'stewardship' agents. Questions about individual privacy are gaining prominence as companies increasingly mediate interpersonal communication. In many countries, judicial decisions increasingly favour stronger privacy protection, although such decisions may not rest on a common regulatory framework offering effective guarantees.[193]

The new phenomenon, which Shoshana Zuboff calls 'surveillance capitalism' offers no guarantees of democratic control and tends to concentrate political and economic power at the expense of individual freedoms and the future of humankind.[194] The international community remains ineffective in tackling this major challenge through binding, enforceable guarantees. At least, such concerns are beginning to take shape at international intergovernmental fora. The UN Global Digital Compact (2024) – a non-binding text – stipulates 'that common data standards and interoperable data exchanges can increase the accessibility and sharing of data and help close data divides. We will enable open data initiatives that are created and managed by all stake-

190 Watch the documentary directed by Jehane Noujaim and Karim Amer, *The Great Hack* (Netflix 2019).

191 For example, with the implementation of the EU's General Data Protection Regulation (Regulation (EU) 2016/679) in May 2018, all companies operating in the EU are bound by the same set of rules, regardless of their headquarters' location.

192 Damania et al. 2025: 178.

193 Munier et al. 2013. Regarding the use of metadata: <http://bit.ly/3p5tYmc>.

194 Zuboff 2019.

holders, including communities and individuals, to utilize and leverage data for their development and well-being' (para. 46).[195]

[*Peer-to-Peer Production and Creative Commons Licences*]
Creators or groups of co-creators may share creation rights through a 'patent pool'. In such an arrangement, the rights holders agree to share their patents via reciprocal use and exploitation licences. However, there is an important distinction between 'peer-to-peer production' and 'community-based peer-to-peer production'. Digital peer production takes place on platforms such as TikTok, Facebook, or YouTube, even though these platforms themselves do not constitute commons.[196] Content may be jointly produced by their communities of users, but not by the platforms themselves, which lack participatory modes of organisation and do not allow users to decide how the platform operates. Equally critical are the status of the 'pool' and the conditions under which it was designed and now operates. Similarly, joint-stock companies may accumulate a shared reserve as the basis for peer-to-peer production, but they do not constitute commons, since the common good, the community, and the community-defined regulatory framework do not co-exist.

In interpersonal and commercial relations, the development of peer-to-peer public creation demonstrates that another paradigm can emerge in the production of knowledge and goods – one not driven solely by financial profit. Although profit is not excluded as a possible outcome, the equal relationship between the parties shifts the paradigm toward social common profit. In peer production, work is freely chosen. It does not involve the production of commodities but of use-values, which can also be shared globally. Whereas wage–labour relations accumulate capital, 'peer relations of production reproduce and accumulate commons'.[197]

There are numerous examples of the joint production and redistribution of knowledge and information. As early as the late seventeenth century, the 'Republic of Letters' emerged among intellectuals who shared their ideas through correspondence, forming a network. One of the most notable examples is the Manufacturers Aircraft Association (MAA), a private cooperative in the United States, which, after its creation in 1917, undercut major

195 UN, Office for Digital and Emerging Techonologies, Global Digital Compact, September 2024, at <https://www.un.org/techenvoy/global-digital-compact>.

196 It can be based on the commons, in the sense of using (exploiting) digital commons. Bauwens, Kostakis & Pazaitis 2019: 13.

197 Papanikolaou 2017.

industrial producers of the time and spurred wartime aircraft production. Participants in the MAA made their patents available to one another without remuneration, thereby rapidly expanding the project's success by combining profit and capital accumulation.[198]

Peer-to-peer production has since extended across many sectors of the economy and the digital sphere. Peer-to-peer networking between two or more computers, allowing equal data sharing, has significantly contributed to the establishment of this new paradigm. GNU/Linux is perhaps the most emblematic example of creating, continuously improving, and adapting freely available computer software. Other examples include, among many others: open electronic encyclopaedias (e.g., Wikipedia), audiobook libraries (e.g., LibriVox), web platforms (e.g., Archive.org), voluntary activism and investigative journalism based on open information sharing (e.g., Bellingcat), as well as professional news-sharing organisations (e.g., the Associated Press).

In Open Source Software products, each participant makes their code publicly available free of charge, subject to the restriction that it may not be redistributed under the same licensing terms. Relations between producer and intervenors are governed by both formal and customary – or 'vernacular' – law. Quality control is often maintained through routine procedures. For example, content posted on the open encyclopaedia Wikipedia is subject to a dispute-resolution mechanism designed to maintain its reliability in the spirit of peer-to-peer production.[199]

Open access to and investment in knowledge provide a sustainable response to the enclosure of knowledge and technology, resources vital for economic growth. Major research programmes rely on open scientific data, such as that produced by the European Organization for Nuclear Research (CERN) microparticle accelerator.

The medical commons have a special place in this debate, as they concern human life itself. Many digital databases aggregate research results and make them accessible to the medical community, often through collaborations among pharmaceutical companies, researchers, and government agencies. In producing, gathering, and sharing medical knowledge, the state may act as guarantor, financier, coordinator, partner, or manager.[200] Numerous examples demonstrate the effectiveness of medical commons in advancing

198 Madison, Frischmann & Strandburg 2010, 660–661. For alternative entrepreneurship models, see Chapter 6.4.

199 Madison, Frischmann & Strandburg 2010: 662.

200 Contreras 2017.

research and improving treatment outcomes – such as databases of microbes and rare diseases, the human genome commons, the Covid-19 treatment (see Chapters 4.8 and 5.6), open-access medical and biological journals like the Public Library of Science, and initiatives of researchers and physicians who collaborate to produce drugs and provide treatment in the field, such as the Drugs for Neglected Diseases Initiative and the International AIDS Vaccine Initiative, among many others. These digital commons are typically hybrid in nature, involving commoners from diverse categories: intellectual property holders, material producers, and professional cooperative organisations.

The creations mentioned above belong to each person individually and potentially to all collectively, reflecting the coexistence of the individual within the collective and vice versa. Ultimately, the goal of peer creation is to produce knowledge based on an original idea and a collective purpose that mobilises commoners worldwide.

To guard against the enclosure of the commons, legal tools have been established to ensure open access to and availability of intellectual creations. Creative Commons or General Public Licences support personal autonomy and protect creators' values, without enclosing their work.[201] Open licences rely on the contractual freedom of the parties involved, enabling users to utilise works in ways that would otherwise be prohibited. These licences were first developed by free software advocates led by Richard Stallman.[202] With the establishment of the Free Software Foundation in 1985, they laid the groundwork for a new legal regime that protects open-source software as a common good.

Open licences now cover hundreds of millions of digital creations, marking a shift in open knowledge and its dissemination. They are defined as private agreements in which the creator specifies the terms of access and any restrictions. Each user or new creator becomes a contracting party bound by the licence terms. In practice, these licences have flourished in various forms since the late 1980s and have been integrated into domestic commercial law. Further research is needed to clarify the cartels and enclosures that have developed around Creative Commons licences and the policies promoted by relevant international organisations (see WIPO, above).

Protecting open licences could help ensure the sustainability of creative communities – for example, by returning a portion of profits to the community when an intangible product is commercially exploited. A global Chamber

201 Kostakis 2012; Bauwens 2010; Barnes 2006.

202 Cf. <https://www.gnu.org/>.

of the Commons[203] could manage such licences within existing national legal frameworks and support commons partnerships at both national and international levels. Moreover, new institutional structures and rules are needed at the international level, both within and beyond the WTO, to enshrine digital data as a common resource. Lastly, the measures introduced during the 2020 health crisis have already shaken the international trade system and underscored the need to renegotiate the rules governing digital trade.[204]

The decentralised peer-to-peer production process and the emergence of a new governance paradigm are crucial to understanding how data are produced and classified. One tool that facilitates peer-to-peer production is *blockchain* technology,[205] a form of Distributed Ledger Technology. The blockchain ecosystem – still in its early stages – aims to bypass traditional relations of production. Many protocol designs are being developed to decentralise storage, law, information, governance, security, economics, and ultimately the market itself. With blockchain protocols, digital data could become public and universal, and the generation of computing power could become a redistributive shared resource. This would enable the creation of new entities, products, and services with added value.[206]

Each blockchain can constitute a commons, provided that a corresponding community of commoners is established – one that shares management responsibilities and not merely a set of disconnected individuals. The transparency, security, speed, and distributed nature of blockchains allow small communities, globally allocated though, to establish new forms of consensus and self-governance without requiring physical space. Blockchains thus enable decentralised production and control at the level of individual users-commoners. Each member retains autonomous decision-making authority, akin to that of a public body. In the blockchain context, abundance does not lead to resource depletion; rather, it reduces scarcity and exclusion in both material and immaterial intellectual production. Nevertheless, the unresolved issue of

---

203 For the idea of creating chambers for the commons – rooted in twentieth-century developments – cf. <https://wiki.p2pfoundation.net/Chamber_of_the_Commons>.

204 A 2020 letter from 315 organisations, both international and national, to the WTO is indicative of the intensity and significance of this negotiation. Cf. Civil Society Letter Against Digital Trade Rules in the WTO, at <https://bit.ly/2JW6jVT>.

205 The blockchain is the registration of a certain transaction or (more generally) information in a public ledger. Each new group of records ('blocks') is connected to the previous ones, forming a 'chain' of entries in which the blocks are connected in linear order.

206 See also the development of *backfeed*, an advanced form of blockchains, in: Pazaitis, De Filippi & Kostakis 2017; Bauwens & Niaros 2017. For the development of blockchains into *holochains*, cf. Bollier & Helfrich 2019.

disproportional energy consumption raises major environmental concerns that undermine their character as 'commons'.[207]

8.3 Internet: A Digital and Tangible Limitless Commons

As Yochai Benkler observes, the myriad changes in technology, the economy, and social practices related to the production and dissemination of information have created new possibilities and relationships in how knowledge and culture are produced, exchanged, and received. Many of these changes reinforce the role of individuals who operate outside market dynamics and relations of appropriation. This reinforcement occurs through various forms of collaboration among individuals, collectives, and legal entities. The emergence of such practices, as well as a new ethical attitude towards the commercialisation of knowledge, has been particularly successful across a range of fields, such as free software, open journalism, and the availability of a wide range of applications.[208] As this new information environment develops through the internet, driven by the free will of individuals and groups, it gives rise to exceptional possibilities that did not exist at the end of the twentieth century. Individual freedom encourages democratic participation, greater criticism of authority, and the spread of information – true or fake – beyond the market-based media industry.

Cyberspace has a dual character in terms of the space it occupies. First, in digital form, it constitutes a virtual space made up of innumerable web pages on the internet. It also occupies real space in its physical form – in the cables running between continents on the ocean floor and on land, through all the countries of the world, and the devices at both central and peripheral nodes, up to the terminal computers. It forms a digital universal commons, subject to national jurisdictions but requiring central governance to ensure accessibility, privacy, and technological neutrality. It can facilitate universal access regardless of geographical boundaries. Its decentralised nature enhances the free exchange of information, while the interactive capabilities of digital technologies enable users to act as both producers and consumers of content.

Cyberspace constantly fosters new relationships among commoners, redefining existing dynamics. Every transfer of information and its content is based on codes that are written and then secured or left open, and these codes can also be continuously rewritten. The development of the internet

207 Bauwens, Kostakis & Pazaitis 2019: 38.

208 Benkler 2006.

through open protocols (HTTP, DNS, TCP/IP)[209] has shaped the new condition of information, alongside the commercialisation of home computers and telephones. Decentralised production and the universal dissemination of information, together with the growth of the digital industry, create a dual system of conflicting interests that often coexist within and beyond the market. It is evident that, for the first time, non-commercial social production plays a significant role in modern democracies, through a universal commons of information and culture produced and shared by commoners.

Homogenising ownership of the internet would require comprehensive political or economic management and control over the entire network and its access points. Control can already be exercised within state borders, as is the case in many regions of the world. Similar considerations also apply to the cloud, which represents the storage capacity provided by digital service companies to users. If this capacity is understood as integral to cyberspace, similar questions arise regarding access to digital infrastructure, management, decision-making, and, above all, energy consumption, ownership, and maintenance of the tangible infrastructure. As Kotsaka questions: If public funding for the infrastructure (cables, hubs, data centres, energy) required to develop digital technology is substantial, should the public not have ownership and control over the resulting product? If the internet is so vital to our survival, should it not be treated as a non-profit utility?[210]

The internet, as a mixed resource, faces a significant threat from 'closed appropriation' and political control at the three levels of its construction, as Lessig notes:[211]

A. The first level consists of cables and computers, over which users have control and ownership.
B. On this substructure, the protocols that govern the internet's functioning operate.
C. This infrastructure exists inside a 'box' containing the TCP/IP; websites, emails, advertisements, etc. move from user terminal to user terminal.

This complex system forms a global common resource – one of the most remarkable innovations yet seen – founded on the principles of jointness, (non)exclusion, and indivisibility,[212] and, at last, a universal commons. Currently, internet operating protocols adhere to the principle of content neutral-

209 Hypertext Transfer Protocol, Domain Name System, Transmission Control Protocol/Internet Protocol, respectively.
210 Kotsaka 2022: 254.
211 Lessig 2002a: 182.
212 Holman & McGregor 2005: 267–268, 287; Lessig 2002b.

ity, i.e., refraining from any inequitable or discriminatory measure that might increase or reduce, even indirectly, the accessibility of particular websites.[213] The question that remains, however, is which body will be able to impose international legal standards to defend the principle of neutrality and, more generally, shared rules regarding the accessibility, connectivity, and use of the internet?

In the European Union, Regulation 2015/2120 established measures to protect free access to the internet and to create the conditions necessary for safeguarding the principle of neutrality. Furthermore, the Office of the Body of European Regulators for Electronic Communications[214] (BEREC) assists national regulatory authorities in standardising practices and exchanging information.

[*On Security*]

Cyberspace security may, in part, serve to protect users, but it may also be shaped by policies that seek to suppress and restrict users' rights. In practice, both states and companies – particularly those that manage vast amounts of information and communication channels, such as social networks – can create oligopolies that exert significant control over the market and seek to influence users' preferences as customers and voters.[215]

The concept of security in cyberspace is inherently controversial, depending on one's perspective – whether defending an existing order or advocating for greater freedom and the exchange of information. In this context, security implies safeguarding pluralism while respecting privacy and the shared right to information. Moreover, it is in the area of security that the true extent of democratic participation and the democratic capacity of the body supervising the common resource can be assessed. Relevant rules derive from treaty law, such as the Council of Europe's 2001 Budapest Convention on Cybercrime, and from non-binding recommendations, such as NATO's Tallinn Manuals 1.0 and 2.0 on cyber warfare. Moreover, after years of negotiations, the UN Convention against Cybercrime was adopted by the General Assembly on 24 December 2024 (Res. 79/243), and opened for signature on 25 October 2025. The Convention is the first international binding text that provides a framework for investigating and prosecuting crimes committed on the internet, such as ransomware, financial fraud, and child sexual abuse. It aims to establish inter-

213 Wu 2003; Lessig 2002b.

214 Cf. <https://berec.europa.eu/eng/berec_office/tasks_and_role/>.

215 Rifkin 2017.

national cooperation, exchange of electronic evidence, and provide assistance for capacity building.

Another aspect of security concerns the physical infrastructure of the internet, such as submarine cables, especially those located on the international seabed. To date, there has been no thorough discussion of who is responsible for their security, nor of how the international community's responsibilities should be defined to ensure that the world's web infrastructure functions smoothly.

[*Management and Openness*]

The regime governing cyberspace is imperfect and determined by state policies. As a result, the internet – a technological resource – is at once unified and highly fragmented. The Internet Corporation for Assigned Names and Numbers (ICANN), an American non-profit company based in Los Angeles,[216] established in 1998 under a US Department of Commerce contract, is in charge of managing and allocating autonomous number systems, root zones in the Domain Name System, and IP addresses to five Regional Internet Registries. The Snowden revelations in 2013 and the reactions against the US-controlled internet, led by Brazil, pushed the US government in August 2016 to withdraw from ICANN, which transitioned to a global multi-stakeholder community while retaining a strong corporate character with no genuine international accountability. The fact that a company, rather than an international organisation, has assumed crucial responsibilities over the internet has aroused strong suspicion. Russia and China have proposed transferring internet governance to the International Telecommunications Union, which they consider the most competent international body in this field.[217]

The ubiquitous territoriality of the internet and the unique characteristics of cyberspace raise crucial questions about the exercise of state sovereignty.[218] Its increasing use by people in the Global South has added new dimensions to a universal commons that is internationally fragmented yet unified, managed

216 Cf. <https://www.icann.org/resources/pages/welcome-2012-02-25-en>. The Internet Assigned Numbers Authority (IANA), a branch of ICANN, is responsible for allocating IP addresses, Internet numbers, and domain names. IANA performs the technical functions and maintains the registries necessary for the internet to operate as a single, interoperable network. At the same time, ICANN provides the organisational structure and policy framework within which the IANA services are provided.

217 Costalli & Fasani 2013: 50. See also joint statement issued by China and Russia in February 2022, at <http://en.kremlin.ru/supplement/5770>.

218 Liaropoulos 2017.; See also: Joseph & Bhaskaran Pillai 2020.

yet ungoverned. As Tim Berners-Lee notes, 'the Internet is dominated by the self-interest of several corporations that have eroded the web's values and led to breakdown and harm. Now the rapid advancement of AI has exacerbated these concerns'.[219] A group of leading internet experts has intervened, pointing out that:

> The internet is an unusual technology because it is fundamentally distributed. It is built from all participating networks. Each network participates for its own reasons according to its own needs and priorities. Furthermore, this means, necessarily, that there is no centre of control on the internet. This feature is an essential property of the internet, and not an accident.

They also called on the UN and states 'to ensure that proposals for digital governance remain consistent with the enormously successful multi-stakeholder internet governance practice that has brought us the Internet of today'.[220]

Sharing these concerns, the UN has initiated efforts to establish a unified policy framework for the internet. The Global Digital Compact, adopted in September 2024, sets a series of goals such as closing all digital divides and delivering an inclusive digital economy; building an inclusive, open, safe, and secure digital space; and strengthening international data governance and governing AI for humanity. Among its central topics are digital public goods and digital public infrastructure, both of which are considered 'key drivers of inclusive digital transformation and innovation' (para. 16).[221]

However, these initiatives lack enforceability, and the legal texts formulate recommendations. One of the main unresolved issues regards free accessibility to the internet. Would it be possible to circumvent the commodification of internet access by using independent networks developed by commoners? For example, the Reasonable Optical Near Joint Access network is a low-cost system that enables data transmission over more than a kilometre, demonstrating that it is technologically feasible to create a wireless network comparable to the internet. This technology could not have been developed if the same regulatory framework that for decades has restricted access to the ra dio spectrum had also applied to light.[222] Other applications with the characteristics of a commons have become a reality without requiring 'heavy' te-

219 Berners-Lee 2024.

220 *An open letter to the UN*, 1 July 2024, <https://open-internet-governance.org/letter>.

221 UN, Office for Digital and Emerging Technologies, Global Digital Compact, September 2024, <https://www.un.org/techenvoy/global-digital-compact>.

222 Cf. <http://ronja.twibright.com/>.

chnological innovation. All that is needed is a political decision in favour of sharing.[223] Increasingly, municipalities worldwide are installing Wi-Fi in public spaces or providing free server space to host web pages.

As with the radio spectrum, it is difficult to associate the digital ecosystem with the idea of something wholly subject to authority and, therefore, to ownership. Both have already become partly subject to ownership. However, the total homogenisation of the internet as an appropriated resource would also mean its demise as a universal commons – or as a free space for browsing, to use a Grotian analogy.

223 Bollier & Helfrich 2019: 309.

CHAPTER 5

Commoning as a Right

> Everyone is entitled to a social and international order in which the rights and freedoms set forth in this Declaration can be fully realized. (Universal Declaration of Human Rights, art. 28)

Common goods, resources, or spaces on the global scale may be subject to an unspecified duty of care by those who have the capacity to provide stewardship. One could argue that this duty of care is interconnected with the intergenerational pursuit of sustainable development of life and wellbeing through the precautionary and preventive principles. Is this duty of care resulting in an emerging right for every human being as a member of the global community of commoners? Certainly, we cannot argue that an enforceable individual right is universally grounded in the commons today.

Conversely, there is an urgent need to develop the established rights that correspond to the collective interests of individuals, communities, and states related to global common resources. These rights are linked to obligations and, above all, to the need to regulate people's relationships with any entity that may influence the fate of the commons. The primary objective of this role should be to ensure the sustainability of the commons, as this is a fundamental precondition for human wellbeing and existence. In this case, shouldn't the rights of people regarding the universal commons be defined and institutionalised? First, however, we need to clarify the position and role of commoners as subjects of rights and obligations.

1 Which Subjects?

The terms of the compromise between state sovereignty and the sustainability of shared resources, goods, or spaces for the benefit of humanity are constantly up for renegotiation. Using the legal tools currently available, achieving this objective remains challenging, except in a fragmented form. However, in recent years, legal arrangements that favour claims for sustainable universal commons have been increasingly adopted. Given the diverse nature of the commons, various legal approaches are emerging within international law.[1]

1 Bodansky 2012: 651–668.

 HTTPS://DOI.ORG/10.1163/9789004764118-006

Likewise, the subjects of international law and the rights and obligations which have developed in relation to the commons are mostly 'rigid', such as the state, but also 'emergent' or 'mobile', as is the case with the individual and collectives.

The universal commons are caught in a double tug-of-war: between national and international law, and between private interests and the need for protection of shared goods, resources, and spaces. In this double-contradictory approach, a series of questions arises: How is the position of communities and commoners as subjects of rights over the commons established? Which subjects retain the power of decision-making – the *demos* of the commoners, the state, or an international body? By which procedures, and with what legitimacy? Who will determine which procedural rules should be followed?[2] Indeed, not all subjects have the same objectives, power, or legitimacy in the commons. The struggle among different groups of commoners acting for the common good can often set the stage for direct or indirect multilateral conflict.

Clearly delineating the rights and obligations of all subjects through international norms is a complex task that extends beyond the recognised subjects of international law. The crucial aspect to address is the identification of the commoners of the universal commons and the subjects who bear the rights and responsibilities associated with these commons, whether in fact or in potential. As stated in the Introduction, these subjects constitute communities of commoners that coexist and often form mixed communities comprising two or more types of subjects: human beings and associations, peoples, states, and intergovernmental organisations. The diverse, overlapping, and changing composition of these communities also poses a significant challenge when formulating international legal norms relating to the universal commons.

1.1 From the Individual to the People: From Humankind to the Earth

In terms of human rights, new subjects endowed with rights emerge in the interactions between commoners and commons. The dynamics between the commons and commoners shift across historical periods and modes of production. While the subjects involved may not fundamentally differ from those already recognised, their circumstances are redefined in light of the evolving significance of global common resources to people's lives and wellbeing. Individuals, groups, communities, indigenous peoples, states, and international organisations all serve as actors who, from different perspectives, influence

2 Shaffer 2012: 669–693.

legal relations with the global resources and, therefore, the universal commons. Their impact varies, contingent on different perspectives, the subjects involved, and the intensity and density of their involvement. There is no predetermined list of subjects or commoners constituting the community at any given time. However, the composition of the community of commoners can be discerned by examining the nature of the commons in any given context.

In recent decades, two rights-related super-subjects have been taking shape: humanity and nature-Earth. Although they come from different backgrounds, they follow a trend of convergence. Both lack a solid legal framework to be considered subjects of international law. However, they have strong potential to support a comprehensive and integrated theory and practice of the universal commons. State sovereignty over the planet as a whole cannot be achieved; therefore, humankind could be seen as the only beneficiary community and steward of the planet, which is, in fact, a *res communis omnium*.

The individual has already acquired the status of a subject of international human rights law and, indeed, as a rights-bearer acting without the paternalistic mediation of diplomatic protection – i.e., the state's mandatory representation of citizens in proceedings before international courts. Individual litigant status has been vested primarily in the European Court of Human Rights (ECtHR) and the Inter-American Court of Human Rights (IACtHR).

Rarely is a community, from the perspective of the commons, recognised as a subject of rights. The European Union Directive 2018/2001 on the promotion of the use of energy from renewable sources, as revised in 2018, according to which 'renewable energy communities', consisting of natural persons and local authorities, acquire legal status as bearers of a right. More than 3,400 renewable energy cooperatives operate in Europe, governed by European and national laws that are developing in parallel.[3] The pioneering recognition of energy communities can serve as a guide for establishing the legal status of communities in other areas, related to water, air, food resources, or the internet.

The collective rights set out in international instruments are exercised either individually and collectively or through collective subjects. In fact, indigenous peoples and local communities have begun to acquire legal personality by enjoying special rights, such as those related to biodiversity, traditional knowledge, and land exploitation. For example, both the Convention on Biological Diversity and the Nagoya Protocol recognise indigenous peoples as rights-holders in relation to biodiversity resources. Moreover, the 1989 Inter-

3 REScoop MECISE 2019. A relevant legislative framework has been developed in the UK, the Netherlands, Denmark, and elsewhere.

national Labour Organization Convention No. 169 concerning Indigenous and Tribal Peoples recognises the rights of indigenous communities to access, manage, and protect natural resources (art. 15.1). The 2007 Declaration of the UN General Assembly also recognises collective rights for indigenous peoples, while similar negotiations are being conducted within WIPO regarding the intellectual property rights of indigenous peoples and local communities in the field of traditional knowledge and genetic resources.[4] However, it is questionable whether these arrangements reflect a newly emerging right for commoners to exploit natural resources or merely a relic of the end of colonialism.[5]

The content of the political agency of the individual as a legal subject-commoner is of significant importance to this discussion. Whether acting alone or collectively, the individual establishes relationships involving the use, stewardship, production, or management of a common good, resource, or space. After all, people, as members of a political community – that is, the *demos* of each state – in theory, convey rights and duties of stewardship to their respective governments for the public interest or for the sustainability of the common resources at the local level. At the same time, they co-constitute, consciously or unintentionally, the universal political community of human beings, the *universal demos*, i.e., the fictitious concept of 'humankind' as a community with common interests,[6] which can be granted the role of commoner in the universal multiple commons. However, can humankind be a subject in the sense of being a commoner of the whole of the universal commons? How can humankind assume stewardship responsibilities without being subject to any liability? As Erin Daly and Dina Lupin put it, humanity in the Anthropocene is corporate in nature, which obscures from view the small group of individuals who make the key decisions and eventually cause disproportionate harm to the rest of humankind.[7]

The *multitude*, local and universal, according to Michael Hardt and Antonio Negri, is a changing unit of people, not identified as such nor uniform. It is mobilised on a case-by-case, segmented basis for the *common interest*. The *multitude* could be seen as a form of organisation, constantly ready to exist as such, yet ultimately not expressing itself in any particular form.[8] Besides,

4 Philips 2016.
5 Armstrong 2017: 163.
6 Simma 1994; Hofbauer 2022.
7 Daly & Lupin 2023: 229.
8 Hardt & Negri 2004.

the people who make up the universal multitude are occasionally active or potential commoners of a universal commons.

'The individual has duties toward the community within which the personality can fully develop', according to Article 29 of the Universal Declaration of Human Rights. This formulation could not describe more fittingly the role of each society, at the local, regional, or universal level, not as a passive recipient of external events but as a subject endowed with rights and responsibilities towards its fellow members. It rejects the notion of societies as impersonal entities within an undefined whole, highlighting the position of individuals instead as subjects of duties. In the context of community management of commons, the term acquires predominant meanings and legal connotations.

Recognising 'the people' as the subject of rights is a major challenge for international law, especially when applied in relation to universal commons. The term 'people' is often tied to the right to self-determination and, in the case of indigenous peoples, to rights over ancestral lands. The acknowledgement of rights for indigenous peoples has direct implications for initiating actions and asserting rights. It also influences how corporations and other non-state actors fulfil their obligation to avoid causing harm to common goods and resources linked to indigenous peoples and to contribute positively to the realisation of these rights.[9] Among many jurisprudential examples, the IACtHR upheld that the Sawhoyamaxa community in Paraguay is a collective subject of rights, that they had been unlawfully evicted from their land for the sake of a meat production development project, and ordered that the land be returned.[10]

A growing number of states have recognised Nature or Earth as a subject of rights and are adopting ecological economics for a sustainable, equitable and prosperous future for all. Earth is gradually acquiring the normative foundations of human development, budding Earth-centred approaches.[11]

The trend to assign rights to nature or the Earth creates a surrogate subject for people, often with reference to indigenous peoples. For example, in 2008, the Constitution of Ecuador was amended (arts. 71 and 72), enshrining the right of the Earth itself to protection, recognising Mother Earth (Pacham-

9 Cosentino 2015.

10 The Court emphasised the importance of women's role in the community's relationship with the land in terms of food production, IACtHR, *Sawhoyamaxa Indigenous Community v. Paraguay*, 29.3.2006. See also, among many others: African Court of Human Rights, *African Commission on Human Rights v. Republic of Kenya*, 26.5.2017. Also: IACtHR, *Saramaka People v. Suriname*, 28.11.2007.

11 UN Secretary-General, *Harmony with Nature,* Report 2022, at <https://bit.ly/44l9eyi>.

ama)[12] as a quasi-subject of rights, and establishing government obligations to protect non-renewable natural resources from overexploitation and destruction. Similarly, a 2010 Bolivian law recognises Mother Earth as a collective subject of public interest. This *sui generis* legal construction creates a fictitious legal person that refers to human society as a primordial collective subject of rights. In New Zealand, a legal personality was granted to the Whanganui River in 2017, in line with Māori tradition. The river was deemed 'an organism and a living whole', granting the local population the right to steward the riparian ecosystem as a common good under state protection.[13] Concurrently, in 2017, India recognised legal personality in the Ganges and Yamuna rivers. Nevertheless, nature is not a subject related only to indigenous legal cultures. In 2022, Mar Menor (Murcia, Spain) was recognised as a subject with rights – the first ecosystem in Europe to have its own rights. The law allows citizens to seek legal protection for the ecosystem and establishes three bodies to serve as stewards of the Mar Menor. In all these examples, establishing enforceable rights for citizens to bring claims on behalf of nature before national courts is consistent with the idea of effectively protecting common resources. People and the state act as mediators or representatives of nature.[14]

Together with 'humankind', present and future 'generations' are given a voice or are at least recognised, as quasi-subjects of rights, but also holders of obligations on behalf of the commons. In particular, environmental law explicitly refers to intergenerational equity, the 'right of future generations to enjoy a just level of the common heritage', as well as intra-generational equity – the right of all people of the present generation to fair and equitable access to natural resources.

Thus, the concept of environmental equity holds the present generation accountable for the long-term consequences of its activities and imposes on it the obligation to act to protect the global ecosystem and its resources for the benefit of future generations.[15] From an egalitarian perspective, therefore, equality should not only encompass current generations' relationships with one another but also future ones.[16] Thus, it could be said that the 'generation' emerges as a quasi-subject of rights – for example, in Article 1 of the Aarhus

12 The principle of protecting Mother Earth was central to the indigenous mobilisation against the proposed highway through Bolivia's TIPNIS National Park in 2011. In contrast, non-indigenous farmer groups supported the road's construction, viewing it as a means to facilitate the transport of agricultural goods.

13 Bollier & Helfrich 2019: 309.

14 Forsyth, Pali & Tepper 2022.

15 Scholten & Bresson 2016.

16 Armstrong 2017: 78–80.

Convention, which states that every human being has a duty, individually and collectively, to protect and improve the natural environment for present and future generations.[17]

The legal recognition of future generations is indeed a complex and evolving concept. However, the increasing emphasis on the term 'generation' at the regulatory level marks a positive step towards acknowledging their importance. The challenge lies in granting subject status to individuals who are not currently alive and have no physical existence. However, the key to understanding this lies in recognising children. They are an existing group of people who garner special attention from a significant portion of society, particularly their parents and guardians. Children are considered a distinct category of subjects, entitled to special rights enshrined in both national and international law. Each child, viewed individually or collectively, represents the beginning of a new generation, even though a generation lacks a concrete beginning or end.

1.2 The State

The state, as the classic and fundamental subject of international law, possesses exclusive powers based on the sovereignty it exercises over its territory. It also bears responsibilities for specific global common spaces that have been normatively defined by international treaties: Antarctica, the seabed and subsoil of the open sea, outer space, and the Moon. In these four domains, where accessibility requires advanced technology, the state clearly occupies a privileged position. Access to certain commons often raises concern, as states with greater financial capacity, political power, and technological resources are better positioned to exploit them. In a few cases, the legal regime provides for the redistribution of benefits to weaker states within the framework of universal stewardship of the commons exercised by an international body (see Chapter 6.2).

Enforcing standard rules among states is crucial to preventing the overuse and misuse of exhaustible resources. The self-interest of any state exploiting a resource is naturally stronger than that of states that remain indifferent. International cooperation governed by shared rules of conduct, reciprocity, trust, and fair sanctions can effectively promote the *common good* and *community*

---

17 See the Preamble to the International Whaling Convention (1946), which first refers to the intergenerational obligation: 'the interest of the nations of the world in conserving for future generations great natural resources…'. The Convention on the Conservation of Migratory Species of Wild Animals (1979) also refers to the obligation to bequeath the protected natural resource to future generations (cf. Preamble, para. 2). Also: UNESCO Declaration (1977) on the Responsibilities towards Future Generations.

interests. Thus, shared interests and benefits may serve as stronger incentives for states than mere rational behaviour.[18]

States are increasingly assuming obligations that support the rights of people forming the global community in relation to health, climate, nutrition, air and water quality, forests, and biodiversity. Rules are emerging at various levels that govern state conduct regarding the production and dissemination of knowledge and information. In such cases, states' exclusive competences will not align horizontally unless an international arrangement is established to harmonise law and behaviour.

Indeed, the role of the state is crucial, since it is the competent power under the social contract. Given that this competence is perpetuated transgenerationally through the people who constitute the political community, the state represents and guarantees the 'public interest'. By extension, it is the guarantor and bearer of the obligation of 'stewardship', aiming to protect the universal commons in the name of the common interest of the people. The state itself may also be regarded as a subject of commoning *rights* over the global common resources, in relation to which it holds the status of commoner.

Today, under the ubiquitous hegemony of the 'free market', the state is far from neutral; rather, it frequently shows bias towards practices and regulations that promote capital accumulation for individual and corporate profit. Nevertheless, the state continues to shape the regulatory framework governing the universal commons through international law. States also retain a central role in the activities of international organisations, which they have themselves created and endowed with institutional autonomy.

Consequently, states assume multiple roles with respect to the universal commons: as commoners and members of the international community; as bearers of obligations to people both within and outside their territory; and as actors in ongoing negotiations with other states, international organisations, international non-governmental organisations and movements. Finally, states act as sponsors of resource-extraction companies – setting the terms of the market while simultaneously participating in it as customers.

1.3 Intergovernmental Organisations

Intergovernmental organisations often function as engines of international law-making and as 'fire brigades' responding to global emergencies. Since the 1950s, they have contributed to the development of what may be regarded as the international law of the commons.

18 Like the Kyoto mechanism for environmental protection: see van Aaken 2018.

Given the conflicting interests and asymmetrical aspirations among states, international organisations frequently serve as mediators, absorbing tensions and fostering new approaches. At other times, they become entrapped or manipulated by powerful member states. The autonomy of these bodies – depending on their legal status – can facilitate the consolidation of their role as *guarantor*s and *overseer*s of stewardship over global common resources. Numerous examples demonstrate their evolving levels of engagement and commitment to the universal commons. In some instances, international organisations act as custodians of the commons, becoming meta-subjects themselves, with multiple roles as *both* commoner *and* guarantor. In others, they promote the rights of other subjects or commoners, such as individuals, peoples, or non-governmental organisations, thereby enabling global consultation and negotiation processes leading to new law-making initiatives. This occurs mainly through the agencies of the United Nations, which plays a central role in adopting regulations governing the management of global common resources.

The International Seabed Authority (see Chapter 3.1) is one of the most comprehensive examples of an international organisation exercising stewardship over global common resources. The World Meteorological Organization exercises partial and incomplete stewardship by coordinating the collection and dissemination of meteorological data, though not extending to climate management. Similarly, the International Telecommunication Union allocates radio frequencies for satellite use but is not involved in licensing satellite orbits (see Chapter 4.6). Other international organisations lack substantial political power. Although the Amazon Cooperation Organization[19] aims to promote sustainable development and social cohesion through cooperation among member states, it has failed to effectively prevent widespread deforestation and biodiversity loss in the Amazon region.

The management of knowledge commons is also an international concern, though it faces contradictions and limitations stemming from economic pressures and the conflicting claims of private profit versus public benefit. Such tensions are evident in the activities of the World Intellectual Property Organization and the European Patent Organisation, particularly in matters of copyright.

Other, more flexible forms of interstate cooperation have developed without establishing a formal international organisation. In the Arctic, for instance,

---

19 Based in Brazilia, founded in 1978, at <http://www.otca-oficial.info/>. Its goals are being redefined in response to the 2015 Paris Climate Agreement, the 2015–2030 Sendai Framework for Disaster Risk Reduction, etc.

eight states have established a special regime administered by a permanent conference. The Arctic Council, founded in Ottawa in 1996 and based since 2013 in Tromsø, Norway,[20] manages this regime. It is complemented by conventions regulating search and rescue, scientific cooperation, and fisheries.[21]

International organisations also play a vital role in promoting international cooperation with regard to global public goods. In recent decades, issues such as public health, education, reducing inequalities and poverty, and access to drinking water have become central global objectives, alongside the imperative to address the climate crisis. These efforts bring together states, non-governmental organisations, and citizens from around the world, often under the coordination of the UN or other international organisations, in a global, polycentric – though often ineffective – attempt to govern the commons.

1.4 Non-governmental Organisations and Social Movements

The assertion of rights and the protection of global resources have been largely driven by the concerted action of non-governmental organisations operating internationally across thematic areas. Such organisations emerged primarily after the Second World War and span a broad and diverse range of global concerns. The environment is the most prominent field of their activity.[22] Many operate in areas directly related to human rights – both individual (life, health, nutrition)[23] and collective (such as the right of peoples to transparency regarding the financial terms of investment agreements between governments and multinational corporations, or the management of revenues derived from such agreements).[24]

Corporations accused of harmful practices sometimes retaliate against activist groups. For instance, in September 2018, Monsanto demanded that the online platform Avaaz disclose the databases of those who voted against the

20 Cf. <https://bit.ly/3auHgEG>. For the regime governing natural resources in the Arctic and the rights of indigenous peoples, see: Cambou & Smis 2013.

21 See: Nuuk Agreement on Cooperation on Aeronautical and Maritime Search and Rescue in the Arctic (2011), Agreement on Enhancing International Arctic Scientific Cooperation (2017), Agreement to Prevent Unregulated Fishing in the High Seas in the Central Arctic Ocean (2017). The first of its kind was the Agreement on the Conservation of Polar Bears (1973). Cf. <https://bit.ly/3auHgEG>.

22 For instance: WWF (<www.wwf.org>), Global Biodiversity Information Facility (<https://www.gbif.org/>).

23 Amnesty International (www.amnesty.org), International Federation of Human Rights (www.fidh.org), SEEDS (https://www.seeds-ngo.org/), Human Rights Watch (www.hrw.org), La Via Campesina (https://viacampesina.org/en/).

24 Extractive Industries Transparency Initiative (<https://eiti.org>), Publish What You Pay (<www.publishwhatyoupay.org>).

company's health-endangering activities. The Manhattan Supreme Court rejected the claim, reasoning not only that it would violate data protection but also that it would unduly restrict the capacity of citizen movements to exercise public scrutiny and advocacy on urgent issues.[25]

More broadly, the term 'organisations' encompasses international social movements, as well as ad hoc fora and gatherings. One example is the coalition of over 900 organisations that participated in the 1992 United Nations Conference on Environment and Development in Rio. Other examples include alliances of groups advocating for the democratisation of the internet and digital communities, or those opposing the monopolistic exploitation of planetary resources by multinational corporations.[26]

International NGOs are often invited to participate in consultation processes organised by intergovernmental bodies. As a result, they contribute to law- and policy-making procedures, defending rights associated with the universal commons. Through assertive activism, such organisations sometimes create jurisprudential precedents that shape international practice and raise public awareness in support of the commons. A notable example is the initiative of Pacific Island Students Fighting Climate Change, supported by other civil society organisations and governments such as those of Vanuatu and other Small Island Developing States, which led to the unanimous UN General Assembly resolution 77/267 (March 2023). This resolution requested an advisory opinion from the ICJ on the obligations of states under international law with regard to climate change and the legal consequences of non-compliance. The ICJ delivered its landmark advisory opinion in July 2025 (see Chapter 5.3.2).

Thus, civil society organisations and movements can be powerful actors in asserting claims to common resources.[27] They represent commoners seeking to mobilise states and international organisations to recognise their stewardship obligations. They often succeed, intentionally or not, in cultivating a sense of global solidarity and shared responsibility. Social movements, as well as influential individuals, empower communities to defend their rights and (re) claim the common goods, resources, or spaces with which they are associated.

Groups of activists, individuals, social movements, and organisations constitute the militant wing of the *universal demos*, aspiring to emancipatory solidarity. They continually seek to infuse new meaning into the 'fertile idea' of the commons.[28] The political pressure exerted by such organisations and

25 Supreme Court of New York, 6.9.2018, at <https://bit.ly/3PcaAlW>.

26 See <https://justnetcoalition.org> and <https://bit.ly/3IDi2XQ>.

27 Klein 2001.

28 Karitzis 2016: 276.

movements can be decisive in shaping attitudes and policies. The Reclaim the Commons Manifesto, presented at the 2009 World Social Forum, articulated the hope that participatory, collaborative, and transparent management of the commons could lay the foundations for a just and sustainable world.[29] Similarly, initiatives such as the Earth Charter have mobilised individuals, organisations, and universities for a just and peaceful world through shared responsibility.[30] Other participatory institutions, such as 'citizens' assemblies', operate at both the national and international levels.[31] Initiatives like the World Wide Web Consortium and the Internet Engineering Task Force have pioneered polycentric governance of the internet.[32] The list of initiatives aimed at developing and protecting the commons is extensive.

As a result of such efforts, numerous legal and constitutional provisions have been adopted in dozens of states, guaranteeing rights over the commons and protecting them from enclosure.[33] In recent years, more hybrid collectives – combining activist and entrepreneurial features – have emerged, expanding the scope of their action. In this spirit, several members of the European Parliament from different political groups formed the Commons Intergroup.[34]

1.5 The Corporations

In contrast to the protection of the wellbeing of all humankind through the development of common goods, resources, and spaces stands the limitless expansion of individual and private profit. Since the advent of modernity, the position of the corporation has gradually gained particular importance as interest in managing and accessing common resources has grown. Legally, corporations safeguard their own economic interests vis-à-vis individuals, communities, and the state.[35] In some cases, corporate interests are protected

29 Reclaim the Commons Manifesto, World Social Forum 2009, Brazil, at <https://bit.ly/3GNB2m4>.

30 Cf. <https://earthcharter.org/>.

31 White 2022.

32 Berners-Lee 2024.

33 Gellers 2015.

34 The Commons Intergroup was created in 2015. In 2019, it tabled an amendment to have the European Parliament adopt the view that energy is a common good. It was not adopted by just 5% of the votes. Cf. <https://bit.ly/3nBCVTN>. It faded out at the beginning of the 2020s.

35 The arbitral award (René-Jean Dupuy), *Texaco/Calasiatic vs. Libya*, 1977, recognised the legal personality of multinational corporations under international law and their ability to claim compensation. It is regarded as the beginning of the internationalisation of investment treaties between companies and states. See: Cantegreil 2011: 456.

under international law; for example, the interests of energy companies are guaranteed by the Energy Charter Treaty in the context of arbitration (see also Chapter 5.4).

Multinational companies that possess the technological capability and financial capital – often supported by loans from multinational banks – to exploit natural resources have, for several decades, operated as monopolies, politically supported by states. Their activities extend across national territories, the lands of indigenous populations, and even areas that are *terra communis*. They can also act extraterritorially and within commons not associated with specific geographical spaces but with networked, intangible, or ubiquitous resources such as the internet, intellectual heritage, and the genome.

The uncontrolled exploitation of productive resources in a region or country, together with the erosion of local relations and modes of production driven by corporate interests, and the exclusion of local societies from sharing in the benefits, often produces violent transformations in productive relations. It frequently results in the impoverishment of local productive classes and the enclosure of shared resources. Ultimately, the corporation becomes a privileged partner of the state, as the state often protects the corporation rather than the common good or its own citizens. A corporation may be entrusted with the management of a resource – ostensibly for the public's benefit – without relinquishing the terms of the market. In either case, it is exercises power over the commons without the legitimisation of the commoners, since the statutory requirement of profit-making minimises the likelihood of promoting the common good. Corporations, therefore, can be regarded as subjects of obligations rather than as holders of rights concerning the commons.

Three examples illustrate this dynamic: one from the colonial era, another from the modern neo-colonial era, and one projecting into a future post-colonial context. All three reveal how powerful national or multinational corporations penetrate and subvert the commons-commoner relationship for their own economic benefit, undermining concern for the public interest and local communities.

A. The first example concerns a commercial company,[36] whose interests were intertwined with the political and geostrategic ambitions of a state and which acquired a leading role in governing a common good (spices and seeds). The

36 As early as 1346, a Genoese company, Maona, acquired the rights to exploit the island of Chios in the Aegean Sea and the port of Phocaea. The company exerted quasi-sovereignty for two centuries, exploiting the region's resources (such as mastic trees) under a monopoly.

East India Company was a driving force behind the consolidation of British colonial rule, which was ultimately imposed in its classical territorial form through military force. The Company left an enduring mark on the dawn of modernity as a striking example of private corporate interests flourishing under the patronage of a major colonial power. The British Empire supported the Company financially, protected it militarily, and, after almost two and a half centuries of coexistence, absorbed it.

After Queen Elizabeth I granted the Company a licence in 1600 to trade in India, it competed fiercely with companies from Holland, Portugal, Denmark, and France. Its shareholders were initially aristocrats and merchants, and later the British government itself. During its first century, it engaged primarily in commercial activities, but from 1730 onwards, it became involved in military conflicts. It clashed with its French rival, the *Compagnie française des Indes orientales*, in the Carnatic Wars of the 1730s and 1740s, and with the Mughal Empire. The Company expanded territorially at the expense of the Mughals, particularly in the Bay of Bengal, pursuing an aggressive policy aimed at securing agricultural production and exploitation, which eventually came under its direct control.

Its army, in addition to English and other mercenaries, included Indian Sepoys, who were less costly to maintain. The Company consolidated its position in Bengal when, through the Treaty of Allahabad (1765), it acquired the right to collect taxes. Using the capital thus accumulated, it extended its influence – and indeed its dominance – across the rest of India. It brought enormous profits to its shareholders and became politically, militarily, and economically powerful, attaining near-sovereignty over the territory and complete control over agricultural production, bolstered by new weapons and transport technologies.

In the ensuing years, the Company expanded its rule across much of the Indian subcontinent, often exercising indirect power through local feudal lords and rulers. By 1803, its army numbered 260,000 – larger than the British army itself.[37] By the mid-nineteenth century, the Company wielded immense authority, controlling agricultural production across much of India and extending its activities into Japan and China.

The Company's rule relied on coercion, bribery, and war, encountering both resistance and collaboration from local Mughal elites. Corruption and the plundering of food resources led to extreme poverty, especially in eastern India. Famines, such as that of 1770 in Bengal, were frequent because agricultural policies prioritised commercial profit over local needs. For example, the

37 Dalrymple 2015.

enforced cultivation of opium instead of grain and rice – against the will of the indebted farmers – enabled the Company to export opium to China, triggering the Opium Wars (1839–1842 and 1856–1860) and consolidating Western economic and political control over China.[38]

The East India Company thus stands as one of history's most powerful and enduring private enterprises, having appropriated and plundered common goods on a massive scale. The transformation of economic power into quasi-sovereign dominion ultimately brought it into conflict with the British Empire itself. In 1858, after the failed Sepoy Rebellion, the British Crown assumed direct rule over India as a colonial possession (the British Raj). The Company was dissolved in 1873 for financial reasons and due to growing resistance from local communities to the continued depletion of India's resources. Yet its replacement by the Empire in 1875 did not improve the situation for farmers. The Company's private army was absorbed into the colonial administration, continuing to serve as an instrument of coercion and extraction until Britain's withdrawal in 1947.

B. The second example concerns the present-day activities of Monsanto (since 2018, Bayer-Monsanto), a multinational corporation that exercises near-monopolistic control over agricultural production through pesticides and genetically modified seeds. The enforcement of its aggressive policies has led to the homogenisation of crop production in dozens of countries, price manipulation, severe environmental pollution, and biodiversity loss, to the detriment of small farmers – many of whom have been driven to economic ruin.

An unofficial extraordinary tribunal 'tried' the 'Monsanto case', aiming to raise public awareness and clarify key legal issues. The tribunal represented a unique instance of individuals and organisations establishing an ad hoc 'court', with 'judges' who were distinguished jurists having served in international bodies. It followed the procedural rules of formal jurisdictions.[39] The corporation was invited to defend itself, but refused to participate. The two-day hearing in The Hague featured testimonies from victims of the company's chemical agents and from expert witnesses. The tribunal's opinion addressed the gaps in current law and the asymmetry between the freedoms enjoyed by multinational corporations and the restrictions imposed on them to protect local communities and future generations.

The tribunal underscored the lack of corporate accountability and the insufficiency of human rights law in controlling multinational activity. It stressed

38 Beeching 1975.
39 International Monsanto Tribunal 2017.

the primacy of international human rights and environmental law over investment contracts. It also observed that a large body of international law protects investors' rights – under the framework of the World Trade Organization, bilateral investment treaties, and free trade agreements –[40] but these often undermine policies and laws that safeguard human rights and the environment. This imbalance risks widening the gap between human rights protection and market regulation.

Ultimately, the 'tribunal' concluded that multinational corporations should be recognised as subjects of international law for liability arising from violations of fundamental rights – especially in relation to environmental destruction, life, and the genome. The 'judges' identified 'a glaring disparity between the rights of multinational corporations and their obligations. Therefore, the advisory opinion encourages authoritative bodies to protect the effectiveness of international human rights and environmental law against the conduct of multinational corporations'.[41]

C. The third example concerns Japan's Shimizu Corporation, which has planned investments in areas outside state jurisdiction – namely, the oceans, the international seabed, outer space, and the Moon.[42] In these environments, the corporation envisions establishing autonomous human colonies. These would be created by exploiting previously inaccessible areas and transforming them into habitable spaces. With technological support from the Japanese government, the corporation proposes to establish colonies in regions that are part of the 'common heritage of mankind', exploiting food resources likewise considered the 'common property of mankind'. In doing so, common spaces and resources would be transformed into private property.

The resulting private habitats would not only be commercially exploitable but would also catalyse new ventures by other companies and states seeking to exploit the associated energy, food, and mineral resources.[43] The company has declared its intention to harness the limitless possibilities of the oceans by vertically integrating the air, water surface, ocean depths, and seabed.

---

40 See: the procedures for reaching the TAFTA/TTIP agreement, which would deprive states of initiatives that would run counter to 'security of investment' and 'freedom of trade'. The massive reaction from civil society, as well as EU Member States, has halted negotiations on the agreements, which, among others, set new priorities at the expense of the measures needed to reverse climate change. At <https://corporateeurope.org/en>.

41 International Monsanto Tribunal 2017: 45.

42 For the company's projects in the ocean and outer space. Cf. <https://bit.ly/3pmvykq>.

43 Ranganathan 2019: 573.

Such ventures would, in effect, convert common spaces into zones of unilateral private annexation. Enclosures would multiply within the global common resources, where legal frameworks remain undeveloped. Those wielding technological and financial power would dictate the terms of the new order, transforming the already proclaimed *res communis* into *res nullius* in a future post-colonial context. This usurpation occurs before the eyes of potential inhabitants, captivated by the seductive promise of technological progress. As in the colonial and neo-colonial cases above, corporate expansionism once again seizes and appropriates resources and spaces, alienating millions from the commons to which they belong – actually or potentially – as commoners.

Yet pressing questions remain. How can a profit-oriented corporation be compatible with the stewardship of common goods? Is a symbiosis between private interest and the development of universal commons conceivable? How far can unilateral corporate appropriation extend? What are the limits of corporate freedom – and what possibilities exist for commoners of the oceans and other global spaces to establish rules defending their rights?[44] Insight may be gained by considering the rapid expansion of SpaceX and its Starlink program (see Chapter 4.6), which aims to monopolise global communications data. The provision of satellite services to Ukraine during the Russian invasion in 2022, and its temporary shut-offs, reveal how corporate use of global common space can create unprecedented military dependencies, putting international law under stress.[45]

2 *Commoning* and Commoners' Rights

The rights associated with common goods, resources, and spaces at the global scale can be understood as aspects of the *right to commoning*, which entails expectations for safeguarding a legal relationship with a universal commons or global public good. However, the heterogeneity of the commons and of commoners makes it challenging to establish fixed classifications of rights. Often, it is not so much the right to access and manage the common resource itself that is at issue, but rather the right or obligation to safeguard the resource's sustainability. Moreover, the subjects' willingness to assume the role of commoners is

44 For example, according to Article 87.1 of the Convention on the Law of the Sea, the freedom to build artificial islands in the ocean is established, but not the installation of underwater structures.

45 Sharma 2025.

a crucial aspect of the debate over the rights to the commons, as well as of what makes a common good, resource, or space amenable to such rights.[46]

Rights are guaranteed to states and to international organisations at levels and through modalities different from those applicable to individuals, groups, or peoples. At the individual – and partly at the collective – level, existing human rights already provide the normative foundation upon which these concepts can evolve and acquire shape and substance in the legal landscape, viewed from the perspective of asserting, by all and for all, the right to manage the universal commons; that is, the assertion of a universal right of all people, beyond conventional and essentialist interpretations.

2.1 Rights Provided for by International Legal Instruments

Many international treaties seek to regulate relations among the commoners of universal commons with respect to their rights and freedoms. For example, access to the open sea, in the sense of freedom of navigation, is guaranteed by the Montego Bay Convention and the relevant customary international law to anyone who owns a seaworthy vessel (see Chapter 3.1). Similarly, in outer space, states' rights to use satellite orbits are established by the relevant law (see Chapter 4.6). On the open sea, rights to exploit fisheries and marine resources are held by states, individuals, corporations, and coastal indigenous peoples. Likewise, international organisations can restrict such rights in favour of preserving the sustainability of a common resource, as illustrated by the moratorium on whaling imposed by the International Whaling Commission (see Chapter 4.3).

The ocean floor and subsoil, Antarctica, the Moon, and outer space – the areas requiring advanced technology for the extraction and processing of raw materials – remain largely inaccessible to individuals. Indeed, multinational companies often enjoy greater access than states. Rights, therefore, pertain to the relationship between states and the companies engaged in resource exploitation vis-à-vis an international authority assigned the role of coordinator and administrator of such exploitation (see Chapter 3.1 on the International Seabed Authority). In particular, with regard to the use of the radio spectrum in outer space, states hold several rights arising from the management of the International Telecommunication Union (see Chapter 4.7).

Rights relating to climate and the natural environment are enshrined either as individual rights related to health, water, and food, or as collective rights concerning access to information and participation in decision-making pro-

46 Marmor 2001.

cesses (by groups, non-governmental organisations, etc.) regarding projects that cause significant changes to the natural environment (see Chapter 5.3.2). Over time, there has been growing recognition of the rights of peoples, tribes, communities, and individuals in relation to the economic aspects of their living conditions, which may be adversely affected by international investment (as explored in Chapter 5.4).

The commons that are a product of human creativity – such as culture, knowledge, the digital world, and the use of the radio spectrum – relate to the rights to freedom of expression, the reception and transmission of information, and, by extension, the rights to privacy and to personal and economic development. A second set of rights and restrictions concerns the exploitation and access to knowledge resources reserved exclusively for the benefit of their creators or users (see Chapter 4.8.2).

The protection of biodiversity and seed reproduction is linked to the protection of health, that is, protection from genetically modified foods and, above all, from harmful substances (such as herbicides). It is also connected to the guarantee of stable and sustainable food supplies for all and to the right of farmers to economic development. The rights associated with the protection of biodiversity are set out in a series of international treaties (see Chapter 4.2). These rights pertain to states' access to the protected seed gene pool, the patent rights granted to seed companies, the general right of people to the protection of biodiversity, and the facilitation of access to seeds through the establishment of a common fund.

An alternative perspective on rights emphasises the safeguarding of global common resources from enclosure and misuse by commoners and free riders. This perspective is best understood through the legal obligations of the subjects involved. The obligations of commoner-subjects are just as significant as their rights, as they delineate relationships that may develop positively or negatively. In essence, these obligations define what a commoner should or should not do to prevent the 'tragedy of the commons'. Thus, a specific body of rules emerges, constituting the normative content of stewardship. Subjects often assume parallel social roles and thus acquire obligations alongside the rights that accrue to them. States' obligations have developed particularly within the field of international environmental law (see Chapters 3.1, 4.1, 5.3.2). The extraterritoriality of liability has already been recognised in cases where victims of damage caused by transboundary environmental pollution have gained access to appropriate legal remedies under certain conditions. In this case, rights and obligations related to commoning are seen through the lens of human rights.

In the context of land exploitation and ownership, the rights of indigenous peoples have evolved in ways that preserve cultural heritage.[47] These rights are exclusive to indigenous peoples and are not extended to other individuals or groups who may have established connections to land vital for their livelihood. This exceptionalism rests on a contradiction: Positive discrimination is implemented exclusively in favour of a people through the quasi-revival of a right rooted in tribal continuity with the territory, resulting in minimal recognition of land rights focused on the pre-modern commons of indigenous peoples.

This narrow perspective was broadened by the 2018 Declaration on the Rights of Peasants, adopted by the United Nations after two decades of consultations. The Declaration links farmers' rights to land within the framework of the commons, thereby conflicting with provisions of international economic law.[48] Accordingly, the right to sovereignty over the land for the creation of a state is linked to the right of peoples to self-determination, including the right to exploit the natural resources therein (see Chapter 4.5.2).[49]

Other quasi-rights attributed to indigenous peoples concern the enshrinement of intellectual property rights over their culture, genetic resources, and biodiversity, which are territorially connected to their lands. The relevant Declaration of the UN General Assembly has already laid the groundwork for the development of international norms[50] and practices,[51] while the Nagoya Protocol (in force since 2015) has gone much further by advocating the participation of indigenous peoples in the benefits arising from the exploitation of these resources by third parties – that is, the right to self-management rather than appropriation by others.

Rights related to the natural commons are fundamentally concerned with preserving life itself and ensuring the health of both individuals and societies. This overarching right gives rise to additional rights, including the rights to access food, clean water, and clean air. In the following discussion, we will explore the legal relations that evolve among commoners regarding a shared

---

47 See: ILO Convention No. 169 and the UN Declaration on the Rights of Indigenous Peoples; Stamatopoulou 2024.

48 Errico & Claeys 2017: 13. The Declaration was adopted in the form of a Resolution by the United Nations General Assembly on 17 December 2018. As Cogolati (2020: 243) reports, peasants produce 80% of the world's food but, paradoxically, they also make up 80% of the population facing the spectre of hunger.

49 Stamatopoulou 2024.

50 UN General Assembly, A/RES/61/295, 2007, Article 31.

51 For example, the development of the antimalarial drug Coartem, based on traditional medical knowledge, was made available free of charge to developing countries by the company Novartis.

good, facilitated by a series of human rights. These cases, directly or indirectly, involve interactions among subjects – including individuals, peoples, indigenous peoples, non-governmental organisations, international organisations, and states – in relation to universal commons, encompassing accessibility, management, governance, and decision-making processes.

2.2 Established Human Rights

Human rights, originating in the 'traditional fields' of civil and political rights, have gradually intertwined with economic and social rights. This fusion unfolds along three dimensions when rights are viewed through the lens of claims associated with global common resources.[52] Materially, civil, social, economic, and cultural rights have entered the agenda of global justice, mobilising people and institutions alike. Temporally, rights represent a common good that reflects universal justice and concerns both past and future generations (see intergenerational justice; rights related to gene management). Territorially, human rights have acquired an extraterritorial dimension beyond state jurisdiction, particularly when international bodies assume responsibility for the management of rights related to common resources. A series of human rights already enshrined in international instruments is of vital importance for defining the position of commoners vis-à-vis the commons and for the emergence of a right to commoning.

The **right to life**, enshrined in Article 3 of the Universal Declaration on Human Rights and a number of human rights treaties,[53] is recognised as an inherent right of every human being. Respect for, protection of and fulfilment of this right may depend on measures taken by states concerning global common goods and resources.[54] Moreover, article 25 of the Universal Declaration provides that 'everyone has **the right to a standard of living adequate for the health and wellbeing** of himself and of his family, including food, clothing, housing and medical care…'. Complementary aspects of related rights can be identified as individual or collective, specifically concerning global resources that serve as prerequisites for life, health, and well-being. These aspects will be further explored below.

52 Francioni 2014: 446.

53 See Article 6 of the International Covenant on Civil and Political Rights.

54 Among many other references, see: Human Rights Committee, *Teitiota v. New Zealand*, (24.10.2019), para. 9.11.

The **right to food** is explicitly affirmed in the Universal Declaration of Human Rights (art. 11) and in international conventions,[55] which recognise the right of every human being to adequate food, in terms of both quantity and quality. In fact, 'the right to adequate food is realised when every man, woman and child, alone or in community with others, has physical and economic access at all times to adequate food or means for its procurement'.[56]

International institutions emphasise that this right must be effectively realised. The FAO underscores the importance of conditions essential to human livelihood – such as soil, water, forests, fish, and livestock – and calls upon member states to implement measures addressing the root causes of hunger.[57] The commodification of food results in multiple enclosures of food raw materials and products. It denies the non-economic attributes of food – 'as vital fuel for our bodies, as a human right, as a product of Nature, or as an element of our culture in favour of an exclusive focus on its tradable features'.[58]

It is increasingly clear that the duty to protect rights related to nutrition and food production must also extend to corporations. For instance, the OECD's Guidelines for Multinational Enterprises and the UN's Guiding Principles on Business and Human Rights[59] emphasise corporate obligations to ensure food sufficiency.

The right to food is directly related to access to the exploitation of land. Its content, in principle, aims to ensure effective access to food and to counter the widespread commercialisation of food resources, which generates exclusions with grave consequences for large segments of the world's population.[60]

55 Article 11 of the International Covenant on Economic, Social and Educational Rights, article 24 para.2 and 27 para. 3 of the Convention on the Rights of the Child and articles 25(f) and 28.1 of the Convention on the Elimination of All Forms of Discrimination against Women.

56 General Comment No. 12 of the Committee on Economic, Social and Educational Rights, UN (1999), at <https://undocs.org/E/C.12/1999/5>. See: Ziegler 2008.

57 Food and Agriculture Organization, Voluntary Guidelines to Support the Progressive Realisation of the Right to Adequate Food in the Context of National Food Security, 2004, and FAO, Voluntary Guidelines on the Responsible Governance of Tenure of Land, Fisheries and Forests in the Context of National Food Security, Committee on World Food Security, 2012, at <https://bit.ly/3uCVnAU>.

58 Vivero-Pol et al. 2019: 2.

59 Resolution 17/4, 16 June 2011, Human Rights Council, UN. Also: the Maastricht Principles on Extraterritorial Obligations in the Area of Economic, Social and Cultural Rights, adopted in 2011 by a group of experts (Maastricht University and the International Commission of Jurists).

60 Cogolati 2020: 239.

As discussed in Chapter 4.2, small farmers are often compelled to purchase genetically modified seeds together with accompanying pesticides. Jean Ziegler, UN Special Rapporteur, stated in his 2008 report that regardless of how much the agri-food multinationals may improve production efficiency, the centralised mode of seed production creates a monopoly that endangers small producers and consumers. The design of genetically modified seeds has generated vertical interdependencies among seed supply, pesticides, and agricultural production – all aimed at maximising corporate profits. Already, soybeans, corn, and cotton dominate crops by reducing production costs, but 'with no intention of feeding the world or improving food quality'. For this reason, the Special Rapporteur urges states to meet their responsibilities to ensure food for all, recalling that 'hunger is not an inevitable situation'[61] and that it can be eradicated. Yet, international, local, and regional practices reveal that hunger continues to be used as a tool of economic subjugation, as long as food remains commodified and its price is determined solely by market forces.

The **right to water** encompasses access to drinking water – in peacetime, in war zones, and under conditions of widespread drought, desertification, pollution, and acidification. It is also under stress due to the ongoing appropriation of water supplies. The absolute dependence of life on water, combined with accelerating pollution and over-extraction, renders it a critically protected resource.[62] The UN General Assembly has recognised 'the right to safe and clean drinking water and sanitation as a human right that is essential for the full enjoyment of life and all human rights'.[63]

Nevertheless, millions die annually from diseases linked to inadequate water supply and sanitation.[64] The increasing commercialisation of water – both locally and globally – and the intensifying political competition over the exploitation of springs and rivers raise pressing questions about the role of

61 Ziegler 2008: 17.

62 Kotzé 2014; Brown Weiss 2007.

63 UN General Assembly, Decision 64/292, 2010, at <https://bit.ly/3IheKrg>. Moreover, according to the UN Sustainable Development Goal No. 6, clean drinking water is indispensable for human life. Also see: UN Office of the High Commissioner for Human Rights, 2010.

64 At least 1.8 billion people use drinking water contaminated with faeces, 2.4 billion people lack access to basic sanitation, and about 70% of the planet's fresh water is used for irrigation (UNESCO 2019).

states and corporations in water abstraction, distribution, and service privatisation.[65] The role of both is crucial to achieving 'water justice' – ensuring affordability, access, sustainability, social control, and accountability. The UN Committee on Economic, Social and Cultural Rights has stressed that 'agreements related to trade liberalisation cannot limit or suspend a country's ability to ensure the full implementation of the right to water'.[66] Furthermore, EU Directive 2000/60[67] calls for deepening states' responsibilities, extending beyond environmental concerns to water pricing policies and public awareness of water consumption. The Directive links cost recovery, affordability, and the 'polluter pays' principle.

Rising water prices often discourage the socially disadvantaged from accessing daily water supplies, while the lack of quality controls in privatised systems creates major public health and safety risks.[68] Therefore, private companies managing water supply networks and sewage systems must, like public municipal utilities, commit to serving the common good (see Chapter 5.4).

Managing water as a common resource has yielded successful results. The case of Cochabamba, Bolivia, is emblematic. In 2000, then President Hugo Banzer, following the World Bank's directives to renew a loan, privatised water services, promising improvements in quality and distribution. However, the poorest residents lost access due to price hikes exceeding their meagre incomes. The people of Cochabamba asserted their right to water through sustained mobilisation, forcing the government to reverse the privatisation. This also overturned the argument that water can be treated as a tradable good in the name of 'economic efficiency'. Thus, the market principle of efficiency gave way to social necessity and the common good.

As discussed in Chapter 5.4, national and international courts have recognised water as an essential public good. For example, the US Court of Appeals for the State of Michigan held in *Nestlé Waters v. Township of Osceola* that pumping water for bottling – which alters surface water tables and depletes groundwater – cannot be legally assigned, rejecting the corporation's claims. The decision ended a long dispute between the company and local residents, who, under US law, possess riparian rights to water adjacent to and beneath their property.

65 For the privatisation of water in the UK, as well as many other examples of the seizure of the commons, see: Standing 2022.

66 Committee on Economic, Social and Educational Rights, 20.1.2003, General Comment No. 15: The Right to Water (arts. 11 and 12), at <https://bit.ly/2UkpKK5>.

67 About the Directive and the implementing texts, see <https://bit.ly/3ppI9Dt>.

68 Ziegler 2008: 18. There the results of the investigations of WaterAid and Tearfund.

Indeed, drinking water is neither a simple commodity nor an inexhaustible resource. Access varies across communities, shaped by geographical, social, historical, and economic conditions.[69] Achieving equality in access to drinking water requires targeted measures that reinforce and guarantee fair practices and legal frameworks, enabling the universal realisation of the right to water recognising its unique value for life and well-being.

The right to the highest attainable standard of health for every person, and especially children, is expressly guaranteed in international law. The right to health has three dimensions: mental, physical, and social. Its implementation requires access to sufficient food, clean water, appropriate medical care, and a healthy environment. In fact, the founding treaty of the World Health Organization (1946) declares in its preamble that the highest attainable standard of health is a fundamental right of man, to be enjoyed without discrimination. Article 25 of the Universal Declaration of Human Rights recognises health as part of an adequate standard of living, including medical care and necessary social services. Article 12 of the International Covenant on Economic, Social and Cultural Rights requires governments to take all necessary measures to improve environmental and industrial conditions, thereby safeguarding the highest attainable standards of physical and mental health. It also outlines specific state obligations, including the prevention, treatment, and control of epidemic diseases, the creation of conditions for access to medical services, and the improvement of environmental and industrial hygiene.[70]

Recent global health challenges have highlighted both the importance and the limitations of international health law. The Covid-19 pandemic demonstrated how health emergencies can strain international cooperation mechanisms while emphasising the interconnected nature of global health security (see Chapter 5.6). Climate change has also emerged as a fundamental threat to the right to health (see Chapter 4.1).

The right to health in international law thus represents a complex and evolving framework. The multitude of legal norms enshrining public health protections does not appear commensurate with the realities on the ground, as significant challenges remain in ensuring universal access to the highest attainable standard of health. Industries can seriously harm public health when they are not subject to standards and protocols, whether due to ineffect-

69 Prieto 2021.

70 Also, among other international instruments: the Convention on the Rights of the Child (art. 24), the European Social Charter (art. 11), or the African Charter on Human and Peoples' Rights (art. 16).

ive regulation, weak enforcement, or corruption. The undermining of public health in pursuit of corporate profit creates a profound conflict of interest. Multinational corporations often promote controversial arguments and practices, claiming that the chemicals they use are non-hazardous, frequently on the basis of studies they themselves sponsor. The involvement of international organisations and courts underscores the complexity of the conflict between public and private interests in public health.[71]

Directly related to the general right to health is **the right to a healthy, safe, and clean environment**, which was articulated at the United Nations Conference on the Human Environment in Stockholm in 1972. The recognition that the environment is a prerequisite for the realisation of fundamental human rights marked the dawn of a new era in international law. Today, more than 140 states have acknowledged the right to a healthy environment at the constitutional level, contributing decisively to the formation of relevant international legal norms. The United Nations Special Rapporteur on Human Rights and the Environment, John Knox, identified in 2018 the threats to environmental rights and proposed ways in which the international community could respond. In his report, the Special Rapporteur formulated certain principles regarding states' obligations to ensure a healthy, clean, safe, and sustainable environment.[72]

At the normative level, the San Salvador Protocol (1988/1999) incorporated into the American Convention on Human Rights the right of every person to live in a healthy environment and to have access to basic public services (art. 11). For the first time, this right thus became enforceable at the regional level. Moreover, the Regional Agreement on Access to Information, Public Participation, and Justice in Environmental Matters in Latin America and the Caribbean, which entered into force in 2021, enshrines rights relating to environmental management and even establishes protection mechanisms.

---

71 Among many other examples: Glyphosate, a component of the herbicide Roundup, is considered a carcinogen in some studies, though the European Food Safety Authority and the European Chemicals Agency have both advised that it is not carcinogenic (European Chemicals Agency, Opinion of 15.3.2017). In national courts, glyphosate has already been ruled as a dangerous substance, and the corporation has been found to inadequately warn users of its potential harmful effects on health. There have been approximately 11,000 cases worldwide involving claims for compensation for cancer caused by the use of Roundup, see <https://bit.ly/3lrbNpJ>. See also the detailed report, *Merchants of Poison* (2022), on the use of glyphosate, the scientific data, and the court battles, at <https://bit.ly/3VSxX5q>.

72 Knox 2018.

A year later, Resolution 76/300, adopted by the UN General Assembly in July 2022, recognised 'the right to a clean, healthy, and sustainable environment'. It also highlighted that climate change, the unsustainable management and use of natural resources, the pollution of air, land, and water, the mismanagement of chemicals and waste, the resulting loss of biodiversity, and the decline in ecosystem services interfere with the enjoyment of a clean, healthy, and sustainable environment, and that environmental damage has both direct and indirect negative implications for the effective enjoyment of all human rights.[73]

In the 2001 *Ogoniland* case,[74] the African Commission linked the public interest to the protection of a 'healthy environment' and mandated the Nigerian government to take measures to prevent pollution and ecological degradation, and to ensure ecologically sustainable development and the rational use of natural resources. It also called on Nigeria to ensure the protection of the right to health and a healthy environment in which every person can develop their personality. In essence, the state is required to take measures against any threat to public health and the natural environment. The Commission outlined the state's obligation to respect the individual's integrity by refraining from harmful actions and by preventing third-party actions that may cause harm.

In 2020, the IACtHR held that the Argentine government had violated the autonomous right to a healthy environment of 90 indigenous tribes in Salta Province, as well as their rights to their cultural traditions, food, and clean water. According to the Court, the natural environment must be protected not only for its importance to the livelihood of human communities but also for the value of the ecosystem itself.[75] It late 2023, the Court went further, establishing the parameters of state obligations regarding the prevention and remediation of environmental pollution, as well as the substantive content of the right to a healthy environment in relation to individual fundamental rights. The judgment in *Community of La Oroya v. Peru* constitutes an important pre-

73 These developments stem from the Global Pact for the Environment, launched by France in 2017 and aimed at becoming a UN treaty. The UN advanced this idea through multilateral negotiations. It was Resolution 48/13 of October 2021, adopted by the UN Human Rights Council, that recognised for the first time at the global level 'the right to a healthy environment'.

74 African Commission on Human and Peoples' Rights, *The Social and Economic Rights Action Center for Economic and Social Rights v. Nigeria*, Comm. No. 155/96, (27.10.2001).

75 IACtHR, *Indigenous communities of the Lhaka Honhat Association v. Argentina* (6.2.2020), para. 208–209.

cedent for the protection of the right to a healthy environment and for adequate state oversight of corporate activities. The Court highlighted the government's failure to protect the inhabitants of the Andean city of La Oroya, who had been exposed to toxic pollution for a century.[76] In 2024, in *Rama and Kriol Peoples et al. v. Nicaragua,* the Court explicitly applied the obligations arising from the right to a healthy environment, illustrating the relevance of the principle of prevention.[77] A year later, in Advisory Opinion No. 32, initiated by Chile and Colombia, the IACtHR took the decisive step of affirming that states have obligations under *jus cogens* norms when they cause irreversible damage to the climate and the environment. This was the first time that an obligation relating to a universal commons was identified as a peremptory norm of international law:

> The existential interests of all individuals and species of all kinds – given their temporal and geographical importance – whose rights to life, personal integrity, and health have already been recognised by international law crystallise the obligation to abandon anthropogenic conduct that poses a critical threat to the equilibrium of our planetary ecosystem. The prohibitions arising from the obligation to preserve our common ecosystem, as a precondition to the enjoyment of other rights that have already been identified as fundamental, are of peremptory importance and are, therefore, of a *jus cogens* nature.[78]

At the same time, the ICJ ruled that 'a clean, healthy and sustainable environment is a precondition for the enjoyment of many human rights, such as the right to life, the right to health and the right to an adequate standard of living, including access to water, food and housing'.[79]

The right to the allocation of natural resources and natural wealth is recognised by the twin international human rights covenants of 1966. The right is attributed to peoples and is understood as the right to participate in, and directly or indirectly benefit from, the exploitation of resources. It is both a central condition and a result of the right of peoples to self-determination, which is linked to the right of each people not to be deprived of their own

76 IACtHR, *La Oroya Community v. Perú* (27.11.2023).
77 IACtHR, *Rama and Kriol Peoples, the Black Creole Indigenous Community of Bluefields et al. v. Nicaragua* (1.4.2024).
78 IACtHR, *Climate Emergency and Human Rights*, Advisory Opinion 32/25 (29.5.2025), para. 291.
79 ICJ, *Obligations of States in Respect of Climate Change*, Advisory Opinion (23.7.2025), para. 393.

means of economic development. The question of incorporating this right into international law as an expression of state sovereignty and power over natural resources and economic hegemony has long been an international source of tension and conflict – between states and companies, or between governments, corporations, and communities – both before and after colonialism.[80]

The case of the Belo Monte dam in Brazil is an illustrative example of the conflict between economic interests and human rights regarding an inland common resource of global importance. The construction of the dam, in which the Brazilian government was the main investor, was expected to cause significant environmental degradation and damage to the Amazon forest and river system, forcing tens of thousands of people to migrate. Following extensive campaigning, the case was examined by the Inter-American Commission on Human Rights, which ordered the government to suspend the project and initiate consultations with indigenous communities in the area after determining that a violation of the Convention had occurred. It also called on the government to adopt measures to protect residents' lives and to grant access to vital information on the project's effects.[81] The case was also brought before the ILO Committee, which, in March 2011, confirmed the Brazilian government's failure to hold prior discussions with indigenous communities about the project, as required by ILO Convention No. 169.[82] In response to international pressure, the Brazilian government withdrew its delegation from the Organization of American States. The question of the rights of the indigenous peoples of the Amazon was eventually examined by the IACtHR, which found violations primarily of a procedural nature and ordered the return of property to the affected persons and the payment of one million dollars towards the further development of the indigenous tribes.[83]

Directly linked to the right to natural resources is **the right to individual and collective development**, which is 'inherent in every person and every people in the sense of the right to participation in economic, social, cultural and political life'.[84] According to the 1986 Declaration of the UN General Assembly, the right to development is both individual and collective, ensuring 'equality of opportunity for all and access to health, education, food, shelter, employment and income distribution'. Moreover, both the Rio Declaration on

80 Gilbert 2013.

81 Inter-American Commission on Human Rights, Precautionary measures 382/10, *Indigenous Communities of the Xingu River Basin, Para, Brazil* (1.4.2011).

82 ILC, Observations, 2011, at <https://bit.ly/38CruXi>.

83 IACtHR, *The Xucuru Indigenous People v. Brazil* (5.2.2018), at.

84 UN General Assembly decision, 4/128, 4.12.1986.

the Environment (Principle 3, 1992) and the Vienna Declaration on Human Rights (para. 11, 1993) stress that the right to development must be implemented in a manner that equally respects the principles of development and environmental protection for present and future generations. As individual and collective development is a prerequisite for the realisation of all human rights, states have an obligation to ensure the equal enjoyment of this right by adopting specific measures to eliminate social inequalities.

These findings are little more than wishful thinking and lack immediate practical feasibility. Nevertheless, they can serve as a significant ethical and political reference point for law-making. Enforcing such regulations would undoubtedly challenge the established global economic structure, necessitating a substantial redistribution of wealth between developed and developing nations and reshaping interactions between states and global common resources. However utopian such a perspective may seem, certain aspects of it can be identified in international legal practice, which increasingly acknowledges the interdependence between the right to personal development and environmental protection.

For example, in 1997, the ICJ referred to the 'need to reconcile economic development with environmental protection, which in practice is expressed through the concept of sustainable development'. Indeed, it ruled that 'the protection of the environment is a vital part of human rights theory, as it is a *sine qua non* for a series of rights, such as to health and to life'.[85] In 2010, the Court underlined the 'interconnection between equitable and reasonable use of a shared resource and the balance between economic development and environmental protection that is the essence of sustainable development'.[86] These judgments take an important step towards delimiting state sovereignty, as they impose restrictions to protect common resources on which the sustainability of human communities depends.

The ECtHR has examined **the right to private life in relation to environmental protection.** In the *Hatton* case, concerning night flights at Heathrow Airport in 2003, the Court held that invoking the country's economic development cannot outweigh human rights, especially in the sensitive area of environmental protection. In their joint dissenting opinion, five judges argued that protection from environmental pollution is supranational, beyond the limits of national sovereignty, and that 'this concern for environmental protec-

85 ICJ, *Gabčíkovo-Nagymaros Dam Case* (*Hungary v. Slovakia*), 25.9.1997, paras. 140 and 88, respectively.

86 ICJ, *Pulp Mills on the River Uruguay Case* (*Argentina v. Uruguay*), 20.4.2010, para. 177.

tion shares common ground with the general concern for human rights'.[87] The Court has accepted, in other judgments, that the right to private life (art. 8 ECHR) can apply where the state causes environmental pollution or where the state's liability arises from its failure to regulate private industry. In *López Ostra v. Spain,* the ECtHR held that the protection of family life may encompass the right to protection from severe environmental pollution, as pollution can affect people's well-being and deprive them of the enjoyment of family life even if their health is not threatened.[88]

It is worth noting the *Cordella* judgment, in which the Court found a violation of the right to family life. One hundred and eighty residents of the Taranto region took Italy to court over the effects of toxic pollution from the Ilva steelworks, which had caused the deaths of many people, and the polluter's failure to comply with relevant regulations. The judgment found that toxic pollution had caused direct harm to local residents' health and disrupted their lives. It also demonstrated the state authorities' lack of effective protection, despite the Council of Ministers' decisions to implement the relevant environmental law.[89] However, the Court once again refrained from finding a violation of the right to life (art. 2).

The ECtHR used to be particularly reluctant to recognise the importance of environmental protection through the rights enshrined in the Convention, asserting that it is necessary to demonstrate an immediate, concrete, and personal risk, as in the case of the establishment of a thermonuclear plant in Switzerland or the destruction of a small ecosystem on the island of Tinos.[90] The Court thus sought to limit the establishment of an *actio popularis* to cases in which serious environmental risks affect large sections of the population.[91]

However, in April 2024, the Court took a decisive step forward in the case *Verein KlimaSeniorinnen Schweiz and Others v. Switzerland,* initiated by four women and a Swiss association whose members were concerned about the consequences of global warming on their living conditions and health.

---

87 ECtHR, *Hatton and Others v. the UK* (8.7.2003), dissenting opinions from Costa, Ress, Türmen, Zupančič, and Steiner.

88 ECtHR, *López Ostra v. Spain* (9.12.1994), para. 51.

89 ECtHR, *Cordella and Others v. Italy* (24.1.2019).

90 ECtHR, *Balmer-Schafroth and Others v. Switzerland* (26.8.1997); *Kyrtatos v. Greece* (22.5.2003). Indeed, in certain cases, the Court, although finding a violation of the ECHR, did not award compensation to the victims of the violation (*Tătar v. Romania*, 27.1.2009), nor did it oblige the state to restore the prior state of affairs before the environmental harm occurred. Pavoni 2014: 346.

91 ECtHR, *Sdružení Jihočeské Matky v. Czech Republic* (10.7.2006).

The Court held that there had been a violation of the right to respect for private and family life under Article 8 of the Convention and a violation of the right to access a court. It found that the Swiss Confederation had failed to comply with its duties ('positive obligations') under the Convention on Climate Change. There had been critical gaps in the process of implementing the relevant domestic regulatory framework, including a failure by the Swiss authorities to quantify, through a carbon budget or otherwise, national greenhouse gas (GHG) emission limitations. Switzerland had also failed to meet its past GHG emission reduction targets. While recognising that national authorities enjoy broad discretion in implementing legislation and measures, the Court held that the Swiss authorities had not acted in time or appropriately to devise, develop, and implement relevant legislation and measures in this case. It has to be noted that the Court considered global developments regarding climate protection:

> In line with the international commitments undertaken by the member States, most notably under the UNFCCC and the 2015 Paris climate Agreement, and in the light of the compelling scientific advice provided, in particular, by the Intergovernmental Panel on Climate Change (IPCC), States need to put in place the necessary regulations and measures aimed at preventing an increase in GHG concentrations in the Earth's atmosphere and a rise in global average temperature beyond levels capable of producing serious and irreversible adverse effects on human rights under Article 8.[92]

The right to participation, consultation, and information in relation to environmental projects is a precondition for the realisation of other relevant individual or collective rights. When a state faces complex environmental and economic policy issues, competent authorities must first conduct appropriate research and studies to anticipate and assess the potential environmental and health impacts of projects that may harm the environment and residents.

This group of rights consists, first of all, of the right of each person to be informed about the plans of governments and corporations that may bring about drastic changes detrimental to health, the environment, and the quality of life. The right to information also applies where such changes have already taken place. States are even obliged, as case law has shown, to keep the local population informed as a necessary condition for carrying out the consultation process before implementing such a plan. Information has another

92 ECtHR, *Verein KlimaSeniorinnen Schweiz and Others v. Switzerland* (9.4.2024), paras. 546, 555, 558, 573.

important aspect, which is directly linked to the commons itself: the exchange of information, figures, and data between different states in a transparent, direct, and reliable manner is essential for the effective management of the global common resources, as in the case of pollutant emissions into the atmosphere, the laying and removal of submarine cables on the international seabed, scientific research in Antarctica and the Arctic, biosafety or the protection of biodiversity.[93] Indeed, from another perspective, shared information is a global public good.

The 1998 Aarhus Convention[94] (in force since 2001) enshrines both the duty to consult and the right to be informed on issues of environmental protection. In particular, it guarantees individuals and non-governmental organisations the right to:

A. Receive information promptly from public authorities regarding environmental policies, the state of the environment, and related risks to public health.
B. Participate in debates and decision-making processes on environmental issues. The views of citizens and of organisations should be considered in the final decision-making process, with explicit reasons provided.
C. Have decisions reversed that are taken without respecting the aforementioned rights through judicial or administrative channels.

Indeed, the ECtHR took account of the Aarhus Convention in *Taşkin v. Turkey,* even though Turkey was not a party to it. The Strasbourg court linked the obligation to include in the decision-making process those likely to suffer environmental interference (art. 6 of the Aarhus Convention) with the protection of private life (art. 8 of ECHR). It held that 'where Article 8 does not expressly include procedural requirements, the decision-making process which produces intrusive effects must be fair, so as to respect the interests of the individual, in accordance with what Article 8 provides, in the context of the public interest'.[95] The ECtHR has also addressed the obligation to inform from

---

93 For example, see Article 17 of the International Treaty on Plant Genetic Resources Conservation: 'The Contracting Parties shall cooperate to develop and strengthen a global information system to facilitate the exchange of information, based on existing information systems, on scientific, technical, and environmental issues relating to plant genetic resources for food and agriculture'. This is similar to Article 20 of the Cartagena Protocol on Biosafety. See: Article 20(4) of the Protocol on Biosafety.

94 Convention on Access to Information, Public Participation in Decision-making, and Access to Justice in Environmental Matters, at <http://www.unece.org/env/pp/treaty text.html>.

95 ECtHR, *Taşkin and Others v. Turkey* (10.10.2004), para. 50 and 118. See also: *Okyay v. Turkey* (12.7.2005), para. 65; *Öneryildiz v. Turkey* (30.11.2004), para. 41; *Guerra v. Italy and Others* (15.2.1998), para. 357.

a particularly narrow perspective. According to the Court, the state's obligation to provide information upon request should not be confused with the obligation to disseminate information on environmental risks.[96]

More open to recognising the right to information in cases of environmental risk, the Council of Europe's Social Charter Committee found a violation of Article 11, para. 2, of the Charter in the Asopos River and lignite mine cases in Greece. The violation involved failing to provide adequate information to the inhabitants of an area that was systematically polluted, resulting in considerable damage to public health, while the government failed to inform residents of the pollution's effects.[97]

The right to participation risks being a procedural pretext for the pursuit of extraction projects: participation 'often is used to legitimize rather than challenge the actions of development agents'.[98] Therefore, participation should involve people who can stand up for their rights and have their views considered.

The right to a healthy environment is accompanied by a secondary obligation: that **scientific research must be independent** and not inextricably linked to economic interests. In many areas of the universal commons, technology plays a key role in providing scientific evidence. The 1966 UN Covenants enshrine the right to freedom of thought and expression, with reference to academic freedom and, by extension, to the production of technology.[99] The 'freedom necessary for scientific research' is closely linked to freedom of thought and expression and the right to information. Thus, independent scientific research is a prerequisite for protecting other rights, such as the rights to a healthy environment, water, and food. Conversely, the obstruction of scientific research or the misleading publication of research results commissioned by a multinational corporation undermines the protection of the rights to food, water, and a healthy environment. The lawsuits brought against Exxon, for example, by environmental organisations and scientific bodies for tampering with scientific findings are typical of the struggle over scientific integrity. These cases began after 1977, when the corporation concealed and then denied

---

96 ECtHR, *Steel and Morris v. the United Kingdom* (15.2.2015); *Vilnes and Others v. Norway* (5.12.2013).

97 European Committee of Social Rights: *International Federation for Human Rights v. Greece*, 72/2011, (23.1.2013); *Marangopoulos Foundation for Human Rights v. Greece*, 30/2015, (6.12.2006).

98 Daly & Lupin 2023: 238.

99 See: International Covenant on Economic, Social and Cultural Rights, Article 15, para. 3, and International Covenant on Civil and Political Rights, Article 19.

the findings of a study it had itself commissioned, which demonstrated the entirely adverse effects of fossil fuels on the environment.[100]

It is worth mentioning the African Charter (arts. 16 and 24), which stipulates that states must ensure that independent scientific studies of environmental impacts are carried out before any project likely to cause environmental changes is undertaken. States must also ensure that a public consultation is held with affected communities, which should be involved in decision-making (para. 54–59).[101]

Biocultural rights pertain to the environmental commons from the perspective of the rights of indigenous peoples living according to traditional ways, political organisation, and economies. These rights are interwoven with the protection of ecosystems and local communities from the threats posed by the unequal imposition of global trade conditions. As David Bollier observes, biocultural rights are still in their infancy, yet aspects of the central idea underlying them are already embodied in certain international treaties.[102]

These rights derive, in principle, from the 1993 Convention on Biological Diversity, which commits state parties to consider the culture and modes of governance of indigenous communities within the environment in which they live. This perspective was further developed during the negotiations of the Nagoya Protocol (2010)[103] on access to genetic resources and equitable benefit-sharing in the implementation of the Convention. The principle of access and sharing, as codified in the Protocol, has an important cultural dimension, as it recognises the role and rights of indigenous communities and peoples with regard to genetic resources.

According to Kabir Sanjay Bavikatte and Tom Bennett, biocultural rights refer to a community's long-established rights to stewardship over land, water, and natural resources, which are not linked to property claims in the modern legal sense:

> Within a rights discourse, biocultural rights can be contextualised as a subset of the third-generation group solidarity rights. The notion of stewardship is critical to a discourse of biocultural rights, for it provides the ethical content for these rights – whereby rights to land, culture, traditional knowledge, self-governance,

---

100 'Exxon Mobil sued for decades of lies', 24.9.2020, at <https://bit.ly/3E0Vok9>.

101 African Commission on Human and Peoples' Rights, *The Social and Economic Rights Action Center for Economic and Social Rights v. Nigeria*, Comm. No. 155/96 (2001), at <https://bit.ly/2UhIXw2>. See: Coomans 2003: 749.

102 Bollier 2015b.

103 Cf. <https://www.kuleuven.be/english/research/integrity/nagoya>.

> etc. are informed by a set of values that are not anthropocentric but biocentric.[104]

However, reading these rights in this way involves an essentialist and static view. It assumes that the natural environment and human communities are eternally unchanging. Consequently, communities can only have the right to preserve the environment in an archaic state of 'indigeneity'. In a rapidly and violently changing world, this approach can only lead to piecemeal solutions.

Lastly, digital commons relate to the **rights to privacy and to ownership and management of digital data**. Data are variously characterised as club goods, commons, infrastructure, labour, or capital.[105] Personal and non-personal data constitute a global common resource that can be used for a range of public-interest applications. However, these digital data are collected by large technology companies without the genuine consent of internet users, are privatised and processed, and are used for private profit (see Chapter 4.8.2). Beyond concerns about private or public profit, the arbitrary use of these data violates and endangers fundamental rights. Personal and non-personal data become commodities, and then future behaviours and predictions are commodified. In fact, future preferences, feelings, and intentions – commercial or political – are marketed.

It is highly questionable whether data-driven businesses based on surveillance are compatible with the right to privacy and with other rights, including freedom of opinion and expression, freedom of thought, the rights of the child, and the right to equality and non-discrimination.[106] As Zuboff aptly puts it,

> We thought we were searching Google, but now we understand that Google searches us. We assumed that we use social media to connect, but we learned that connection is how social media uses us. We barely questioned why our new TV or mattress had a privacy policy, but we have begun to understand that 'privacy' policies are actually surveillance policies.[107]

By providing data and allowing large corporations to engage in unaccountable practices such as facial or voice recognition, people lose control over the data they produce. The ceding of privacy is gradually becoming a prerequis-

104 Bavikatte & Bennett 2015.
105 Purtova & van Maanen 2024: 2.
106 Amnesty International 2019.
107 Zuboff 2020.

ite for accessing cyberspace, with free choice being manipulated and channelled towards commercial and political interests.

Regulations could put limitations on algorithms which entrap attention or 'brain hack', establishing addictive behaviours through the continuous use of social media platforms. The openness and transparency of these platforms' modes of operation should be accompanied by restrictions on their capacity and scope of applicability.[108] In a largely unregulated digital environment, the EU has taken the lead by adopting a series of legal instruments.

In 2022, the Digital Services Act (DSA)[109] imposed obligations on corporations to ensure respect for human rights. The DSA requires very large platforms and search engines to assess and mitigate systemic risks arising from the 'design, including algorithmic systems, functioning and use made of their services'. The Act prohibits targeted advertising practices on online platforms based on profiling using special categories of sensitive data, as defined under the EU General Data Protection Regulation (in force since May 2018). Strict rules apply to online platforms and search engines, which must analyse the systemic risks they create – namely, risks related to the dissemination of illegal content, adverse effects on fundamental rights, electoral processes, gender-based violence, and mental health. The DSA also forbids 'dark patterns', meaning interface designs that manipulate uses' future decisions, and it establishes a monitoring body empowered to impose sanctions. However, as Amnesty International highlights, the DSA did not go far enough to phase out all intrusive, surveillance-based advertising practices.[110]

Taking an additional step, the Data Act[111] clarifies who can create value from data and under which conditions. Finally, the Artificial Intelligence Act, adopted by EU,[112] prohibits specific AI applications that threaten citizens' rights, such as remote biometric identification systems (RBI). The use of RBI by law enforcement is prohibited, except in exhaustively listed cases. Real-time RBI can only be deployed if its use is limited in time and place and subject to specific prior judicial or administrative authorisation. Post-facto RBI is

---

108 Kotsaka 2022.

109 Regulation (EU) 2022/2065. On 25 August 2023, it came into effect for very large online platforms and search engines. It became fully applicable to other entities on 17 February 2024.

110 Amnesty International 2022, What the EU's Digital Services Act means for human rights and harmful Big Tech business models, at <https://www.amnesty.org/en/documents/pol30/5830/2022/en/>.

111 Regulation (EU) 2023/2854, entered into force on the 11 January 2024, applicable in September 2025.

112 Regulation (EU) 2024/1689, in force on 1st August 2024.

considered a high-risk case, requiring judicial authorisation linked to a criminal offence. According to Dragos Tudorache, Civil Liberties Committee co-rapporteur:

> We have linked the concept of artificial intelligence to the fundamental values that underpin our societies. However, much work lies ahead that goes beyond the AI Act itself. AI will push us to rethink the social contract at the heart of our democracies, our education models, labour markets, and the way we conduct warfare.[113]

In late 2025, industry pressure led the European Commission to propose delaying the implementation of AI and data acts and passing amendments on personal data and AI that would favour entrepreneurship.[114] On the other hand, public awareness of the utility and importance of personal data has led to the emergence of movements calling for transparency and fair compensation in relation to data control by large technology companies.[115] Therefore, despite the stewardship exercised by international organisations, movements created by the commoners of cyberspace could establish twofold norms: for human rights protection and for their own control over the data they produce. What is needed is to confront the shortcomings of the dominant system and to consolidate new forms of polycentric management that enable data management by internet users.

Platforms, such as the Solid Protocol,[116] can provide users with their own Personal Online Data, through which they decide how their data are managed and shared. Decentralised data management, based on users' free will, is already being implemented in Belgium (Flanders) and the Netherlands, offering a model for the future of data ownership and control. This is 'an example of the emergent movement that is poised to replace the outdated incumbent system'.[117]

113 European Parliament, at <https://bit.ly/3AyoxXK>.

114 See: Crowell, *EU AI Act, GDPR, and Digital Laws Changes Proposed*, Nov. 2025, at < https://bit.ly/4rMhVvk>.

115 Among others: The Data Union (https://thedataunion.eu/) and the Free Software Foundation (https://www.fsf.org/).

116 See <https://solidproject.org/>.

117 Berners-Lee 2024.

3 The Obligation of Stewardship

We have already considered the idea that the commons presuppose a structured, formal or informal organisation of relations between subjects, aimed at ensuring the sustainability of communities associated with common goods, resources, or spaces. In other words, an entity must provide effective governance of global common resources and an active role for commoners. Usually, a single entity does not assume this role alone; instead, multiple guarantor relationships are developed, with varying degrees of consequence for individuals, groups, states, and international organisations in protecting the commons. However, is there evidence in current international law of the emergence of such rules for assigning the guarantor role for each of the universal commons? If so, where does the responsibility for undertaking such a task arise?

3.1 Establishing an Obligation

According to the 'public trust doctrine', the state, as custodian, is charged with maintaining and preserving common goods, resources, and spaces.[118] While this may make sense for common resources within a state, at the international level, things become more ambiguous, as there is no solid political or normative basis to prevent the displacement of common resources into the realm of private or state interests, where the universal *demos* is excluded.

The 'responsibility to protect' emerged as a global commitment endorsed by the international community at the 2005 UN World Summit. It concerns a series of international crimes, such as genocide. However, the drafters initially included 'overwhelming natural or environmental catastrophes, where the state concerned is either unwilling or unable to cope, or call for assistance, and significant loss of life is occurring or threatened'. The core idea is to link state sovereignty with global oversight through a 'residual responsibility' vested in the broader community of states. Thus, the international community can be activated when a particular state is unable to provide effective protection.[119]

If we go a step beyond the idea elaborated by the UN, the principle of responsibility, as formulated by Hans Jonas, includes life itself and its material conditions – namely, the environment that sustains the development of eco-

118 Hudson 2024; Bollier 2014: 131. See also Bosselmann (2015: 180–181) with reference to the work of Josef Sax.

119 For the genealogy of the principle, see: UN Office on Genocide Prevention and the Responsibility to Protect, at <https://www.un.org/en/genocide-prevention/responsibility-protect/about>.

systems in which humans also live.[120] Responsibility in this sense motivates individuals and groups to act, especially when a grave danger is imminent. From this point of view, communities of people, states, and international organisations can understand their responsibility as the obligation to take action – that is, is, as an impetus to develop or adopt policies and laws, even at the last moment, in the face of threats to vitally important universal commons, for the common good or common interest, in the name of 'humanity'.

The issue of responsibility transformed into a legal obligation already arises in the field of environmental protection and, according to Joseph Raz, highlights the notion of interest as the substrate of any right associated with parallel obligations.[121] On the other hand, human rights, as discussed within the framework of the commons, presuppose obligations corresponding to concrete needs shaped by relations among actors in real life.[122]

A sense of obligation can be created within any community of commoners through a political culture. That is, the commoners *must* receive the direct guarantee that the benefits derived from the use of common goods, resources, or spaces are shared and reinvested on behalf of the common good or public interest. The analogy between the legal entity of a trust and the normative content of trusteeship can be useful for understanding legal relations among subjects-commoners and the universal commons, and for establishing a clear horizon for multi-layered governance to the benefit of commoners.[123]

Such cases can be seen from the state's perspective. Aiming to exploit energy resources in Norway, the government established corporations that extract, process, and sell oil and gas, placing the profits in a fund for the benefit of the Norwegian people (Sovereign Wealth Fund).[124] Another similar case concerns the Alaska Permanent Fund, established by the state of Alaska in 1976 to manage and invest the state's revenue, primarily derived from oil and gas production. The fund provides equal annual payments to all residents, alleviating poverty to some extent.[125]

---

120 Jonas 2019.

121 Raz 1986.

122 Birrell & Matthews 2020.

123 For an extensive analysis, see Bosselmann 2015 (145–155), where the genealogy of trusteeship in international law is traced from the League of Nations to the United Nations, and models for the governance of global environmental commons by states or international organisations are examined (155–267).

124 Overland 2018; Takle 2021.

125 Berman 2024.

State responsibility cannot be effective unless it acknowledges its role in relation to the common good on a global scale. Indeed, this responsibility, in the sense of an obligation to exercise stewardship, can be identified at two levels: first, at the domestic level, where states have exclusive jurisdiction over a universal resource; and second, at the international level, where this obligation is shared with other states. Here, however, the capacity of state institutions to safeguard these rights is crucial.[126]

The quality of democracy is usually correlated with the widest distribution of rights over common resources, as determined by processes of accountability, transparency, and representation, as well as by the protection of human rights. Therefore, it could be argued that democratic institutions and laws can guarantee an equitable relationship between people and the commons, especially when mechanisms of a distributive economy are enshrined in law. However, states typically do not ensure their citizens' participation in decisions concerning the exploitation of resources, nor does international law point the way in this direction.[127]

Similar responsibilities are held by international bodies that exercise stewardship over the universal commons. Here, limited responsibilities imply less responsibility and greater inefficiency in managing the commons and in redistributing direct and indirect benefits to the community of commoners, states, individuals, or peoples.

Numerous proposals have been discussed in international fora and among the academic community, focusing on centralised or decentralised approaches to local, regional, or universal commons.[128]

The key feature of mechanisms for the stewardship, supervision and protection of multifaceted global resources is fragmentation across tools, enforcement, sanctions and dispute resolution. Consequently, effectiveness is reduced. Already, a series of mechanisms, varying in their degree of commissioned oversight competence, can be identified in treaty texts:[129]

---

126 See the Wellbeing of Future Generations Act adopted by Wales in 2015, which explicitly aims to contribute to global wellbeing. Morrow 2023: 223.

127 A unique example is the African Commission on Human and Peoples' Rights, which promotes this idea. See: Decision 224/2012 on the Human Rights-Based Approach to Natural Resource Governance.

128 For instance, the 1995 report 'Our Global Neighborhood', drafted by the Commission on Global Governance, proposed converting the obsolete UN Trusteeship Council into a UN Trusteeship of the Global Commons, at <https://bit.ly/3TV3yoG>. See Westra (2011) or Bosselmann (2017), among others.

129 More examples in Schrijver 2016: 1261–1262.

– The Montreal Protocol (1987) to the Convention for the Protection of the Ozone Layer established the Assemblies/Meetings of the Parties and the Implementation Committee.
– The Kyoto Protocol (1997) to the Convention on Climate Change established the Compliance Committee.
– The 1982 Convention on the Law of the Sea established the Assembly of Member States and the International Seabed Authority.
– The Antarctic Treaty (1959) established the meetings of the members.

However, the term 'stewardship' is rarely used in legal instruments. In the preamble to the 2023 High Seas Treaty on marine biodiversity, for example, the signatory states explicitly refer to their role as 'stewards of the oceans in areas beyond national jurisdiction on behalf of present and future generations'.

In addition, many committees of the UN and other international organisations have been set up ad hoc or pursuant to a respective legal instrument to promote cooperation between states and to exercise certain powers, control, and supervision – therefore, a certain degree of stewardship. They perform an important task of informing and consulting with other subjects-commoners of the universal commons. The means available for them to implement their objectives effectively are even rarer and more piecemeal, and include:

– Moratoria (imposed by the International Whaling Commission).
– Establishment of an international court (such as ITLOS).
– Imposing fines (under the Montreal Protocol on the Montreal Convention for the Protection of the Ozone Layer).
– Quotas (on fishing, imposed by the UN Food and Agriculture Organization).
– Issuance of certification of goods (by the International Tropical Timber Organization).
– Freezing sovereignty claims (under the Antarctic Treaty).
– Sourcing products (from non-deforested areas, EU, 2022).

This indicative list reflects the progress – albeit limited – that has been made towards laying the groundwork for effective management of global resources, in other words, effective governance of the universal commons within the international system.

The seventeen goals set out in the 2030 UN Agenda for Sustainable Development[130] require dynamic and effective stewardship. It should be noted that most of the goals pertain to all sectors of human activity and, therefore, to all universal commons (Table 6). They also propose a legitimate project that envi-

130 UN 2015, Sustainable Development Goals, at <https://sdgs.un.org/goals>. See also Commission on Global Governance 1995.

TABLE 6. Goals of the 2030 UN Agenda for Sustainable Development

1. Ending poverty everywhere;
2. Ending hunger and achieving food security;
3. Ensuring healthy lives for all at all ages;
4. Ensuring inclusive and equal quality education;
5. Achieving gender equality;
6. Ensuring the availability and sustainable management of water;
7. Ensuring access to cheap and sustainable energy for all;
8. Promoting inclusive and sustainable economic growth, and decent work for all;
9. Building resilient infrastructure, promoting inclusive industry, and fostering innovation;
10. Reducing inequalities within and between countries;
11. Making cities and villages inclusive and safe;
12. Ensuring sustainable models of consumption and production;
13. Taking urgent action to combat climate change;
14. Conserving and sustainably using the oceans and marine resources;
15. Protecting, restoring, and sustainably using ecosystems, combating desertification and biodiversity loss;
16. Promoting peaceful and inclusive societies with access to justice for all, and creating effective and accountable institutions at all levels;
17. Forming an alliance to achieve the goals.

sions the global community as a viable entity, suggesting that it necessitates the overthrow of the prevailing economic model and the current legal framework.

Certainly, there is much more work to be done to legitimate and transform the foundational principles of commons governance into a tangible reality. Effective global stewardship would require the engagement of all subjects of universal commons – especially the *universal demos* of human beings – together with states and international organisations, to exert a collective and multilateral *agonistic commoning*.

The commoners of universal commons – namely individuals, communities, states and international organisations – are likewise subject to a moral, political and statutory obligation to respect the common goods, resources, and spaces. The commoners who bear a quasi-right to the commoning only rarely assume specific obligations under international law. These obligations, still in the process of formulation, relate, for example, to the pollution of a resource such as the sea or the air, and are based on general principles that, by analogy, bind the members of a community of commoners according to the specific features of each universal commons.

Lastly, stewardship-based obligations must be understood in the context of the resource's sustainability (obligations to protect), respect for other commoners (obligations of solidarity), and the resource's enhancement (obligations to contribute). These obligations are rooted in a hyper-duty to respect society that stems from the human condition of political organisation.

3.2 The Obligation to Protect the Environment

The normative approach to international justice, grounded in the equality of states, is increasingly challenging the established practice of powerful states imposing aggressive, interventionist, and hegemonic policies. Although force often prevails over law in the international arena, the crucial role of stewardship for the 'common good' cannot be ignored when the environment is at stake.[131] As concerns about the trajectory of environmental protection indicators have grown amid globalisation, political and legal interactions between states have intensified, giving rise to both synergies and conflicts.

The emergence of a global ecological consciousness first found institutional expression in the 1972 Stockholm Conference on the Human Environment. The Final Document declares that it is the obligation of states to protect and improve the human environment (Principle 4). It takes an anthropocentric approach by defining the right to freedom and equality in a way that enables people to live with dignity (Principles 1–3). Accordingly, states are required to develop international law recognising international responsibility and the payment of compensation for harm (Principle 22). At the same time, the 1970s saw the rise of the ideas of 'cosmopolitan solidarity' and the 'common heritage of mankind' (see Chapter 3), which helped to consolidate the emerging field of environmental international law (Chapter 4.1). These concepts shaped the competencies of international supervisory bodies, yet they remain largely ineffective at protecting natural common resources and, at times, even facilitate new enclosures.

The International Court of Justice and the Inter-American Court of Human Rights have developed the view that ecological balance constitutes a fundamental matter of interest for *all* states.[132] Consequently, states are gradually

131 Bosselman 2015.

132 ICJ, *Obligations of States in respect of Climate Change*, Advisory Opinion (23.7.2025); IACtHR, *Climate Emergency and Human Rights*, Advisory Opinion 32/25 (29.5.2025).

assuming collective 'stewardship' in matters of environmental protection, acting from the perspective of pluralistic international coexistence and solidarity through cooperation. Stewardship also implies compliance with the principle of good faith, requiring commoners (states, individuals, and others) to refrain from acts or omissions that undermine the implementation of international obligations serving the *common good.* This goal will only be achieved when reflection on the common destiny of humankind becomes deeply embedded. Yet, the shift towards international collaboration through a universal ethic is constrained by market pressures and the uncooperative aspects of state sovereignty.

ICJ Vice-President Christopher Weeramantry, in his separate opinion in the *Hungarian-Slovak Dam* judgment, articulated the principle of stewardship of natural resources:

> There is a duty lying upon all members of the community to preserve the integrity and purity of the environment. Natural resources are not individually owned; they are collectively owned, and a principle of their use is that they should be used for the maximum service to people.[133]

The cosmopolitanism of human rights and the obligation to steward or to act as a trustee of the commons imply the establishment of guarantees for environmental security – that is, ensuring the capacity of the environment to sustain human civilisation.[134] Such guarantees correspond to an obligation on states to cooperate in achieving a common goal through appropriate methodologies and measures.[135] Extending this reasoning to all universal commons, the obligation of states to cooperate is linked to the right of human beings to the protection of the conditions under which life can be guaranteed and qualitatively enhanced, both socially and ecologically. The protection of this global good – life and wellbeing – places states' stewardship under constant scrutiny by diverse actors: individuals, civil society organisations, international organisations, and other states representing the global interests of 'humanity'.

States have gradually acquired a commitment to manage the resources within their territories for environmental protection under the principle of 'common but differentiated responsibilities', as formulated in Article 3(1) of

133 ICJ, *Gabčíkovo-Nagymaros Dam Case* (*Hungary v. Slovakia*), 25.9.1997, Weeramantry, separate opinion, p. 110.

134 Falkner & Buzan 2018; Bosselman 2015; Westra 2011.

135 Such an obligation for cooperation between states is explicitly stated in Article 6.1 of the World Heritage Convention (1972) and in Article 19.2 of the Convention for the Protection of Intangible Cultural Heritage (2003), among others.

the UNFCCC. The principle exempts or eases the obligations of developing states under the treaty – for example, in the 1997 Kyoto Protocol, which exempts them from restrictions on pollutant emissions. It seeks to reconcile stewardship with the inequalities between the Global North and South and with the rigidities of state sovereignty. International political processes have redefined globalisation in terms of shared ecological risks, now regarded as 'common' to all states and peoples. Yet this ambiguity persists, as states that invoke the principle retain the exclusive right to produce international law while failing to construct an effective global system for monitoring compliance.

A telling example of ineffective regulation is the trading of pollution rights under the Kyoto Protocol, which permits states with unused emission allowances to sell them to other states. Although designed to reduce greenhouse gases, this market-based arrangement is of dubious compatibility with the protection of the environmental commons.

As responsibility for combating global warming has been extended to more states, the legal regime has confined 'environmental stewardship' to contractual obligations. The 2015 Paris Agreement exposed the limits of voluntary, decentralised self-commitments by states,[136] given the ambiguous legal character of the obligations[137] and the lack of effective sanctions.[138]

China aligned itself, as far as possible, with the new restrictions,[139] while the United States, under the Trump administration, withdrew from international climate agreements and challenged emission limits. Following the change of administration in the US in 2021 (Biden), the United States re-entered the global process, and the 26th Climate Change Conference (COP26), held in Glasgow, reaffirmed the UNFCCC's goals, declared the beginning of the end of the fossil fuel era, and reiterated the commitment to minimise global warming. Yet no breakthroughs were made regarding the binding nature of commitments, leaving developing states dissatisfied with the lack of specific guarantees and financial assistance. Subsequent unilateral declarations to reduce emissions and reverse deforestation have not inspired optimism that global warming will be slowed,[140] especially after Russia's invasion of Ukraine in 2022.

At COP27 (Sharm el-Sheikh, 2022), states agreed to establish a $100 billion fund to compensate vulnerable countries for 'losses and damage from envir-

136 Falkner & Buzan 2018: 21.

137 Bodansky 2016: 297.

138 Okonkwo 2017.

139 McEldowney 2017: 232.

140 See <https://unric.org/en/cop26-a-snapshot-of-the-agreement/>.

onmental disasters'.[141] The re-election of Trump in 2024 once again reversed progress on global climate measures. COP28 reiterated the call for a 'transition away from fossil fuels', and the UN Global Stocktake assessed progress towards the Paris Agreement's goals, including Article 2.1(c). Yet the tens of trillions of dollars required for an effective energy transition remain unfunded.[142]

At COP29 in Baku (2024), states agreed to triple climate finance for developing countries – $100 billion to $300 billion annually by 2035 – and to mobilise $1.3 trillion per year from public and private sources. Many observers regard this new target as both inadequate and vague.[143] In Belem (2025), COP30 was marked by the absence of the US. The conference, ten years after the Paris Agreement was adopted, fell short of achieving the fundamental goal of effectively tackling the climate crisis. Although the conference avoided mentioning deforestation or fossil fuels, it launched a 3-year negotiation on environmental protection and trade.

We remain far from the situation envisioned by Hedley Bull, where states would act as 'local agents of the common good'.[144] As he observed in 1984, 'the greatest ambitions of cosmopolitan environmental solidarists are limited to state-centred solidarism'.[145] Therefore, stewardship duties have not developed to a degree sufficient to produce substantial results.

Nevertheless, obligations on states to protect the commons increasingly appear alongside individual and collective rights. For instance, in international fisheries, the duty of due diligence – requiring preventive measures to prevent the destruction of resources – has been recognised as a principle of environmental protection. The 1999 Southern Bluefin Tuna case before the International Tribunal for the Law of the Sea established that states must act prudently and cautiously to ensure conservation measures, even amid scientific uncertainty.[146] The precautionary principle was later articulated by the ICJ in the *Pulp Mills on the River Uruguay* case.[147]

In a landmark Advisory Opinion, the International Tribunal for the Law of the Sea affirmed that state parties to the UNCLOS, including Part XII (on marine pollution), have concrete and positive obligations to prevent global warming and protect the marine environment from greenhouse gas emissions. The

141 See <bit.ly/3guxvf9>.

142 World Resources Institute, at <https://bit.ly/4ci2Hpy>.

143 Centre for European Policy Studies 2024, at <https://bit.ly/3IOTyLb>.

144 Bull 1984: 14.

145 Falkner & Buzan 2018: 26.

146 ITLOS, *Southern Bluefin Tuna Cases* (New Zealand v. Japan; Australia v. Japan), 3 and 16.8.1999, para. 77, 79, and 80, respectively.

147 ICJ, *Pulp Mills on the River Uruguay* (Argentina v. Uruguay), 20.4.2010, para. 164.

Tribunal emphasised that 'the standard of due diligence is stringent, given the high risks of serious and irreversible harm to the marine environment from such emissions'.[148]

Several national courts have also addressed the protection of natural resources from a human rights perspective,[149] often invoking the concept of stewardship. The 2018 *Andrea Lozano Barragán v. President of Colombia* decision held that Colombia had violated the right to life and breached its obligations under the 2015 Paris Agreement, ruling that 'the deforestation of the Amazon causes direct and serious harm to all Colombians for present and future generations, as it is responsible for massive emissions of carbon dioxide into the atmosphere, causing global warning, which in turn disrupts ecosystems and degrades water sources'. The Supreme Court of Colombia also declared in this decision: 'Without an equitable and careful consumption framework, the future of humankind may be jeopardised by the scarcity of vital resources. Solidarity and environmental consciousness must be correlated to the point that they become identical'.[150]

In 2019, the Dutch Supreme Court, in *Urgenda Foundation v. Netherlands*, held that inadequate government action to reduce emissions violated Articles 2 and 8 of the European Convention on Human Rights. The court ordered the government to reduce emissions by 25% from 1990 levels by the end of 2020, reasoning that the failure to act effectively on climate change posed a serious risk to life and family life.[151] The ECtHR later endorsed this line of reasoning in *Verein KlimaSeniorinnen Schweiz* (see Chapter 5.2.2).

The UN High Commissioner for Human Rights welcomed the *Urgenda* judgment, noting that 'climate change is already seriously affecting human rights, and its effects are rapidly growing [...]. The recognition by the highest Dutch court that the Netherlands' human rights obligations provide a legal basis to compel stronger and more rapid action by the Government is vitally important'.[152] The judgment exemplifies stewardship in practice and affirms the role of civil society in asserting stewardship rights over the universal commons.

In July 2025, the ICJ issued its first Advisory Opinion on climate change, following advocacy by civil society organisations and supportive governments (see Chapter 5.1.4). The ICJ confirmed that states have legal obligations under

148 ITLOS, *Request submitted by the Commission of Small Island States on Climate Change and International Law*, Opinion, 21.5.2024, pp. 147–153. See also: Taylor 2023.
149 For an indicative presentation of cases, see <https://bit.ly/2Uiq1NJ>.
150 On the judgment, see <https://bit.ly/3pmXm8n>.
151 For a summary of the judgment, see <https://bit.ly/38OE7Pt>.
152 UN High Commissioner for Human Rights, UN, Press Release, 20.12.2019, at <https://bit.ly/3njpXtr>.

international human rights law and environmental treaties, including the UNFCCC and the Paris Agreement, to protect the climate and ensure a clean, healthy, and sustainable environment as a precondition for human rights and intergenerational equity. The Court underscored the continuing obligation of developed states to provide financial support to developing countries for mitigation and adaptation 'in a manner and at a level that allows for the achievement' of these objectives.[153]

The ICJ also ruled that all existing international treaties – including those on human rights, the law of the sea, and other environmental regimes – as well as customary international law, govern climate-related obligations. These obligations apply to all states, regardless of treaty participation. Furthermore, the Court found that fossil fuel production and consumption, the granting of exploration licences, and the payment of fossil fuel subsidies can all constitute breaches of customary international law on climate protection. States also bear an obligation to regulate private-sector polluting activities. These findings may form the basis for future claims seeking reparations from states that fail to fulfil their climate obligations.

4 Stewardship on Common Resources and International Investments: Between Rights and Obligations

Policies developed in relation to the universal commons shape governance and compel us to question the position of commoners, both individually and collectively. This issue is particularly relevant in the context of the exploitation of natural resources in developing countries by multinational corporations investing large amounts of capital. In such cases, the livelihoods of local communities are often determined by decision-making processes that exclude the commoners of these resources. There are countless examples of asymmetric, excessive, and unilateral exploitation of natural resources by multinational corporations.

In such situations, the rights at stake concern three issues: the right of people to participate in procedures of environmental management and resource exploitation; property rights over land and soil, including resource management, particularly water; and the repression and criminalisation of active opposition to the exploitation of these resources. However, the right to devel-

153 ICJ, *Obligations of States in respect of Climate Change*, Advisory Opinion (23.7.2025), para. 265.

opment is crucial in determining the context of rights and obligations relating to the commons.

[*Sustainable Development and Stewardship*]

The obligation of states to oversee the global common goods, resources, and spaces must be precisely specified, together with the parallel retreat of sovereignty in both industrialised and developing states. Two decades after the Stockholm Conference, the UN Conference on Environment and Development (Rio, 1992) defined the term 'sustainable development'. In distinct fields, states assumed the political and moral commitment to pursue stewardship policies for the common good and shared interests. However, there is no guarantee that each state will cooperate with others by moving away from its own autonomous policy of overusing a resource or under-providing a public good for its own benefit and development, thereby disregarding *common sustainable development* objectives and confirming the prisoner's dilemma.[154] This situation can be avoided if a culture of cooperation for the common good is politically established as a shared assumption.

Indeed, the incentive to achieve the maximum collective benefit at the lowest individual cost in economic terms can also work in favour of the common good, as a group of researchers demonstrated mathematically by disproving Hardin's theorem. The model also applies to large social groups, particularly when information about the benefits of the commons in which they participate is shared, thereby fostering the creation of active, participatory bonds.[155]

As discussed in Chapter 1, 'sustainable development' is used as a concept without a precise meaning, shifting with the political direction of the economy, as it has always meant everything and nothing, often implying contradictory aims. Even with definitions imposed by the UN, mainly as political compromises, the concept remains politically ambiguous. At least some rudimentary features of sustainable development are a common goal (see the UN 2030 Agenda, Table 6), without being subject to rules regulating states' economic policies. The free market demands immediate gains, while sustainable development requires long-term planning and, at a minimum, a participatory process involving subjects-commoners when it concerns common resources.

---

154 The *prisoner's dilemma* considers the strategic choices of rational players involved in competitive situations.

155 Hauser, Hendriks, Rand et al. 2016.

[*Right to Development and Multinational Corporations*]
Governments make commitments to corporations that invest in resource exploitation. They must respect the terms of the development contract and, when applying restrictive measures, comply with the principles of proportionality, necessity, and appropriateness.[156] However, the state party to an investment contract is also the guarantor of the public interest. It must protect the rights of the people whose lives and wellbeing depend on the resource and ensure the resource's sustainability and non-exhaustion.

Important decisions on international investments are often made far from where they are implemented, and the specific factors relating to the exploitable resource or the needs of local societies are rarely considered. Access rights for other potential users are often disregarded as well. However, Lorenzo Cotula notes that, since the beginning of the twenty-first century, the gradual democratisation of many developing countries has empowered citizens to demand sustainable natural resource management policies and to participate in public debate, thereby enhancing transparency and accountability.[157] Indeed, the increase in interventions by communities and organisations in international investment cases before arbitration tribunals demonstrates the growing influence of civil society on natural resource management.

These developments have moral and normative value, as the obligations of states and corporations are already enshrined in positive law. In practice, however, matters are more complex. Pressure from large multinational corporations to invest, coupled with the capital inflows needed by developing countries, has led to the establishment of a special category of 'flexible' treaty. Examples include Bilateral Investment Treaties (BITs) and broader thematic framework agreements such as the Energy Charter Treaty. Contracts negotiated between a state and a corporation occupy a unique position within the international economic system, particularly when they concern the exploitation of significant natural resources. Disputes between corporations and states are often intertwined with broader political tensions and economic dependencies and are subject to international arbitration. This system consists of Investor-State Dispute Settlement (ISDS) tribunals rather than the national courts of the state.[158] The arbitral tribunals operate by applying the

156 ECtHR, *Levages Prestations Services v. France* (23.10.1996), para. 40; *Runkee and White v. UK* (10.7.2007), para. 40; IACtHR, *Ricardo Canese v. Paraguay* (31.8.2004), para. 132.

157 Cotula 2017: 21.

158 See in this respect <https://icsid.worldbank.org/en/Pages/about/default.aspx>.

rules of the UN Commission on International Trade Law or under the auspices of the World Bank's International Centre for the Settlement of Investment Disputes (ICSID).[159]

However, the rules applied by arbitral institutions to resolve disputes are usually those set out in the investment agreement rather than those of national or international law on environmental protection and human rights. In this way, the legal architecture of international investment results in a transfer of jurisdiction that bypasses national and international law – especially in matters of public interest – to an extraordinary, non-accountable jurisdiction.[160] It is not uncommon for arbitrators to act as defenders of corporate interests, in flagrant violation of the independence of arbitral institutions.[161] Thus, contracts become detached from the social and legal context and are treated as sacred instruments that may be opposed to the general interest. The *lex mercatoria* is flexible and evolves much faster than international human rights law. The applicable law itself has become a negotiable commodity, as the parties have the right to choose the law governing dispute resolution (forum shopping), making it easier to avoid the guarantees offered by the rule of law.[162]

A regulatory framework is gradually being developed within the United Nations, establishing an obligation on states to prevent their corporations from violating the rights of individuals and communities in the countries where they operate. The Committee on Economic, Social and Cultural Rights has linked the obligation to monitor corporations with the right to health.[163] Similarly, the Committee on the Elimination of Racial Discrimination has expressed strong concern about the activities of multinational corporations based in Canada that extract natural resources from third countries, calling on the Canadian government to take legislative and administrative measures to monitor these corporations effectively.[164]

---

159 The Centre was established by the Convention on the Settlement of Investment-Related Disputes (Washington, 1965). See: Schreuer et al. 2009.

160 Bohoslavsky, Martin & Justo 2017: 77–78.

161 See: related complaints on <https://isds.bilaterals.org/?-the-basics->.

162 Dardot & Laval 2014: 483.; Delmas-Marty 2006.

163 CESCR, General Comment No. 14, The Right to the Highest Attainable Standard of Health (Article 12); Ruggie 2008.

164 CERD, Concluding Observations, CERD/C/CAN/CO/18, Canada, 25 May 2007, para. 17. Meanwhile, international outcry has been caused by the excessive violence used against local communities when they reacted against Canadian mining corporations. The proposed legislation was introduced in 2010 and eventually defeated by a narrow majority in the Canadian House of Commons. Comisión Ecuménica de Derechos Humanos & Fédération internationale des ligues des droits de l'Homme, 2010: 7.

In 2008, the UN Secretary-General's Special Rapporteur on human rights and transnational corporations noted the 'fundamental responsibility' of corporations to respect human rights, 'irrespective of the obligations of states'. He stressed that corporations bear an autonomous obligation to exercise due diligence to avoid rights violations.[165] How, then, are human and social rights to be applied in the conflict between 'protecting natural resources' and 'safeguarding international investment'? How can the following conclusion, reached in 2015 by the UN Human Rights Council's Special Rapporteur on Human Rights, de Zayas, become part of political culture?

> Every State under the rule of law [...] cannot divest itself of human rights obligations by outsourcing or privatising activities that are fundamentally State functions. Before and after entering into international investment agreements, States should conduct human rights, health and environmental impact assessments.[166]

In this regard, Resolution 25 of 2021, adopted by the UN Human Rights Council, underscores the obligation of states to protect rights from violations arising from the activities of third parties, usually multinational corporations. The ECtHR has ruled that compliance with the provisions of an international agreement cannot justify a violation of contractual human rights obligations.[167] Similarly, the Inter-American Court of Human Rights found that:

> The application of bilateral trade agreements does not justify non-compliance with State obligations under the American Convention. On the contrary, their application must always be compatible with the American Convention, a multilateral treaty on human rights that, in itself, creates a normative framework of rights for individuals and does not depend on reciprocity between states.[168]

In another case, the Inter-American Court held that when a state delegates powers relating to the provision of public-interest services to a corporation –

---

165 Ruggie 2008: 55.

166 de Zayas 2015. Also: 'Berne Declaration' at: Canadian Council for International Co-operation & Misereor (2010). Similarly, according to Special Rapporteur De Schutter 2011, states must ensure that the conclusion of any trade or investment agreement does not impose obligations inconsistent with pre-existing international treaty obligations, including those aimed at protecting and respecting human rights.

167 ECtHR, *Pellegrini v. Italy* (20.7.2001), para. 40, *Maumousseau and Washington v. France* (6.12.2007), para. 96, *Bosphorus Airlines v. Ireland* (30.6.2005), para. 153–154, *Woolley v. UK* (10.4.2012), para. 77.

168 IACtHR, *Comunidad Indígena Sawhoyamaxa v. Paraguay* (29.3.2006), para. 140.

such as water supply – there are three distinct legal consequences:[169] (1) The state bears a direct responsibility for the operations of water service corporations, as such services constitute a basic state obligation, even if delegated to a private party. (2) The state has a corollary obligation to oversee the corporation managing the water supply to ensure that the public interest is safeguarded. (3) The state has a responsibility to protect human rights and, therefore, an obligation to establish jurisdictions that guarantee the effective examination of every individual complaint.

Therefore, the rules governing investment must be framed by principles that serve the public interest, from the perspective of the rights of the people directly or indirectly involved in resource exploitation. However, there are numerous examples of arbitral interpretations of bilateral investment agreements focusing primarily on investor protection. For instance, in *Biwater Gauff v. Tanzania*, the corporation contracted to provide water supply and waste collection services in Dar es Salaam, increased prices, and reduced investment compared with the previous public provision. The corporation, which had won the tender with a very low bid, requested that the contract be adjusted to increase state payments. When the Tanzanian government refused, the corporation ceased providing services, and the government re-nationalised them. The investor appealed to the ICSID, and the arbitral tribunal ruled that the nationalisation of the investment was illegal, without justifying the company's loss under the contract, even though the company's value had already been negative.[170]

As a counterweight to the powerful position of corporations, the principle of 'corporate social responsibility' has been incorporated into new investment agreements, introducing the principle of sustainable development. Although often addressed only superficially, it has sown the seeds of a dynamic interpretation of BITs. Consequently, in some judicial decisions, environmental protection and rights have begun to be recognised as legitimate expectations, even when not explicitly provided for in investment agreements.[171] For example, the *Urbaser v. Argentina* arbitral award held that an investor must refrain from actions that might curtail the right of access to water. The decision is a landmark, following the framework set out by the UN Committee on Economic, Social and Cultural Rights, according to which rights correspond to specific, rather than vague, obligations to respect, protect, and enforce.[172]

169 IACtHR, *Ximenes-Lopes v. Brazil* (4.7.2006), paras. 86, 87, 96, 97.
170 DCDDE, (ICSID) ARB/05/22, 2008.
171 Baroncini et al. 2018.
172 Cf. <https://www.iisd.org/itn/2018/10/18/urbaser-v-argentina/>.

Although the decision adopted only the obligation to respect, the investor company was held under international law to bear responsibility for human rights in relation to a global common resource.

Similarly, the *Philip Morris v. Uruguay* arbitral award held that Uruguayan law did not violate the investment agreement, because the state had discretion to restrict investor rights to protect public health.[173] According to the US Supreme Court in *Central Penn Station Co. v. New York City*, measures to protect legitimate public-interest objectives such as public health, safety, and the environment may not impose restrictions on rights that must be protected without alteration.[174]

In Ecuador, the natural environment, soil, groundwater, and air have suffered immeasurable damage as a result of indiscriminate 'exploitation'. The rights of Mother Earth, though enshrined in the constitution,[175] ultimately proved to be no more than words. In the same country, alongside the case of the Yasuni National Park (see also Chapter 6.2.1), the case of the giant El Mirador copper mine, located within a protected national park, illustrates the restrictions placed on rights when powerful economic interests collide with the public interest. As the economic benefits of exploiting the mine are crucial for the country, the government has ceded an even larger area to Chinese corporations.

In response to enclosures restricting access to and management of resources imposed by multinational corporations, interest groups, or states, certain principles and guidelines have been formulated by international institutions, though with limited effectiveness. For example, in international trade, attempts have been made to establish the principle of special and differential treatment and to promote Interstate Commerce Acts to ensure fair prices, enforce principles of conduct for international business, and formulate new rules for technology transfer. These initiatives have collapsed under the power of neo-colonialism, as developing countries – specifically their unaccountable political, economic, and military elites – have broken ranks, pursuing their own self-interest and profiting from dependency. The question, therefore, is not which state will reap the benefits of the resource, but whether the resource and the people who use it will have access to it and on what terms. Thus, the right to self-determination and to the exploitation of one's own resources has often come to mean the privilege of powerful national elites to manage those

173 Cf. <https://www.italaw.com/cases/460>.

174 Supreme Court, 438 US 104, 26.6.1978.

175 Faundez 2017: 133.

resources at the expense of the state's own citizens, the commoners of the resource.

5 Enforcing Security for Common Resources?

In recent decades, the notion of security has been overused and misused through ambivalent interpretations in international law and politics. The security of sovereignty takes precedence over the security of the people, and likewise, the security of private profit takes precedence over the security of common resources. It remains unclear whether transnational solidarity for the oversight and management of global common resources and the legal protection of universal commons can succeed where inter-state cooperation has failed. As discussed in Chapter 4, initiatives undertaken by the United Nations across various fields do not always translate into effective mechanisms for securing the commons. State and non-state actors alike co-construct realities through stark contrasts within multiple, complex, asymmetric, inefficient, and contradictory networks of governance.

The absence of effective sanctioning and deterrence mechanisms to ensure the protection of universal commons has undermined equitable access to and use of resources. For example, the obligation of states not to destroy areas beyond their jurisdiction – such as the atmosphere and the high seas – has been enshrined in law. However, compliance mechanisms have not been developed to guarantee protection-based security.

Indeed, 'security' is associated with 'peace', and the security of common resources is closely linked to the peaceful development of universal commons. The effective protection of global natural resources is a prerequisite for the security of the planetary ecosystem and of human commoners. According to the 1987 Brundtland Report, 'the concept of security, as traditionally understood, must be extended to the growing effects of environmental stress'. Moreover, military conflicts cannot guarantee a prosperous future for common natural resources or protect public infrastructure from destruction.[176] In the field of environmental protection, Principle No. 25 of the Rio Declaration states that

176 States have a legal duty to refrain from such activities. In some cases, the destruction of natural resources and public infrastructure is carried out according to a political project, such as the Israeli operations in the occupied territories of the West Bank of Palestine and especially in 2024–2025 in Gaza (ICJ, Advisory Opinion, *Legal Consequences Arising from the Policies and Practices of Israel in the Occupied Palestinian Territory, Including East Jerusalem*, 19.7.2024; Francesca Albanese, *Anatomy of a Genocide*, Report, UN Human Rights Council, A/HRC/55/73, 25.3.2024).

'peace, development and environmental protection are interdependent and inseparable', and in 1998 the UN Secretary-General emphasised that 'competition for land and water resources is a factor in conflicts in Central Africa',[177] and, one might add, everywhere on the planet.

Already in 1978, the Convention on the Prohibition of Military or Any Other Hostile Use of Environmental Modification Techniques aimed to protect the natural environment from 'any deliberate manipulation of natural processes – the dynamics, composition or structure of the earth, including its biota, lithosphere, hydrosphere and atmosphere, or of outer space' (art. 2). However, this treaty did little to protect the environment during warfare. State responsibility for violations of *jus in bello* can be established in cases of environmental damage. For instance, Iraq's liability for severe losses and damages caused by its invasion of Kuwait was affirmed by Security Council Resolutions 674 (1990) and 687 (1991).[178]

Efforts to protect nature have, in recent decades, produced a penal approach that advances the concept of 'ecocide' as a quasi-crime that infringes the legal interests of nature or human life itself. 'Ecocide' is defined as acts and omissions causing severe damage to or destruction of the environment, resulting in significant or permanent alteration of the global common resources and ecosystems on which the subsistence of human societies depends. A few rules of international law address the issue. Protocol I of 1977 to the 1949 Geneva Conventions (arts. 35 para. 5 and 55) protects the environment in armed conflict by prohibiting methods of warfare that are expected to cause 'widespread, long-term, and severe damage' and by prohibiting environmental attacks as reprisals. Moreover, according to Article 8 para. b.iv of the Statute of the International Criminal Court, a war crime, among many other instances, is the intentional launch of an attack 'in the knowledge that such attack will cause severe damage to the natural environment which would be clearly excessive in relation to the concrete and direct overall military advantage anticipated'.

In 2016, the UN Secretary-General António Guterres underlined the crucial importance of environmental protection and its broader correlation with violent conflict:

> Many conflicts are triggered, exacerbated or prolonged by competition over scarce natural resources; climate change will only make the situation worse.

177 Elliott 2003: 49.
178 Collao 2020: 261.

> That is why protecting our environment is critical to the United Nations' founding goals of preventing war and sustaining peace.[179]

The emerging principle of human security, combined with the right or obligation to humanitarian intervention, creates a conceptual link with factors that undermine international peace and security and could trigger the Security Council's interventionist powers – even by military means – under Chapter VII of the UN Charter. This possibility raises numerous issues that cannot be examined in detail here. The present challenge, however, is whether it is possible to intervene – by peaceful or military means – to deliver assistance effectively to populations in distress and to secure access to essential survival resources.

In this respect, could the Security Council's powers be extended to address threats to vital resources essential to humanity as a whole? For instance, could coercive measures be adopted in response to threats to the planet's water resources or atmospheric oxygen? If states are collectively obliged to safeguard common resources globally, what adequate means are available to ensure effective protection for these resources when they are threatened with extinction, thereby endangering the human community and states themselves?

Ultimately, and in borderline cases, it would make little sense to engage in a rigorous debate over distinctions between the subjects of protection and their inclusion within the categories of 'all states', 'the international community', or 'humanity'. Could one, therefore, legitimise the exercise of compulsory compliance measures against states that threaten to destroy – or have begun to destroy – environmental or other common resources at the global scale massively and irreversibly? Similarly, could one imagine taking action against a corporation or group of individuals committing such acts? Could interventionist measures depend on a penal approach, such that acts resulting in the mass destruction of natural resources would be classified as a 'crime against humanity'? However appealing or controversial the debate on criminalising the destruction of resources may be, it should not be forgotten that the exploration of the limits of legitimate intervention, particularly involving military force, has rarely satisfied the conditions of formal and substantive legality.

---

179 UN Environment, *Annual Report and Programme Performance Report for 2016*, at <https://bit.ly/3puHjWn>. In 2022, the International Law Commission also elaborated a series of principles related to 'Protection of the environment in relation to armed conflicts' (ILC, Yearbook 2022-II, Part Two).

This legal deficiency is especially evident in relation to principles such as proportionality and the appropriateness of the means employed.

In the event of an environmental disaster, the Security Council could deem the consequences of environmental damage a critical threat to international peace and security and order military intervention to protect the environment. Such an interpretation could draw on the 'responsibility to protect' principle. This approach has been advocated by many, some of whom have referred to the right of self-defence under Article 51 of the UN Charter. As Gilley and Kinsella suggest:

> It is at least legally possible for the Security Council to invoke its competence under Article 42 and use military force against states that could be considered a threat to international peace and security based on their non-compliance or failure to stop destructive acts against the environment on their territory.[180]

Under the international political conditions prevailing in the first quarter of the twenty-first century, one could imagine a hypothetical scenario in which the Security Council might have the authority to implement measures to mitigate catastrophic fires in Australia, Siberia, and the Amazon during 2019–2020, or floods in Pakistan in 2022. In particular, could it legitimately take action against Brazil and China, which have agreed to turn a large part of the Amazon ecosystem into a soybean production and shipping hub, with the soybeans transported down-river to China?[181] The construction of 49 dams, the clearing of millions of acres of rainforest, and the incessant river traffic pollute water and air, drastically reduce oxygen replenishment flows in the ocean and atmosphere, and destroy an ecosystem that has already suffered enormous damage over the past 30 years. Bearing in mind that oxygen production in this region makes a vital contribution to the global supply of clean air, could a right to collective intervention on behalf of the oxygen we all share be established?[182]

The question is certainly hypothetical and perhaps irrelevant, since the application of the UN Charter in matters of collective security remains subordinate to the political objectives of the Security Council's permanent members. On the other hand, security can be understood, in the narrowest sense, as the use of global common resources in the interests of the state. According to

180 Gilley & Kinsella 2015.

181 The Guardian, 5.10.2017, at <https://bit.ly/3ngoWCr>.

182 Walt (2019) even wondered whether a unilateral right to intervene could be established in the model of humanitarian intervention.

this argument, such resources and spaces should be protected for the sake of individual security by any means necessary, including the use of force. The US formulation of the military doctrine of security on the open sea, air, and cyberspace exemplifies this approach:

> The United States will continue to lead global efforts, in partnership with capable allies and partners, to ensure access to and use of the Global Commons, both by strengthening international norms of responsible behaviour and by maintaining relevant and interoperable military capabilities.[183]

Accordingly, ensuring the security of common resources depends on an ostensible appeal to freedom and presupposes military strength, economic supremacy, and control over the commons. The entity possessing the means of enforcement thus dictates the rules and establishes the framework of legitimacy under the guise of a selective freedom that enables exclusions. Preventing the dominance of such policies requires a profound transformation of the international political system and the establishment of a universal collective consciousness committed to preserving the 'common good' as the shared interest of both states and peoples.

6 Securing Healthcare: The Covid–19 Pandemic

Healthcare is a global public good, allocated locally within each national government's area of responsibility. Since the beginning of 2020, each state's public health system has been at the centre of the pandemic crisis triggered by the virus SARS-CoV-2. The scale of the problem, combined with the absence of effective channels of communication and cooperation, has revealed the universal nature of the challenge. The urgent need for a holistic ecosystem approach to public health, or 'ecohealth', has once again become apparent.[184]

Global cooperation was required to contain the rampant spread of Covid-19, necessitating the sharing of knowledge and technology as well as the development of a framework for mutually compatible measures. Therefore, collaboration and the pursuit of coordinated health policies were essential.

Epidemiologists advised the World Health Organization (WHO) to coordinate the imposition of varying levels of restrictive measures by individual states. These measures caused severe disruption to the daily lives of billions of people,

183 Department of Defense, USA, 2012: 3.
184 See Soskoline et al. 2018.

to the economic status quo, and to the daily incomes of the poorest. They also raised concerns about the present and future of fundamental human rights.

In order to assess the complex issues that arose during the global health crisis, we must ask the right questions and seek answers by introducing a different parameterisation of its determining factors: the protection of rights, pluralism, and democracy; the obligation of institutions exercising power to prioritise public goods; the preservation of basic social bonds; and the guarantee of security and safety, especially for those whose material conditions place them in a precarious situation.

Global mobilisation was prompted by the virus's high transmissibility, leading to comparisons with the 1918–1919 Spanish Flu pandemic, which caused at least 50 million deaths. However, the countless victims of disease in developing countries – not to mention those of hunger and extreme poverty – have never elicited a comparable level of action from the international community. One possible explanation is that, immediately after the outbreak in China, the virus spread rapidly to the centres of the world's most powerful economies. If people were mobilised with the same intensity to address diarrhoeal diseases or tuberculosis, it would inevitably lead to severe and disruptive changes in global economic, moral, and political relations between people and states. The same would occur if adequate policies were implemented to combat poverty and environmental degradation, both of which are directly linked to the spread of disease. Such a shift would have enormous implications for the production and redistribution of wealth and for the benefits derived from natural resources.

The travel restrictions imposed during the 2020–2021 pandemic temporarily improved the state of the natural environment – an effect previously unattainable despite decades of global campaigns for environmental protection and waste reduction. During the lockdown, global production slowed to such an extent that it had disastrous consequences for markets and for people living on minimum daily incomes. The international financial system certainly did not intend to suspend growth or stifle production, nor could it claim to have withdrawn from all outward economic activity in order to protect the environment. This unintended global experiment resulted in a temporary 'shutdown' that benefited the planetary ecosystem. However, it is unlikely that this positive side effect will be taken as a precedent for enforcing drastic environmental protection measures to safeguard health and other public goods. The Russian invasion of Ukraine in February 2022 and the subsequent energy crisis, deepened by the US-Israel war against Iran in 2026, have once again relegated both global health issues and the fragile state of the environment to the background.

If we consider that a new model of universal concern for public health and the common good emerged during the pandemic – albeit in an authoritarian form – we might also seek meaningful concern for the public interest in other fields. Alongside the healthcare objective, should we not also aim to preserve social cohesion and protect labour relations and activities? Should appropriate care for vulnerable populations not be a priority? Even when the vital role of public health systems was recognised, most countries made only temporary investments in healthcare.

Furthermore, the ability of governments in the Global South to tackle the pandemic was undermined by their commitments to investment companies. In many cases, governments were obliged to implement costly and unprecedented measures to protect public health and the economy. Yet, in meeting the conventional demands of investors, numerous decisions were adopted by arbitration panels (ISDS) that awarded substantial sums against governments despite the exceptional circumstances in which emergency measures were required to safeguard citizens.[185]

Political conflicts within the WHO have brought the issue of accessible knowledge in vaccine research to the fore, promoting the idea of equitable sharing without excessive profits or exclusion. Such a practice would align with the concept of healthcare as a global public good. Consequently, voices around the world began advocating for the principle of the commons in areas traditionally subject to industrial profit and political control.[186] Organisationally, the WHO's appeal found fertile ground for fundraising by the EU and the G20, which promoted research into the disease and the mechanisms required to develop a vaccine.[187] The Global Covid-19 Vaccine Alliance, 'Gavi COVAX AMC', raised substantial funds from private and governmental donors to develop vaccines and distribute them to developing countries in particular. As WHO Director-General Tedros Ghebreyesus stressed, 'working together through the COVAX Facility is not charity, it's in every country's own best interests to control the pandemic and accelerate the global economic recovery'.[188]

The WHO sought to incentivise pharmaceutical corporations to share their know-how through a data and patent-sharing pool – the Covid-19 Technology

185 See <https://isds-americalatina.org/isds-and-covid-19/>; <https://bit.ly/4pEtymM>.

186 For example, in early May 2020, European Commission President Ursula von der Leyen, French President Emmanuel Macron and many other political leaders declared that the vaccine should be a 'common good for all humanity'.

187 European Commission, *Coronavirus global response*, Press release, 4.5.2020 <https://bit.ly/2K3c4Bl>.

188 WHO, *Boost for global response to COVID-19 as economies worldwide formally sign up to COVAX facility*, at <http://bit.ly/38j5Y8v>.

Access Pool (C-TAP). Participation in C-TAP was intended to expand publicly available research, maximise vaccine production, and reduce costs. However, the major vaccine companies did not participate in the project. A different response came from the Drugs for Neglected Diseases initiative, which produces and distributes medicines where they are needed. In collaboration with the WHO, the initiative activated global synergies with minimal financial resources while mobilising scientific staff to conduct research on the Covid-19 treatments.[189] This represents one of the most significant examples of collaborative use, based on the creation of a mixed commons in terms of community composition, open access to knowledge, and open availability of the product.

In this context, the Parliamentary Assembly of the Council of Europe, in its Resolution 2361 of 27 January 2021, supported equal access to vaccines and the WHO's efforts in this regard. It called on states to remove the barriers and restrictions imposed by intellectual property rights to ensure the widespread production and availability of vaccines in all countries and for all citizens, arguing that vaccines constitute a 'global public good'.[190]

However, by early 2021, it had become clear that powerful states had chosen a path of selfish competition, establishing enclosures around the patents of their respective corporations. In theory, copyright law yields to compelling public-interest considerations. Indeed, TRIPS (see Chapter 4.8.2) allows a government to produce a patented product without the patent holder's consent in cases of national crisis involving urgency and non-commercial use, as enshrined in Article 31. Yet, when the time came in early 2021 to put compulsory licencing into practice, EU leaders clearly prioritised corporate interests over those of their citizens.

Several grassroots initiatives set the tone for an egalitarian fight against the pandemic – through free access to health material production, free use of tests, and the sharing of scientific knowledge. Sharing occurred either through hackers who distributed closed studies within the community or through scientific journals themselves, which temporarily suspended their rights. In both cases, free access to scientific articles was achieved.[191]

Conversely, corporations at the forefront of vaccine production, such as Pfizer and Moderna, received hundreds of millions of euros in funding from

---

189 DNDi, August 2021, *Another triumph for science, but defeat for access?* Available at <http://bit.ly/3Vo7Pjg>.

190 Council of Europe, PACE, Resolution 2361/2021, Art. 7.1.7 <https://pace.coe.int/en/files/29004/html>. Also: PACE, *Covid-19 vaccines: ethical, legal, at and practical considerations*, Report, 11.1.2021, Doc 15212, at <http://bit.ly/3F1GRZg>.

191 Cockroach 2020.

the governments of the richest countries, including the US, the UK, and Germany. These corporations were under no obligation to share their results.[192] Nonetheless, they made enormous profits from vaccine sales without returning any of the public money invested – except for the bare minimum – to those who bore the costs, namely, the taxpayers of these countries. In principle, the states that contributed to vaccine production should have acquired patent rights and ensured proportionately cheaper distribution of the vaccine.[193]

In the race to secure the vaccines, powerful states offered their surpluses to assist developing countries. However, this could not reconciled with 'common interests', as geopolitical ambitions prevailed. Global public health – though solemnly proclaimed to be the highest public common good – was ultimately trapped between the gears of narrow corporate and state interests.

It is evident that in this particular health crisis, an opportunity was missed to develop and consolidate the principle of the commons through international stewardship. The Covid-19 pandemic could have prompted a fundamental reversal of the global pandemic of aggressive profit-seeking, exploitation of people, and the extraction of unilateral surplus value. Changes in values, such as those concerning public health, could establish a human-centred political 'normality' that incorporates all kinds of exceptions in the event of a health, ecological, social, or economic crises. Such a shift would serve as a check on the tendency of political power to appropriate extraordinary control over society and individuals. The negotiations launched in 2021 within the WHO culminated in the adoption of the Pandemic Agreement in May 2025,[194] which, once in force, will legally enhance principles such as equity, collective responsibility and management, sharing of information, and protection of human rights.

7 Towards a Right to Universal Commons?

We have seen that many different rights are attributed to commoners – the subjects of universal commons. These may concern the rights of states vis-à-vis other states, recognised individual or collective human rights, or the competencies of international organisations. These rights vary in meaning and significance and produce differentiated legal and political effects. In each case,

192 't Hoen 2021: 37.

193 See related review at <https://bit.ly/38lgegs>.

194 The Agreement will be open for signature after the Pathogen Access and Benefit-Sharing system is adopted and annexed to the Agreement. See <https://bit.ly/40zyS9a>.

competencies and rights concern the position of commoners in relation to a global common good, resource, or space that constitutes the respective universal commons. Some of these rights may be enshrined in legally binding international instruments, while others may arise through non-binding texts. Many more remain merely aspirations or the object of collective struggles. A crucial but rare property of some is that they are enforceable at the international level, meaning that an individual can claim recognition of a violation of their right before a judicial body. Ultimately, rights are secured by the protection of a public good, such as public health.

One could say that every human being has an inherent right to the essentials required to sustain life – food, water, oxygen, and shelter – and to secure the economic means of subsistence. People's rights in relation to the universal commons should be understood from precisely this perspective. The diagonal that intersects politics and law with regard to people's needs – as actual individuals but also as abstract and conceptually integrated entities, i.e., as acting or potential commoners – defines the field in which the need arises for the universal democratisation of normative guarantees that will ensure a right to commoning, that is, a right to access, govern, manage, or exploit the commons. This right is broken down into a nexus of individual relations of rights and obligations enshrining informal and customary law, positive law, and national and international law between:

- The commoners-users
- The commoners and the guarantor of the commons
- The commoners and the entity exercising power over the commons
- The acting commoners and the potential commoners

The right of every human being to commoning, as the ultimate and absolute subject of protection, can be anchored in Article 28 of the Universal Declaration of Human Rights: 'Everyone is entitled to a social and international order in which the rights and freedoms set forth in this Declaration can be fully realized.' If the commons are a precondition for human life and wellbeing within the social dimension of the international legal order, one can reasonably argue that the rights of commoners should be guaranteed in law. Already, aspects of this super-right can be traced in rights that have been established or are emerging as partial guarantees of the status and role of particular commoners. Depending on the nature of the commons, rights are held by communities of commoners: states themselves, individuals, peoples, indigenous communities, and international organisations.

Conversely, the claim to protection – especially with regard to finite commons – is linked to the obligation to protect the commons and to participate in their governance in ways that sustain the conditions for resource's productivity and ensure commoners' participation. Rights and obligations are thus interrelated aspects that define both the status of the commoner and the nature of the commons. The obligation of *stewardship*, as seen in Chapter 5.3, rests on the shoulders of subjects who possess institutional and political power or economic and technological capacity to determine the fate of the commons, such as states, international organisations, and, from another perspective, corporations. It also falls on subjects who possess a quasi-right to control and the political capacity to claim rights, such as individuals, communities, social movements, and non-governmental organisations.

The *right to commoning* – or the *right to the commons* – presupposes the formation of a right of access, possession, and use that includes everyone. In this sense, it represents a form of cosmopolitan law that transcends national and international law as we know them today, within the political community of all the people of the world, taking into account the future members of this community. The Kantian vision and ideal of a cosmopolitan society would constitute humanity's highest conquest to the extent that *jus cosmopoliticum* is imposed on international law and national laws, with the aim of achieving world harmony and peace. In this way, cosmopolitan law seeks the unification of all peoples through rules of effective communication among them, but not in the sense of creating a global state.[195] Ultimately, the right to social life concerns every human being – directly, individually, or collectively – or legitimates the state to act in his or her name, as the human being is the central subject of the right.

The differentiated frameworks of national and international courts interpreting the autonomy of human action should be developed uniformly 'in a social and international order', as Article 28 of the Universal Declaration requires.[196] Rights in this context are linked to the *cosmopolitan freedoms of* all those who have a stake in the common good and who coexist within the international economic arena. The juxtaposition of the interests of those who seek to harvest or exploit the commons, individually or collectively, lies at the core of the dialectical constitution of people's right to the commons.

[*A New Generation Right?*]

Human rights, as a component of cosmopolitan law, can be schematically classified into generations to elucidate their evolution within the multilayered, asymmetrical global legal order. This trajectory of rights is closely linked to political and economic factors, both domestic and international. Established

195 Kant 1996.

196 Petersmann 2014: 125–126.

rights reflect successful assertions of claims against state power concerning the subjects of rights. These rights are classified into *first-generation* political and individual rights; *second-generation social,* economic, and cultural (or educational) rights; and *third-generation* solidarity rights.[197] Their subjects are the individual, society, or people, even humanity, with blurred distinctions between rights and often overlapping correspondence with their subjects.

It is aptly argued that an emerging *fourth generation of human rights* is linked to the digital revolution and to new relations in the production and exercise of power.[198] The changing relations of production in the economy and the osmosis between the private and public spheres – where power is exercised – already imply a reordering through new rights corresponding to new phenomena and needs.

The rights related to the management of the universal commons are dispersed across different levels of normativity and effectiveness. They represent sporadic and imperfect manifestations of the protection of commoners of a particular universal commons against enclosures through the quasi-right to commoning. The right to commoning of all subjects tends to form a new category of rights that lies beyond the classical categorisation of first-, second-, and third-generation rights. The right to the commons incorporates features of established rights – whether individual, social, or solidarity-based – but ultimately reconfigures and promotes them within a new normative framework. It is a synthetic form of right, lying at the heart of any discussion of humans' place in nature and in economic and social life.

In an ideal state of affairs, the right to commoning would have a universally normative and enforceable form, fostering democratic and participatory governance of common resources. At the same time, it would redefine global economic relations, with the primary goal being the value of the common good rather than individual profit achieved at the expense of common goods, resources, and spaces. Such a right would mark a universal paradigm shift in law, politics, and economics and would greatly alleviate the tensions between national and international law.

The leap to a new generation of rights primarily concerns all members of the *universal demos* as subjects of the right: individuals, communities, and peoples; non-governmental organisations; social movements; or composites thereof, as well as states and international organisations. It concerns the commoners of any commons possessing a universal character. Finally, just as the human rights we know today stand in opposition to state power, so too would the

197 Dinh, Daillet & Pellet 1998: 642.
198 Soh, Connolly & Nam 2018.

right to commoning stand in opposition to the agent exercising managerial power over the commons – and thus, to the community of commoners and, above all, to those imposing enclosures.

The ongoing rise of human rights must be recalibrated to include collective human concerns and the interests of future generations, encompassing a holistic view of nature and all living creatures. Human rights may open the way for a general right of human beings to access and manage common resources on a global scale, a right that is currently in formation. Consequently, could this common concern for the establishment of the right to commoning itself be regarded as a commons subject to international stewardship?

CHAPTER 6

The Paradigm Shift

> When the world we are trying to explain and improve is not well described by a simple model, we must continue to improve our frameworks and theories so as to be able to understand complexity and not simply reject it.[1] (Elinor Ostrom)

States' responsibilities to safeguard the commons are associated with certain norms of international law and human rights, such as the rights to life, health, food, or wellbeing. If the fulfilment of these rights – whether individually or collectively – depends on the management and exploitation of resources in the sense of their appropriation, the concept of 'property' becomes of key importance. What is crucial, therefore, is the search for a conception of 'property' in relation to nature and human creations that are not subject to appropriation. Consequently, it is necessary to identify the legitimating basis for the exercise of power, the management of the resources, the extraction of benefits, and, above all, the capacity to regulate relations among commoners. We return, therefore, to our original question concerning the reform of the relationship between commoners and the commons from a normative perspective.

The ultimate objective of these inquiries is to transform the protection of private property, which is usually not accompanied by guarantees on behalf of the commons and thus functions as an enclosure that restricts access, management, and exploitation of common resources by potential commoners. What we should ultimately seek is a transformation of the legal conditions of the 'ownership' of the global common resources to those who need them, not for enrichment, but as a fundamental guarantee for life and wellbeing.

A paradigm shift would first require rethinking the value of the universal commons, moving beyond the narrow notion of individual, state, or corporate profit towards that of a societal dividend or collective benefit – towards measuring and assessing value according to criteria other than those of a strictly economic hierarchy. For example, the value of nutritional raw materials should be assessed not by their current market price but by their value to human life. A forest acquires economic visibility only when converted into raw material. A whale, which has a certain value when its meat is sold, possesses a far greater value as part of the oceanic ecosystem, as a living carbon dioxide

1 Ostrom 2010: 665.

HTTPS://DOI.ORG/10.1163/9789004764118-007

sequestration unit, and as a critical link in the oxygen production chain.[2] The value of elephants, mangrove forests, Neptune grass, or coral can be understood in a similar way. Calculating the value of a commons is a highly complex task. How can we price the oceans? Should it be based on the value of the total fisheries they contain, the water and salt, or their role as the largest pool of biodiversity and organic carbon on the planet and a crucial reservoir for long-term storage? Such considerations argue in favour of replacing extractive policies with regenerative ones for shared global resources.

The paradigm shift would also require horizontal global governance – possibly polycentric, decentralised, or federated – that would propose, or even impose, models of effective management for matters of central importance with beneficial effects for all, such as improving the natural environment, consolidating individual or collective rights, or eradicating poverty, among others. The categorisation and prioritisation of needs is not definitive; however, since the late twentieth century, the concept of universal governance has gradually been redefined.[3] Centralised or decentralised governance does not, however, necessarily imply that it is or is not democratic.

Contemporary challenges regarding the environment and the management of common resources – in relation to overexploitation and the failure to prevent degradation or destruction – require radical and effective changes in the way international stewardship of the commons is applied. Relevant challenges also concern the knowledge commons. These challenges and needs may serve as the driving force behind broader global transformations, much as nationalism and territorial sovereignty once did. Just as globalised trade, by establishing an extensive market across political borders, has driven change in recent decades, the need to institutionalise the universal commons may likewise trigger new countervailing, holistic, anthropocentric transformations. As Fridjof Capra and Ugo Mattei suggest, such transformations should bring about a shift in paradigm and in perspective, corresponding to the ways people live. The revolutionary aspect of the shift involves changing legal paradigms and concepts by drawing on findings from the natural sciences to bring the legal order into alignment with ecological principles, favouring the sustainability of life. For Mattei and Capra, law can be an essential mechanism and tool in the

2 Medium.com, *Appraising Whales with Ralph Chami*, 9 Feb. 2021, at <http://bit.ly/3GQqzE3>.

3 For a discussion of approaches to universal governance in the first decade of modern globalisation, see: Hewson & Sinclair 1999.

struggle against overconsumption and pollution, so that all actors come to understand our world as a single common good.[4]

After all, certain concepts that surround us have become alienated from what they state. The *free market* is entangled with the freedom of those possessing the power and technology to exploit common resources. The *rule of law*, however developed, does not protect people from extreme inequalities, and thus fails to function as an effective guarantee of freedom and equality. Nor can *human rights*, as we know them today, effectively guarantee livelihood and wellbeing for all through the use of common resources. These concepts can therefore be reborn and endowed with a genuinely global meaning through a new approach. Boldness and imagination are required – not simply through the extension of social and economic rights, but through the emergence of a new law of the commons, in which the relationship between the commons and their commoners produces effective rules serving the principle of sustainability of shared global resources.

Finally, the paradigm shift must rest on overturning the notion of *exploitation*, which is falsely portrayed as exceptional and occasional. Today, exploitation is systemically embedded in international law, central to the discriminatory redistribution of wealth, and serves as a regulator of economic and political relations on a case-by-case basis.[5] A new model governing the regime of the universal commons should eliminate the unequal relations of exploitation that exist to the detriment of certain categories of commoners while favouring others. These relations develop within an asymmetrical and complex pattern of multilevel dependencies and needs. To produce new structures enshrining the commons, a critical level of self-organisation must be reached.

Self-organisational denotes a state in which the subjects of the commons influence one another as members of a system, pursuing the common good and effecting institutional and normative change. Often, this change – such as the establishment of a legal framework governing a universal commons – occurs through a series of avalanche-like events. These systems possess a degree of freedom, but the initial trigger (for instance, the need to protect the environment effectively or to maintain the openness of the internet) is transmitted from one subject to another until a critical threshold is reached. A universal commons is thereby established, and the process begins anew, developing in parallel with regard to other commons and involving both existing and new commoners.

---

4 Capra & Mattei 2015; Taylor 2011.

5 Marks 2008.

1 The Increasing Complexity of Relations

The governance of the universal commons – both finite and inexhaustible – as it unfolds amid the chaotic conditions of global governance and international law, remains more an aspiration than a reality. To comprehend the fluid and dynamic ongoing reordering of policies, ideals, and claims, as well as the limited body of relevant law, one must first distinguish the roles and characteristics of commoners. One must then classify the responsibilities exercised by states and international organisations, and the concern that is beginning to emerge as an obligation of international institutions. This is especially relevant when universal commons are transnational or fall within the territorial jurisdiction of a state, but whose importance for the *universal demos* is such that they arouse international interest and mobilise international actors. Tensions in the relations between commoners and potential commoners are certainly reflected in the way regulatory regimes develop – whether centralised, polycentric, or asymmetrical.

One question, however, remains unanswered: which institution has the right or the obligation to undertake the governance of the universal commons? Numerous theories and approaches have been developed concerning state sovereignty and its possible transformations,[6] since the universal commons possess two contrasting attributes that make them high-stakes issues and the source of conflicts of interest: They are essential to human life and wellbeing, yet they also have significant economic value. In an international system that still revolves predominantly around states, the governance and law of the universal commons is contentious when it comes to assigning new responsibilities to entities that already possess management capacity (states, international organisations, communities, etc.) or to those capable of acquiring it (individuals, non-governmental organisations, indigenous peoples, etc.).

According to Ostrom, at the local level, multicentred systems of commons governance overlap and interact. Most importantly, she demonstrated that polycentric governance tends to work more efficiently than unified systems. Polycentric systems, which may appear chaotic or non-hierarchical, 'tend to promote innovation, knowledge, adaptation, trust, different levels of cooperation among participants and the achievement of more effective, equitable and sustainable outcomes'.[7] This insight may also be confirmed at the international level, where multiple actors seek to contribute to the management of

6 Armstrong 2017: 135–148.
7 Ostrom 2010: 552.

global common goods, resources or spaces – whether under the exclusive jurisdiction of the state or within the international or transnational sphere.

Governance relations 'from below' and 'from above' are complex and interconnected – cooperative or antagonistic – depending on the nature of the commons and the specific level of governance (local, national, regional, or international). Local communities, national and international non-governmental organisations, state authorities, and international inter-governmental organisations make decisions and exercise influence or power within an interactive chain of actions concerning the universal commons and global public goods. Forests, for example, are common resources at the local and regional levels and also have a decisive impact on and contribute to the global quality of air, oceans, and soil. The protection of forests is therefore a matter of concern for local communities, the state, and the international community alike.

The exercise of power in relation to the commons – that is, the power to decide, to set rules, and to sanction rule-breakers or free riders – can be divided into two categories: power-over and power-with. In the commons, the exercise of power is relational, without any absolute ruler, shaped and legitimated through participatory processes, with the possibility of communication and regime change from within. Accordingly, within the universal commons, the exercise of power can occur at multiple levels simultaneously and be co-constituted within the state, between states and communities, and through the activity of international institutions.

The failure of states to protect common resources and secure essential public goods, or to curb free riders, often leads to the conclusion that what is needed is a universal mechanism to control and channel the behaviour of states. From this perspective, a mechanism controlling and imposing policies would operate, in turn, through the mechanisms of a panoptic Leviathan.[8] A fine line separates the powers of coordination and stewardship, consistent with democratic norms, from the powers of authoritarian decision-making and enforcement. This distinction is particularly important regarding the role sought by international organisations, especially the UN. Institutions assuming the role of guarantor of stewardship should ensure the common good of the commoners in an inclusive and redistributive manner, in favour of the *universal demos*.

With regard to the immediacy of governance, the universal commons may be subject to differentiated regimes depending on the nature of the subject-commoner. As governance moves beyond the local level in relation to the individual and society, direct or indirect forms of political representativeness

8 With reference to the 'Climate Leviathan', see: Brando et al. 2019.

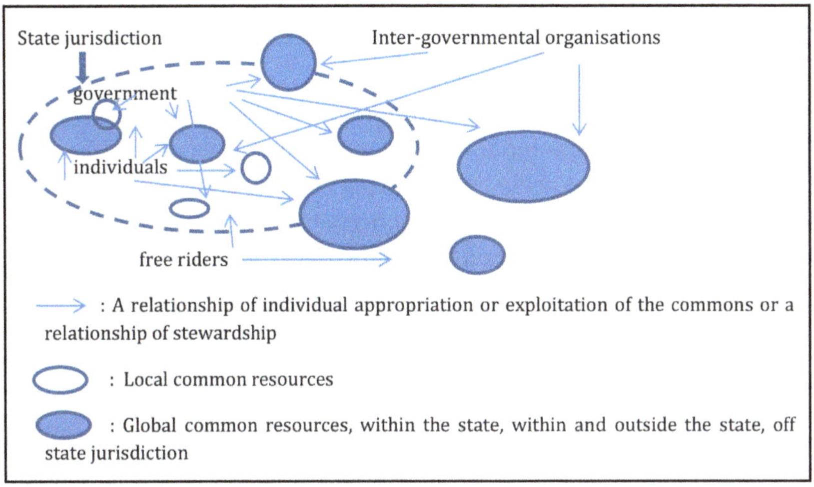

FIGURE 2. Spatial interactions in relation to global common resources

develop. Similarly, states-commoners exercise direct governance over the commons unless they have delegated management and supervisory responsibilities to an international organisation. A rich complexity is constantly being rearranged according to the nature of the commons and the profile of different commoners. These subjects, despite their heterogeneity, are continually negotiating their socialisation through relations of governance or claiming governance of the universal commons through new rules.

Figure 2 and Table 7 attempt to illustrate and schematise the complex relations and tensions that develop within spatial and power relations between commoners, stewardship actors, and those seeking to exploit the universal commons. This 'recapitulation' is followed by a discussion of the need for change in political, economic, and legal paradigms in order to establish a just and sustainable relationship between commoners and the common resources, spaces, and goods at the global scale.

2 Shaping Common Principles of Governance

Models for governing the universal commons influence the identity of commoners and humanity as a whole. Common issues related to livelihoods and wellbeing significantly affect the exercise of power, the application of law, and the functioning of the economy. Depending on the circumstances, participants in decision-making processes and the implementation of policy and law – including citizens, political parties, the military, corporations, states,

TABLE 7. Tensions between subjects-commoners

Key: =>: concession to ←→ : tension between

A. As regards the competence and exercise of management

Individuals, local communities ←→ states, multinational corporations

B. As regards the rights to socio-economic life

B1. Individuals, indigenous peoples, non-governmental organisations, universal demos ←→ states, multinational corporations

B2. States ←→ multinational corporations ←→ International organisations

C. As regards the management regime

C1. Centralised management

C1.1. Exclusivity of the state [state sovereignty] => individuals, indigenous peoples, local communities, multinational corporations

C1.2. Exclusivity of an international body [International concern/ common heritage of humankind] [loose management (seeds, climate, seeds)], dense management (Antarctica, satellite orbits, international seabed)] => states, indigenous peoples, non-governmental organisations

C.2. Multi-centred and asymmetric stewardship [Within the state; In the international (non-state) arena; In a transnational context] => Individuals, indigenous peoples, NGOs, states, international organisations, multinational corporations, multinational corporation

C.3. Unmanaged common resources

C3.1. Absence of a regulatory regime: => free riders/appropriation/ destruction without effective restrictions (fisheries, dumping of pollutants into the atmosphere, oceans, and space)←→ potential commoners

C3.2. Absence of any activity due to inaccessibility (celestial bodies, great ocean depths, Arctic seabed)←→ free riders

---

and movements – propose strategies that either promote co-management or exclude commoners from accessing and managing common goods, spaces, and resources. Similarly, the responses of international actors play a crucial role in determining whether the management of universal commons tends towards authoritarianism and exclusion or democracy and inclusivity, particularly concerning equality and freedom.[9]

Gradually, international practice and sporadically emerging legal principles are seeing to reverse the course towards the depletion of global resources and the uncritical prioritisation of profit. These counterweights are contingent

9 Anderies et al. 2013.

and remain insufficient to offset the persistent tendency to appropriate and alienate resources from the universal community of potential commoners. Certain general principles of international law, such as equity, aim to bridge the gap between the theoretical and actual equality of states while strengthening fairness in conjunction with the right to equitable development.

These principles could provide the theoretical basis for an equitable economic redistribution of the benefits derived from the exploitation of common resources, especially when such resources are material and finite. Yet, how can this be achieved within a dynamic and chaotic model of international governance driven by the hegemonic logic of private profit and ownership? After all, the governance of the universal commons consists of a 'regime complex'[10] of multiple systems of resources, spaces, and goods interacting at differentiated levels. Certainly, there is no single optimal governance model to propose for the universal commons.

The institutional density that results in the establishment of a matrix of governance rules is increasingly influenced by institutional commoners operating at the international level, within a spectrum ranging from integrated governance to outright fragmentation and the absence of governance. Some clusters are cooperative, others antagonistic. Thus, a multifaceted, often contradictory and asymmetrical regime of rules and political-economic interests runs through the public and private domains, both locally and globally.[11]

For example, the UN Forum on Forests, the FAO's Committee on Forests, the International Tropical Timber Organization, and numerous other bodies are active in protecting forest commons, yet without common objectives and certainly with inadequate and ineffective means. In the realm of global public health, national ministries and the WHO operate within a complex framework in which uniform policies must be defined alongside strategies for preventing and treating diseases across 195 countries. Effective medicines must be developed that are both affordable and available, while the exchange of knowledge and information must be secured.

Governance of the commons can only be exercised through participatory processes of democratic pluralism,[12] since relations between commoners are based on mutual responsibility. However, in the asymmetrical ecosystem of the universal commons, how can the reciprocal responsibilities of heterogeneous commoners and communities be respected? For individuals, peoples, states, international institutions, and organisations to attain self-awareness as

10 Orsini, Morin & Young 2013: 29.

11 International Task Force 2004: 33.

12 Kioupkiolis 2014: 174.

commoners, they must first emancipate themselves as entities with rights and obligations formulated within a framework of global quasi-constitutional principles. Achieving effective governance of the commons will thus require a pioneering political effort by collective actors through innovative forms of mobilisation[13] and global cooperation.[14]

According to Pierre Dardot and Christian Laval, the governance of the commons is an act of democracy that can be transformed into a constitutive political principle – 'the commons'. This principle would embody cooperation as a universal goal across all spheres of social life. Though its full application by micro-communities is not yet evident, it could evolve into a new universal political paradigm: a multiple federation of the commons, a 'world democracy'.[15] Pierre Sauvêtre goes a step further, disconnecting the commons from management practices and viewing them as fields of social domination that oppose capitalist domination.[16] Whatever the theoretical approach, the principles underlying the universal commons share certain core values: redistributive justice, effective stewardship, and the cultivation of a democratic political culture.

2.1 Distributive Justice

Governance involving the cooperative management of the global common resources by states and other entities engaged in the international arena leads to post-sovereignty practices, whereby the authority and dominance of the state recede and transform into a new relationship that transcends the traditional hierarchy of subjects in international law. The fair distribution of shared resources fosters the regeneration of social relationships on the global stage, exemplifying new forms of life in common. However, this new paradigm is in constant conflict with the trend towards enclosures and profit-driven motives, which contribute to the de-socialisation of the commons.[17]

If we accept that every human being has an inalienable right or entitlement to access and utilise the universal commons, then the obligation arises to redistribute the benefits derived from the exploitation of the commons from the few actual users to the many potential users. The challenge lies in estab-

---

13 Hardt & Negri 2009.
14 Kiss 1985: 439; Pardo 1993: 68.
15 Dardot & Laval 2014; Dardot 2018.
16 Sauvêtre 2018: 96.
17 Hardt & Negri 2009: 258.

lishing barriers within a framework that prevents free riders from exploiting the commons for their own benefit.

Those assuming the responsibility of safeguarding the global common resources, spaces, or goods, under the concept of 'benevolent stewardship', oversee the conditions necessary for fostering solidarity among commoners. The role of the 'steward' also includes wielding authority to ensure justice and equality among commoners. Stewardship involves implementing practices that fairly redistribute the benefits derived from the commons, ultimately serving the common interest.

To establish guarantees for applied redistributive justice through stewardship,[18] the principle of solidarity and democratic representation, a commonly accepted system of accountability, responsibility, and co-decision, must be ensured among those involved in the management and ownership of global common goods, resources, and spaces. Providing people with the material means to live decently is a partial precondition for achieving redistributive equality. The constant search for adequacy intersects with equality, resulting in a paradox: Although human rights guarantee equality in status, they do not ensure redistributive equality, as rights are not designed to address material inequality effectively.

Distributive justice aims to address power imbalances and hegemonic relationships that benefit certain individuals while excluding others. To understand redistributive justice, we must determine what constitutes an effective and genuine redistribution of common resources and identify the causes of their asymmetric distribution. We must also explore how the redistribution process can genuinely promote equity. Therefore, to formulate a normative question about how to redistribute resources effectively and equitably, we must understand the root causes and mechanisms that sustain inequality.[19]

Achieving redistributive justice, however, requires a radical transformation of the international system, such that it no longer unreservedly serves individual profit. This transformation depends on a re-evaluation of the international legal order. Mechanisms for redistributing capital generated by oligopolistic profits derived from the exploitation of global resources can serve to address exclusion from access to the commons.

While the critical issues of fair access to and equitable distribution of the benefits of a resource between developed and developing states remain unresolved, state sovereignty continues to be regarded as the sole condition for accessing and utilising global common resources. This state-centric approach

---

18 Roberts & Sutch 2016: 240.

19 Prieto 2021.

prevents a broader debate that would include non-state actors such as individuals, the scientific community, social movements, and various organisations or international bodies legitimised to represent 'humanity', i.e., the fullest possible representation of international society. In any case, the needs of those who use common resources are not adequately considered in light of states' obligations regarding the exploitation and management of these resources under their jurisdiction. Therefore, it becomes imperative to establish consistent rules regarding representativeness, legitimacy, and transparency in decision-making, exploitation, and accountability at the international level.[20]

Developing states often strongly advocate redistributive justice without simultaneously proposing a paradigm shift. They adhere to a rigid logic grounded in state sovereignty, thereby neglecting the democratic, fair, and equitable rights of individuals to access and enjoy the benefits of common resources. There has been no shortage of proposals for redistributive compensation for being denied access, or only indirect access, to the resource, articulated by movements and states (the Group of 77) from the 1970s to the present. Their proposals have rarely yielded the expected results. Examples of such efforts – some institutionalised – include the following:

- A regulatory proposal initially established by the Montego Bay Treaty, but later downplayed by the 1994 Agreement on the International Seabed Authority (see Chapter 3), to create a Fund and operate the Enterprise for redistributing revenues and sharing expertise.
- Provision for the redistribution (when technology permits) of benefits from the exploitation of the Moon's subsurface minerals (Moon Treaty).
- A proposal made by the Group of 77 during the Copenhagen climate law negotiations aimed at establishing a Common Fund to consolidate resources from developed countries, channelled towards developing nations to achieve environmental protection goals, prevent ecological disasters, and combat climate change.
- A proposal to impose and extend the minimum amount of money withheld on every stock exchange transaction (Tobin Tax) in favour of environmental protection. The proposal, however, did not gain traction.
- Establishment of a fund under the Plant Genetic Resources Convention (see Chapter 2.4) to support farmers, drawing on contributions from member states and revenues generated from patents and seed marketing.[21]

---

20 Simma 1994: 234.

21 The system of collecting royalties from seed and plant states' revenues derived from genetic plant material originating in the Multilateral System (of plants subject to the Treaty) is based on Article 13.2(d)(ii) of the Treaty (set at 0.77% of the trade value), with exceptions and limitations that make it impractical.

- Implementation of pollution compensation clauses and the buy-back of pollutant quotas (Kyoto Protocol and EU Directive 2003/87/EC) to reduce emissions.
- Provision for the payment of fees due to the Authority in the event of authorisation to exploit the seabed (Annexe III to the Treaty of Montego Bay).
- Establishment of a $100 billion fund for losses and damage caused by environmental disasters in vulnerable states (UNFCCC: COP26 and COP27 decisions), which was not implemented in COP28. At COP29, the fund was increased to $300 billion, but it remains far from a satisfactory measure to mitigate the immense challenges.
- The High Seas Treaty (marine biodiversity) sets obligations for sharing both monetary and non-monetary benefits from the use of genetic resources. A financial mechanism was established to manage potential future funding flows, with developed states obliged to pay a flat rate into the mechanism.

If proposals for universal redistributive democracy were implemented in the economic sphere, states would have to assume obligations as members of a collective entity, rather than as part of an imaginary international community. 'Humankind' is often understood as a community of states that collectively pursue specific objectives, yield tangible outcomes, and are bound by obligations. In this way, it assumes the role of a genuine custodian of the universal commons. This stance represents a paradigm shift from one-dimensional state sovereignty to collaborative, multilateral 'trusteeship' or 'stewardship' of common goods, spaces, and resources. The obligations created are linked to benefits that will be enjoyed not only by current users of the commons but also by future generations. Institutionalising countermeasures in the form of compensation payments or buyouts for damage to common resources allows wealthy states and corporations to pay a small percentage of their profits to retain the right to set enclosures.

Equal access to resources and the redistribution of benefits among commoners remain utopian today. However, certain court decisions are laying the groundwork for the establishment of a legal culture in favour of the commons.

Consider an example from the Americas. A 2012 ruling by the Inter-American Court of Human Rights on the rights of an indigenous community in Ecuador regarding an oil extraction project in the Yasuni National Park[22] led to new national legislation guaranteeing the protection of communities and the natural environment. However, the initially indigenous rights-friendly govern-

22 ICJ, *Kichwa Indigenous People of Sarayaku v. Ecuador* (27.6.2012).

ment denounced the international community, claiming that it was forcing the government to act in a way that would ultimately lead to environmental destruction. Under the auspices of the United Nations Development Programme, a fund was established to solicit donations to strengthen Ecuador's economy and offset the losses caused by the reduced oil extraction in Yasuni National Park. The international community, coordinated by the United Nations, promised to pay financial compensation for the cancellation of the mining project. The Ecuadorian government could expect to receive $3.6 billion in exchange for leaving the oil untapped. However, since the project did not come to fruition, President Correa ultimately authorised oil extraction. He accused the international community of indifference to environmental concerns while emphasising his duty to use the drilling revenues to combat poverty among his citizens. Consequently, a promising plan for compensating the commons through effective redistributive democracy was abandoned.

As we saw in Chapter 5.2, examples of this kind are numerous. All converge on the following: Given the constraints on developing alternative political and economic options, developing countries are compelled, often under varying degrees of pressure, to pursue policies that exploit finite natural resources and access non-exhaustible resources without ensuring human rights or regeneration practices. Governments and corporations intensify control over these resources without establishing sustainable infrastructures or ensuring equitable redistribution of benefits. This is compounded by the absence of coherent policies and effective legal rules guaranteeing or enforcing respect for the commons and their commoners. However, in recent years, victims of such policies have gained more effective means to denounce government and corporate actions and assert their rights by invoking the principle of redistributive democracy.

2.2 The Commons of Governance: Equality and Freedom for the Development of All

The complex principle of equity guarantees real and effective access to common resources, goods, and spaces, especially for individuals, peoples, and states with a reduced capacity to participate in economic life at both the national and international levels. Without effective application, equity becomes a loose and uncertain legal principle that further excludes the economically weaker in favour of those with socio-economic advantages. Ultimately, equality and justice should be applied based on a specific analysis of power distribution to produce tangible outcomes. Those who are disadvantaged in terms of access to and participation in the commons require 'more equality' than those who already participate. For this to occur, there must be an inclusive community of commoners that neither tolerates exclusion nor accepts hegemonic globalisation.[23]

Throughout history, power dynamics and governance structures have evolved alongside ongoing redefinitions of individuals' roles. In the interplay between authoritarianism and democracy, freedom and equality are key indicators of quality governance. The dynamic force that steers change and maintains a constant equilibrium between the qualitative and quantitative aspects of freedom and equality within a given context is the collective will of groups and interests. Conflicting aspirations and goals drive this collective will – either to overturn or to uphold what has already been achieved.

In a democratic configuration, the public sphere is based on the principle of equality, whereby individuals are regarded as equal. In contrast, the private sphere operates according to the principle of differentiation, which acknowledges distinctions between people. Hannah Arendt argues that, contrary to what might follow from the mere existence of human beings, equality does not arise naturally but is the result of a society organised according to the principle of justice.[24] Similarly, equal access to and management of common resources, spaces, and goods on a global scale are not inherent, but rather intended features of the social and political organisation of international society.

The emergence of an international law of the commons should be grounded in respect for the principles of justice and equity, both in procedural and normative content.[25] Furthermore, the successful governance of common goods, resources, or spaces depends on the resilience of the system and its capacity to absorb potential risks. This success also relies on the system's ability to adapt by amending its rules in ways that preserve the sustainability of common resources and protect the commons from enclosure. Therefore, one of the main fields to be tested is the state's sovereignty over common natural resources.

---

23 Santos 2020: 546.

24 Hannah Arendt, in the 9th chapter of *The Roots of Totalitarianism*, entitled 'The Decline of the Nation State and the End of Human Rights' (Baeher 2000: 42).

25 Joyner 2001: 374.

[Permanent Sovereignty over Natural Resources]
The right of states to pursue their own development[26] gradually became established through decolonisation and the granting of autonomy to former colonies with respect to the exploitation of natural resources within their territories, free from economic and political dependency. Yet no explicit guarantees were established to protect those resources. The Calvo Doctrine was the first central legal principle to affirm a state's protection from unilateral and unconstrained exploitation of wealth-producing resources by corporations linked to dominant, often colonial powers.[27] Within the context of newly gained self-determination, the principle of permanent sovereignty over natural resources emerged as a new tenet of international law.[28]

The 1962 UN General Assembly Declaration on Permanent Sovereignty over Natural Resources (Resolution 1803 XVII) refers to the obligation of states and international organisations to respect fully the authority of peoples and nations over resources whose exploitation is directed towards 'national development' and 'the wellbeing of states'. Likewise, according to common Article 1 of both 1966 United Nations International Covenants, 'peoples may freely dispose of their wealth and natural resources, without prejudice to the obligations arising from international economic cooperation based on the principle of mutual interest and international law' (para. 2).[29] The provision establishes permanent sovereignty but does not guarantee satisfactory outcomes.[30] The right of each state to manage its own resources is reflected in numerous other legal texts adopted before the now global predominance of neoliberal policies.

The notion of 'permanent sovereignty' limited foreign economic interests within state territories, particularly in the developing world. However, the interpretation of the 'right of the people' often translates into the exclusive 'right of the state government'. without granting citizens and local communities a genuine legal claim over natural resources.[31] As discussed, international practice also shows that the exercise of sovereignty over natural resources is frequently influenced by economic relations that favour powerful multinational corporations.

---

26 Shaw 1997; Dinh, Daillet & Pellet 1999.

27 In 1868, the Argentine judge Calvo opposed the predatory interventions of France and Great Britain in Argentina.

28 Schrijver 1997. See: ICJ, *Armed Activities on the territory of the Congo (DR of Congo v. Uganda)*, (19.12.2005), para. 244.

29 Shaw 1997: 177. See also: Rio Declaration (1992), Principles 2, 3, 4, and 22.

30 Armstrong 2017: 132.

31 See, for example, the case of the indigenous peoples in the Arctic. In: Cambou & Smis 2013.

Although 'permanent sovereignty' was initially intended to protect new states' rights over their natural resources, it has ultimately come to be exercised in an undemocratic and unjust ways at two levels: Internally, there is minimal redistribution of profits, disadvantaging citizens; externally, wealthy states do not redistribute resources to poorer states, disadvantaging them as members of the international community. Addressing situations of extreme poverty[32] and structural inequality remains an urgent yet unresolved task.

Moreover, international law does not recognise a universal right of people to exploit natural resources directly, nor does it preclude the commercialisation of raw materials by non-democratic governments. Such commercialisation is often conducted in the name of communities of commoners, depriving them of the minimum benefits derived from those resources. Strengthening the accountability of authoritarian governments that expropriate natural wealth on behalf of an economic oligarchy could contribute to a more equitable distributive democracy – but only if accompanied by comprehensive regulations and policies.

Democracy may improve the prospects for combating poverty under certain conditions, yet it does not prevent democratic governments, exercising 'permanent sovereignty', from trading with oppressive regimes, thereby perpetuating the unequal distribution of raw materials. A universal redistributive mechanism between states – such as the one initially envisaged for the exploitation of the international seabed (see Chapter 6.2.1) – or an international redistributive tax would be required.[33] Furthermore, inequality is deepened by the destruction of the commons, such as the natural environment. Poor populations, though least responsible, suffer the most from pollution caused mainly by the rich.

[*Ecological Governmentality and Energy*]

In 1998, UN Secretary-General Kofi Annan observed that 'the global commons is the political field in which the interrelationship between the various actors and institutions is most advanced'[34] – but not sufficiently nor effectively enough, as would become apparent within a couple of decades. It has been

32 Nearly 700 million people live on less than $2.15/day, and 3.5 billion fall below $6.85/day, Damania et al. 2025: 12.

33 Thomas Pogge advocates adopting a 1% global tax on the extraction of critical natural resources, with the proceeds allocated to developing countries. Additionally, Leif Wenar proposes promoting accountability and democratic management of extractive resources. In: Armstrong 2017.

34 UN, General Assembly, A/51/950, 14 July 1997, Fifty-first Session, Report, *Renewing the United Nations: A Programme for Reform*. In the same report (para. 85), the Secretary-

understood that the open sea, water resources, extensive forests, the atmosphere, and the biosphere should be subject to a universal *ecogovernmentality*, implemented through international cooperation and oversight initiatives led by the UN and global citizens' movements.

However, the international system lacks mechanisms capable of reconciling state sovereignty, democratic governance, and the right to development on one hand, with the protection of life's essential preconditions – clean air, food, and drinking water for all – on the other. Such mechanisms would ensure a holistic approach to the protection of nature and to the 'ecological sustainability' or 'sustainable development' of human communities, as opposed to the 'profit sustainability' of corporations or states that enclose common resources. Close to 80% of low-income country residents are exposed to poor air quality, unsafe water, and degraded land.[35] Existing tensions are particularly evident today, as global neoliberal governance increasingly seeks to extract natural resources and control spaces in the name of efficient exploitation with minimal constraints.[36] As Manuel Prieto argues, political ecology invites us to transcend the tension between efficiency and equality by sharing power between international actors and human societies.[37]

The 'green governmentality' promoted in recent years can serve *both* the free market *and* the protection of natural resources in a tug-of-war between profit appropriation and resource preservation. Protecting resources in the name of 'green politics' often alienates them from local communities through strict appropriation measures imposed by the state or corporations. This 'green appropriation' generates new power hierarchies that create tensions detrimental to the commons. Two controversial examples of green practices, often driven by profit accumulation and lacking long-term ecological benefit, are worth noting. First, the large-scale installation of wind turbines or solar panels, while reducing reliance on fossil fuels, if not wisely used, diminishes the productive capacity of fertile soil. Second, although electric cars reduce dependence on petrol and diesel, they have increased global toxic waste and created new demands for electricity generation, with significant environmental implications.

Nevertheless, a comparison of fossil fuels and renewable energy sources indicates that the latter are far more environmentally benign and sustainable,

General proposed to activate the Trusteeship Council to discuss global problems such as the atmosphere and oceans and to link civil society with states and the United Nations.

35 Damania et al. 2025: xv.

36 Adelman 2017: 188.

37 Prieto 2021.

provided that the equipment used is recyclable after several decades. By contrast, fossil fuels require continuous extraction.[38] The mode of use, waste management and holistic economic policy determine whether renewable energy is genuinely 'green'. Another major concern is the intensive mining of key minerals such as manganese, copper, nickel, lithium and a series of rare-earth metals – essential for the 'green transition' – which often causes ecological damage and social problems more severe than those the 'green economy' seeks to address.[39] Mining must therefore be aligned with the goals of achieving net zero and mitigating environmental impacts, in accordance with just and fair governance.

Data from 2024 show that two-thirds of global energy consumption is still based on fossil fuels; globally, 42% of electricity is used in industry, while 65% of oil is consumed by the transport sector.[40] As profits for major oil corporations soar, so does energy poverty – not only in developing countries (where access to electricity remains lowest, particularly in Africa) but also among households across developed countries.

The transition from fossil fuels to renewable energy remains largely controlled by major corporations[41] whose production is still based on extractivism. The key questions, therefore, are: How can fossil capital be transformed into public renewable energy, and how can decarbonisation be channelled through commons-based production? How can access to critical energy sources be made equitable when such resources are concentrated in a few countries (Russia, the United States, Saudi Arabia, Canada, Iran, China, Brazil, etc.) and exploited by powerful corporations?

Energy is a highly complex, tradable commodity composed of heterogeneous resources, networks, and uses. It is subject to market forces, highly centralised, and crucial to human life and well-being, as it underpins every sector of public, economic, and community life. Furthermore, the environmental impact of energy production and consumption is decisive for people's health and living conditions.[42]

The commercialisation of energy has excluded users from communities of producer-commoners, which would play a decisive role in integrating energy

---

38 See <https://bit.ly/478fj2F>; <https://bit.ly/47kAMnN>; <https://bit.ly/3WcxJZG>.

39 Owen et al. (2022). These minerals are primarily concentrated in a few countries: South Africa, China, the Democratic Republic of Congo, Australia, Chile, Indonesia, and others. Buxton 2024: 148).

40 Enerdata, World Energy & Climate Statistics, Yearbook 2025, at <https://bit.ly/3GNF HV1>.

41 Buxton 2024: 149.

42 Giotitsas et al. 2022.

into a holistic framework. The central idea of such a framework is that energy is a common good directly linked to human life and the preservation of the natural environment – a prerequisite for the development and safeguarding of all other common and public goods. From the perspective of commons thinking, energy production and use presuppose non-commercialisation, or at least democratic and equitable oversight of production and distribution, based on the principles of generative and holistic exploitation, accessibility, and use. This approach supports the ecological management of energy production.

Energy statistics for the G20 countries indicate that the Paris goal remains an ambitious one: The objectives reaffirmed at COP28 are insufficient to meaningfully address climate change. Renewables have supplemented, rather than replaced, fossil fuels; improvements in energy efficiency have failed to offset the rise in energy consumption and harmful emissions, which continue to grow. Global energy intensity declined by only 1% in 2024 – a figure far below the decrease required to meet the -2°C scenario.[43]

Protecting the natural environment, ensuring energy security, and making energy affordable are prerequisites for the production and distribution of renewable energy in both the market and within communities of users and producers. The ecological necessity is so urgent, and the social benefits of environmental protection so evident, that the future of humanity depends on energy sustainability as an ecological public good. Eco-policies, viewed through the lens of public goods or the commons, require new modes of producing, distributing, and consuming electricity based on peer production and sharing. Power plants following these principles are already being rapidly developed in response to local climate conditions.[44]

Pressure groups' campaigns for energy production and distribution by energy communities – conceived as commons – found statutory expression in the EU in Directive 2018/2001 on the promotion of renewable energy and the establishment of 'renewable energy communities'.[45] These communities operate alongside or within an increasingly commercialised energy market governed by stock-market imperatives. The state plays a crucial role in ensuring energy justice. If it remains passively neutral, the potential for energy communities to develop will be severely constrained, as they must compete with economic giants on unequal terms.

---

43 Enerdata, World Energy & Climate Statistics, Yearbook 2025, available at <https://bit.ly/3GNFHV1>.

44 Lambing 2012.

45 REScoop MECISE 2019.

The countries of the Global South face energy deficits, foreign debt and food shortages. The stark division between the Global North and the Global South has prevented the world from confronting structural global challenges such as the climate crisis, energy needs, severe pollution of air, soil, and water, biodiversity loss, and armed conflicts over territory and resources. A cosmopolitan culture promoting democratic governance should therefore advocate inclusive and participatory interpretations of the rules governing the international system. This approach implies that the governance regimes for the universal commons should be justified through a cosmopolitan public discourse that ultimately benefits humanity as a whole. In essence, the effective and equitable protection and management of the universal commons depend on the development of a cosmopolitan constitutionalism rooted in coherent interpretations of multi-level arrangements that integrate various elements of international and transnational law of the commons. Such a legal arrangement presupposes corresponding economic relations between the subjects-commoners of the universal commons, within which the sovereign institution of ownership is accordingly redefined.

3 For a New Understanding of the Commons–Ownership Relationship

The institutional features of the universal commons become apparent through patterns such as grids, networks, or islands of commons that emerge from the pervasive realities of the market, private property, and state control. However, the commons can coexist with structures and institutions that are not necessarily favourable to them. Each commons, viewed through the lens of appropriation as articulated by Michel Bauwens, is part of a 'triarchy'. Commons theory introduces a third element alongside the traditional binary of private property (both individual and corporate) and state-owned assets. This addition gives rise to complex relationships between commoners and the commons, extending beyond conventional property dynamics. Governance structures for any form of appropriation are organised at local, national, and even global levels.[46]

Common goods, resources, and spaces placed within the state's jurisdiction often belong either to public property or to the property of private individuals (see Chapter 1). In the case of common resources under state ownership, state

46 Bauwens 2010.

authorities should serve the interests of their citizens. However, state ownership may complement or support private ownership, potentially at the expense of the common resources. Frequently, and subject to the laws of each state, private individuals acquire rights of ownership, use, and exploitation over significant resources that might otherwise be considered common goods.

For example, the status of the subsoil is critical, as it contains water, hydrocarbons, coal, minerals, and gems. In the United States, subsoil is subject to separate *in rem* rights regardless of the status of the land's surface. In the United Kingdom, subsoil is owned by the Crown, as are hydrocarbons and coal. Under continental European law, subsoil resources are usually owned by the state. In most cases, partnerships between the state and private corporations favour the private sector, which does not transfer the surplus value generated from resource exploitation to its natural beneficiaries – the people of the state – but instead retains almost all of it. A partial exception is Norway, as discussed in Chapter 5.3.

The right to private property is widely recognised as a fundamental pillar of legal, political, economic, and social systems, and it enjoys high normative and symbolic significance. Although it is often portrayed as absolute or even sacred, the scope of ownership is not limitless. Questions arise about what can and cannot be owned. Even though the right to property is sometimes considered inviolable, it is subject to restrictions in the name of 'public interest' or 'public necessity'. The jurisprudence of the ECtHR outlines a broad range of justifications for the state to impose restrictions on private property.[47] However, a crucial functional aspect influencing the dynamic between property rights and restrictions – favouring the commoners of a commons – is state sovereignty. Under the current legal framework, states retain ultimate authority, known as *dominium eminens*, exercising absolute control over all things within their territorial boundaries.

Thus, the extent of the right to property and the restrictions the state may impose ultimately dictates the rules. Consequently, *it is* state sovereignty that underlies individual property rights.[48] Can clauses protecting the commons, then, be enshrined within this normative environment? A prerequisite for an affirmative answer would be the appropriate regulation of sovereignty in terms of rights and obligations towards the commons – that is, management, access, withdrawal, alienation, and sharing of the benefits of the commons –

47 See among many others: Grgic et al. 2007.
48 Gutwirth & Stengers 2016: 7.

beyond the private-state property dichotomy.[49] The state, and any other guarantor of the commons, should, as already noted, assume the role of an overarching authority exercising stewardship for the benefit of the commons, rather than sovereign appropriation. The aim, then, is to transform *extractive ownership* into *regenerative ownership*, within a new architecture of ownership.[50] As Ernst-Ulrich Petersmann observes,

> The more 'globalisation' transforms national into transnational public goods whose protection depends on international rules and institutions, the more HRL requires citizens as 'democratic principals' to assume democratic control and responsibility of transnational governance powers and of their 'cosmopolitan property' of international public goods (*res publica*).[51]

From this perspective, the right to property should be harmonised and integrated with the economic aspects of the right of 'commoning'. According to David Bollier and Burns Weston, the right to commoning is not merely another human right; rather, it is a fundamental right with the potential to redefine the relationship established over the past three centuries between state sovereignty and the market.[52] In other words, within the context of the commons, the right to property assumes a collective dimension, signifying shared ownership, use, or possession of a resource, space, or good. Let us not forget that Article 17 of the Universal Declaration of Human Rights enshrines the right to property, both individually and in *common with others*.

For centuries, states have prioritised the 'free market' and the expansion of multinational corporations in appropriating the commons. If states were to demonstrate a comparable commitment to the universal commons, a remarkable improvement in the quality of life and in the prospects for sustainable resources could potentially unfold, benefiting all who share in the commons.

For civic participation to evolve from a theoretical concept into a tangible right, it must be anchored in the legal system and incorporated into positive law. It must become a legally enforceable rule that can stand alongside the right to property and, above all, enter into a dialogue with it, giving it new content. Redefining the dynamics between property rights and limitations

49 Parlance and de Saint Victor (2014) propose a rethinking of legal modernity, which defined the state-market-ownership triptych, from the perspective of relations with the commons.

50 See the relevant discussion in Cogolati 2020: 181–183.

51 Petersmann 2014: 130.

52 Weston & Bollier 2013.

requires a fundamental shift in the concepts, practices, and norms that have historically defined state sovereignty. Understanding ownership of the whole planet as the accumulation of sovereignties could not provide a solution. The concept of *condominium*[53] may be more appropriate when shared responsibility applies to a *res communis omnium*.

To think and act as a 'commoner' does not mean renouncing one's rights to private property and personal interests. On the contrary, it means exercising and enjoying them together with other members of society and the community of commoners – citizens of a state and inhabitants of a region. In our clearly globalised and interconnected world, this is even more pronounced and significant. Universal commons create interdependencies that are preconditions for people's livelihoods, well-being, and survival. Moreover, the commons are often subject to mixed uses of property rights and social relations. For example, the same forest can produce wood for private use and for trade; it can provide recreational space for all, whether privately or publicly owned, while also supplying oxygen for everyone.

The connection between commoners and the universal commons depends on the specific features of property regimes and appropriation dynamics. These are defined through rights and obligations designed to ensure the sustainability of the commons and the benefits they provide. Certain universal commons, particularly those vital for life and in the *general interest* of the human community, should ideally be categorised as inalienable – a concept rooted in Roman law. Alternatively, they should coexist with diverse property modalities and authority structures that uphold the fundamental notion of the commons.[54]

4 The Commons in the International Economic Order

> The Stone Age did not end because the world ran out of stones, and the oil age will not end because we run out of oil.[55]

Having examined various aspects of the universal commons, one may argue that society itself – whether conceptualised as the community of citizens within each state or as the global community – constitutes a common good

53 Like the rights related to floor ownership, see Magalhães 2016: 186–189.

54 Bollier & Helfrich 2019: 232, 226.

55 Attributed to either Ahmed Zaki Yamani, Saudi Arabia's oil minister (2000), or Don Huberts, a senior Shell executive (1999).

comprising networks of political, legal, and economic interdependencies. In this context, the economy functions as a commons, in its own right, with accessibility, management, and the safeguarding of benefits as qualitative factors that affect the lives of commoners. Specific economic commons or global public economic goods can be identified, such as the stability of national economies, economic justice, the reduction of economic inequalities, and tangible resources like money.[56] A crucial criterion for understanding these super-commons is that they are essential to the well-being of the community of commoners in terms of equality and democratic governance, rather than for the purpose of accumulating individual profit. These commons concern the whole of humanity as an unconnected but real community of people.

In a system that focuses on extraction, capital accumulation, and strategic expansion, economic change often results from the appropriation of commons. International investment law structurally privileges corporations over both the commons and human rights. After all, 'the market is structurally biased against the protection of shared wealth as a commons'.[57] Ideally, in a system that prioritises the common interest, changes would be primarily linked to the just economic management of the universal commons.

In this spirit, the founding declaration of the International Labour Organization, adopted in Philadelphia, USA, on 10 May 1944, established the principle of universal social justice by emphasising the dignity of humankind in economic relations.[58] It affirms that labour is not a commodity and emphasises that money and the economy should serve human well-being rather than exist as ends in themselves.[59]

The question under consideration here is whether the economic governance of the universal commons can be brought under a single, uniform international regime. Such a regime would conceive the commons, whether within or beyond state sovereignty or under the jurisdiction of an international body, as 'social goods'. The primary aim of the economy of the universal commons would be the 'common good' of humanity, oriented towards enhancing the well-being of every individual through economic solidarity. To ensure coherent and effective governance of the universal commons, it is essential to secure stable and sustainable economic prosperity and promote social inclusion.

56 See the proposal for the creation of a new global reserve currency, the decoupling of the US dollar, and the exclusion of all other national currencies. See: Zacharie 2012.

57 Bollier & Helfrich 2019: 285.

58 For the text of the Call for Proposals, at <https://bit.ly/2Ui1Ej6>.

59 Sopot 2019.

Indeed, tensions abound as conflicting economic interests manifest in the use of benefits derived from common resources. Achieving sustainable management of the universal commons requires an analytical framework that acknowledges the fundamental institutional characteristics of common-pool resources and the involvement of multiple users. *Degrowth*[60] emerges as a potential overarching strategy, proposing a deliberate reduction in economic activity and a conscious retreat from trends that lead to resource depletion. It can also bring about a shift in the dominant economic paradigm – from perpetual production and wasteful consumption to the rational and equitable exploitation of finite resources. Finally, it can contribute to the democratisation of wealth distribution, countering the massive capital accumulation by a limited number of local and global oligarchies.

Such a paradigm must serve human well-being and be linked to the social dimensions of the economy, guided by the principles of justice, solidarity, social benefit, and the ethics of the 'common good', while respecting individual autonomy. It presupposes, as we have seen, mechanisms of redistributive justice, possibly through taxes and guarantees of good governance by communities of commoners. Finally, it requires redefining 'economic value' in terms of its socio-political significance. Value has one meaning in the market and another in addressing people's needs. For example, the value of wheat and rice should not be determined solely by market price but primarily by the need to feed people without exclusions. Consequently, the criteria used to calculate value play a crucial role in this debate.[61]

New concepts are beginning to challenge the traditional view of sovereignty, emphasising the importance of protecting the 'common good'. Concepts such as the 'green economy', 'sustainability', and 'sustainable development' have acquired a dual meaning and, in practice, often serve market interests and benefit those most adept at exploiting the commons. For example, so-called 'green' practices may not meet the criteria of ecological development and may fail to realise the anticipated social dimension of the economy. Nevertheless, these terms remain valuable conceptual tools reflecting the features that constitute the commons. When commoners adopt and redefine these concepts, they can actively promote democratic participation, accessibility, and the development of the commons as resources, communities, and institutions. Otherwise, they are surrendered to the countervailing forces of enclosures.

---

60 See among others, Kallis 2017.

61 Bauwens, Kostakis & Pazaitis 2019.

According to the UN Secretary-General, Ban Ki-moon:

> Our practical actions for enhancing sustainability should be embodied within the framework of a new economics, addressing market failures that have ignored ecological implications and resulted in the increasing deterioration of nature as well as of the well-being of many human populations around the world. [...] A paradigm for a new economics must go beyond neoclassical and environmental economics and learn instead from the concepts of deep ecology, the rights of nature and systems theory.[62]

The tumultuous era of global deregulated capitalism has given rise to an all-encompassing and borderless market that levels and homogenises the commons and their commoners on the altar of profit. In essence, the enclosures that restrict the universal commons constitute infringements upon the freedom of commoners, extending to the global human community. Therefore, if the free market fails to align with and contribute to the principles of a just society, it becomes an illiberal and undemocratic mechanism of constraint. This mechanism perpetuates privilege and restriction based on oligarchic economic gains, rather than prioritising social profit – namely, the well-being of the *universal demos*, of *all* human beings. As Klaus Bosselmann puts it, 'liberalism mutates into the opposite of its original purpose'.[63]

Effectively safeguarding economic rights and the welfare of citizens, insofar as international jurisdictions permit, requires a constitutional cosmopolitanism grounded in rights, democratic self-governance, and adherence to the international rule of law. The selective strategic support of certain public goods (such as the stability of the international economic system) by international organisations, over others (such as public health and poverty prevention), also reveals a hegemonic globalisation that disproportionately serves the powerful and creates exclusions for the weak, whether states or communities.

The UN Special Rapporteur on extreme poverty and human rights, Philip Alston, observed in 2018 that little progress had been made in combating poverty precisely because the private sector is deeply involved in the global poverty eradication agenda: 'The private sector will not be interested in the less privileged part of the world's population, it will be interested in making a

62 GAOR A/68/325, UN Secretary General, Report August 2013, para. 63–64. Belongs to the *Harmony with Nature Dialogue* initiated by the UN. See all relevant resolutions and reports <www/harmonywithnatureun.org>.

63 Bosselmann 2015: 21.

profit'.[64] Following the first phase of the Covid-19 health crisis in the spring of 2020, UN Secretary-General António Guterres reaffirmed the urgent need to return to the Sustainable Development Goals through systemic economic change in response to the challenges and crises affecting billions of people.[65] Despite the unprecedented mobilisation of the international community and its declared intentions to protect vulnerable groups, global economic disparities rendered anti-Covid measures fragmented and largely ineffective (see Chapter 5.6).

The consolidation of the 'sustainable development' project can be achieved through the fair and sustainable exploitation of universal resources in terms of a 'circular economy', oriented towards social benefit rather than private economic profit alone. The EU defines the circular economy as one 'where the value of products, materials and resources is maintained in the economy for as long as possible, and the generation of waste minimised'.[66] Meanwhile, transformations in production relations brought about by digitisation are ushering in a new paradigm of industrial post-modernity. The paradigm is characterised by micro-units of nomadic entrepreneurship operating within global space. Production costs are frequently minimised, and capital requirements are reduced, laying the economic foundation for the emergence of knowledge commons.[67]

The spirit of solidarity and collective responsibility is a *sine qua non* for transforming political, legal, and economic structures that perpetuate enclosures. Reparative finance would strengthen resource flows from the Global North to the Global South within a framework of equity and distributive justice among individuals, communities, states, and generations. Moreover, multilateral debt restructuring and cancellation could reduce pressure on governments to prioritise export-oriented extractive industries that harm biodiversity, while increasing public resources for essential public goods and services such as health care and climate mitigation and adaptation.[68] Payments for loss and damage could expand public international finance to support commons-friendly policies, partially compensating for the exploitation of global resources and the harms caused by the operations of the global economy that have disproportionately benefited only developed countries. Conversely, states could fund energy production and distribution infrastructure costs in a

64 See <https://news.un.org/en/audio/2018/10/1023692>.
65 Statement of 1 June 2020, at <https://bit.ly/3pGeNku>.
66 See European Commission, *Towards a circular economy*, at <https://bit.ly/2Hpaw3p>.
67 Arvidsson 2019.
68 Dempsey et al. 2024.

manner similar to taxation, ensuring the equitable distribution of public goods. Reorienting subsidies towards the costs of the commons may seem like a basic preliminary proposal, yet it constitutes a sound starting point for further research along this line of inquiry.[69]

Such an approach seeks to ensure the protection and fair utilisation of common resources while promoting equitable development, poverty eradication, and the reduction of inequality. However, it refrains from imposing constraints on states or prescribing a specific economic development. Rather, it serves as an analytical framework offering clear and prudent recommendations.

The economic-political paradigm shaped by strategies of direct profit and capital accumulation is incompatible with an inclusive, pluralist, and participatory democracy founded on decentralised cosmopolitan accountability. The dominant economic elites benefit from the globalisation of capital mobility and from fragmented, largely unchecked state sovereignty. They have taken no initiative to effect meaningful changes that would lead to a redistribution of power and wealth.[70] As a result, the global economy is characterised by a profound democratic deficit and unfair economic growth, whereas equitable development is intrinsically linked to participatory democracy. As Amartya Sen has demonstrated, meaningful economic growth for all is impossible without the enjoyment of fundamental political and economic rights.[71] When international governance, in its present imperfect form, fails to serve the *common good* and the *universal demos,* as it is subordinated to economic oligarchies, the discourse of democracy and commoning becomes hollow.

In environmental commons, social and economic inequalities influence who bears the costs of degradation and the strength of environmental protection measures. When those benefiting from harmful activities hold more power than those affected, environmental safeguards are often weaker. This imbalance can produce environmental injustices across class, race, ethnicity, gender, and age, and can diminish overall environmental quality.[72]

The democratic deficit in the global economy is multilevel and characterised by opacity, lack of legitimacy in decision-making, and the absence of accountability mechanisms for economic authorities. One consequence of this deficit is the persistent disconnection between the global economy and

69 Giotitsas et al. 2020.
70 Papanikolaou 2022: 78.
71 Sen 2000.
72 Boyce 2019.

the needs of commoners-citizens.[73] Consequently, as long as the United Nations and international economic institutions such as the World Trade Organization *tolerate* systemic failures in markets and international governance, and as long as governments *exclude* their citizens from shaping economic policies, the need to reform the content of state sovereignty through forms of cosmopolitan democracy and commoning rights based on economic justice becomes urgent. The UN Secretary-General has referred to studies underscoring the 'urgent need to change destructive economic policies that are wresting control of the natural world to build private wealth for the few at the expense of the many, insisting that the economy must be placed at the service of the greater wellbeing of human beings and the Earth itself'.[74]

New economic and political approaches to 'development' must, therefore, be initiated to restore communities of commons to a central position, emphasising the protection and sustainability of cultural and natural resources.[75]

[*Ecology and Economy*]

In the *Anthropocene*, market mechanisms and privatisation, primarily focused on individual profit, have proven insufficient for preserving global natural resources. Continuous modes of extraction are expanding into new territories. Over the past decades, the extraction of four main material groups – biomass, fossil fuels, metal ores, and non-metallic minerals – has skyrocketed.[76] The big industrial countries consume the vast majority of products made from these materials and capture much of the wealth associated with their production. The impacts of relentless oil and gas extraction, continuous mining, forestry, and industrial agriculture often follow an economic development model based on largely unfettered resource exploitation, with highly unequal distributions of benefits and impacts both between and within the Global North and Global South. Governments around the world continue to expand extractive development that encloses both exhaustible and, in some cases, inexhaustible commons. According to Dempsey et al., domestic policies that support the expansion of the extractive sector are often influenced by the international financial system, which makes extraction necessary to maintain economic stability. The

73 Patel 2017.

74 Ban Ki-moon, UN Secretary-General, *Harmony with Nature*, Report, 17 August 2012, para. 44. For full references, see <https://bit.ly/3UvHwcd>.

75 Giraud, Leyronas & Rota-Graziosi 2016; Leyronas & Bambridge 2018.

76 Fleck 2024.

uneven structure of the global economy constrains what the Global South can do to address both economic development and ecological crises:[77]

a. Governments support extractive sectors, in part, because they seek to attract foreign investment and maintain investability;
b. Governments support extractive-sector expansion and continuity to obtain foreign currency;
c. International financial institutions uphold the unequal structures that subordinate states, while often incentivising and sometimes mandating policy choices that impose austerity and intensify extractivism;
d. The pursuit of financial stability drives states towards extractivism and constrains policy options aimed at ecological stability.

It is widely recognised that there is a pressing need to establish new economic models that prioritise the wellbeing of the global ecosystem. These models place Earth's capacity for recovery at the forefront of economic development, treating it as a fundamental goal rather than a secondary or external concern.[78] From such a perspective, 'economic growth' gives way to 'economic success',[79] with the qualitative criterion being the wellbeing of human commoners and, perhaps, the general happiness of people.

Undoubtedly, the environment and the imperative to reorganise economic relations and modes of exploitation constitute a critical arena for testing new policies. The adaptation of industrial production to environmental protection standards would reshape market conditions. The observance of *planetary boundaries* – which serve as indicators for environmental protection, as noted in Chapter 4.1 – on the one hand, and *economic growth* on the other, form two asymmetric poles of tension. After all, depletion and destruction of natural resources have severe effects not only on biodiversity, the global ecosystem, and the human habitat, but also on economic development.[80]

Ecological integrity as a legal principle and political goal is gradually gaining ground in international fora, legal instruments, and political declarations, pointing the way towards respect for the planetary ecosystem.[81] Moreover, economic policies prioritising *resilience* can strengthen the ecosystem's adaptive capacity to respond to change, serving life and wellbeing rather than capital accumulation. Successful resilience that favours life requires reducing

77 Dempsey et al. 2024: 3–4.
78 Nakicenovic et al. 2016: 40.
79 Bregman 2017.
80 Damania et al., 2025. Especially on the economic impact of water-cycle stress and natural resource depletion, see: Global Commission on the Economics of Water 2024.
81 Westra 2016. See also Bosselmann 2016: 75–76, with reference to the *Earth Charter* and other documents.

pressure on planetary boundary markers. *Stability* is another factor: It means maintaining changes in indicators within planetary boundaries through resilience, rather than succumbing to the tendencies and tensions that push the system into disequilibrium.[82]

As noted above, proposals for a *green economy* and for the Green New Deal permit multiple readings and accommodate significantly different political aspirations and agendas: from the extractive vision of continuing resource exploitation with a 'green face' to the subversive – and possibly only viable – proposal advocating the end of all carbon-based economic activity and the adoption of new socio-political models of development.[83] The existence of fossil fuel reserves valued at trillions of dollars suggests that this conflict will persist. However, renewables are sufficient to meet global development needs, and the required metals are in far smaller quantities than those of fossil fuels. Effective and consistent recycling is a key factor in achieving ecologically sustainable development.[84]

The European Union adopted the Green New Deal in 2019, setting the goal of achieving climate neutrality by 2050 while supporting economic growth.[85] Besides proposing a framework to reverse global warming, the launch of this policy reflects less a democratic reflex than an opportunity for political leaders to adjust their rhetoric to give 'fresh legitimacy to an existing and unpopular model'.[86] After all, the ecological approach alone does not necessarily imply democratic management of the commons, nor does it guarantee resource redistribution or access for communities.

Frequently, the state's implementation of 'green policies' focuses on nature preservation but can inadvertently result in social detachment. This may contribute to the de-communalisation of resources, create inequalities, and impede democratic management. For example, the state, through the monopolistic exercise of market-based power, may transform an open ecosystem into a closed ecotourism park, thereby alienating the local population from a common resource.

In such a context, the demand for 'environmental' or 'climate justice' is constantly intensifying and assuming various forms and meanings. The new terminology seeks to highlight ways to address social injustice in the relationship between the environment and justice. For example, 'environmental just-

82 Nakicenovic et al. 2016.

83 Foster 2019.

84 Damania et al. 2025.

85 European Commission, *A European Green Deal*, at <https://bit.ly/3sgq8eF>; *The Just Transition Mechanism: making Sure That No One Is Left Behind*, at <https://bit.ly/3q69Gv4>.

86 Adler & Wargan 2021: 3.

ice' refers to the material link between human vulnerability and disadvantage on the one hand, and the state of the natural environment on the other.[87] 'Ecological democracy' implies the participatory democratic organisation of the community of (potential) commoners, the effective attitude of the state towards the multi-level challenges of climate change, and the sharing of responsibilities based on the rule of law and human rights.[88] The obligation to repair damage to a common environmental resource leads to the idea of 'restorative justice', whereby those who cause environmental harm are required to make tangible reparation.[89]

In contrast, neoliberal approaches alienate the state from collective responsibility and care, assuming that the market offers more effective solutions than the state's cumbersome and complex mechanisms. As already noted, even promising climate protection agreements often fall short of ecological justice standards. What would be the purpose of moving towards decarbonisation without democracy and justice, without guarantees that the burden of reversing global warming will not fall disproportionately on certain commoners?[90] Jefim Vogel and Jason Hickel have shown that high-income countries, which champion reductions in CO_2 emissions per unit of Gross Domestic Product relative to population, are far from meeting satisfactory levels according to the Paris Agreement's goals for reducing global warming. As they suggest:

> Green growth approaches, understood as pursuing climate mitigation alongside continued economic growth, are inadequate for high-income countries to meet their Paris commitments. Further economic growth in high-income countries is at odds with the climate and equity commitments of the Paris Agreement. Narratives that celebrate decoupling achievements in high-income countries as green growth are thus misleading and constitute greenwashing.[91]

In the post-Covid-19 era, China, the United States, the European Union, and India are among the top emitters of CO_2. When emissions are calculated on a per capita basis, the United States, Russia, and all oil-producing countries in the Middle East rank highest. In general, emissions and living conditions are interlinked. Many of the world's largest emitters today are in Asia. However,

87 Schlosberg 2013: 55.
88 Harvey 1997; Sen 2009.
89 Forsyth, Pali & Tepper 2022.
90 Lyster 2019; Adler & Wargan 2021.
91 Vogel & Hickel 2023: 765.

Asia's rapid rise in emissions has occurred only recently, alongside increased life expectancy and reductions in extreme poverty.[92]

As Felix Guattari argues, the ecological crisis is a single condition with three dimensions, in which extreme environmental, spiritual, and social degradation are experienced.[93] The dyadic confluence of power between the sovereign state and private property – between the Leviathan and *homo economicus*, as Serge Gutwirth and Isabelle Stengers[94] note – plays a crucial role in driving the trajectory towards catastrophe. We should not nostalgically seek a return to nature or look forward to a techno-scientific utopia, but rather establish realistic principles of governance in economics, law, and politics that respect the universal commons: 'to learn to live as commoners, inventing a new world',[95] without allowing the components of nature to become exclusively marketable products transformed into capital once they have been plundered.

Even the preamble to the founding agreement of the WTO (Marrakech, 1994) declares that the relations among states in the field of trade and economy should be developed with a view to raising people's standard of living, and that states should allow for the optimal use of natural resources in accordance with the objective of sustainable development, aiming at the protection and preservation of the environment according to their level of economic development.[96] In practice, however, as the WTO's subsequent work has shown, concern for the shared environment and the wellbeing of human commoners has been diluted in the pursuit of other interests.

Stewardship of the environment is incompatible with war and any extreme man-made destruction of the environment. Consequently, stewardship of the natural commons, in its ideal form, would impose objective constraints and ultimately alter the ends and means of the 'free market' and 'development'. *Ecological justice* and *ecological sustainability* are key concepts for such an approach. The apparent cosmopolitanism of the market and environmental

---

92 Ritchie & Roser 2020.

93 Guattari 1989.

94 Gutwirth & Stengers 2016: 316.

95 Bollier 2014.

96 'Relations in the field of trade and economic endeavour should be conducted with a view to raising standards of living, ensuring full employment and a large and steadily growing volume of real income and effective demand, and expanding the production of and trade in goods and services, while allowing for the optimum use of the world's resources in accordance with the objective of sustainable development, seeking both to protect and preserve the environment and to enhance the means for doing so in a manner consistent with their respective needs and concerns at different levels of economic development', at: WTO, Decision of 1 April 1994, at <https://bit.ly/3kn5TFp>.

stewardship ends where the former threatens the latter – when neoliberalism pursues immediate profit without constraints or concern for the universal commons of shared resources and their commoners.[97]

[*Towards Alternative Entrepreneurship Models*]

Cooperative forms of entrepreneurship embrace participatory decision-making. They oversee and support commons networks by managing licences and infrastructure, and by providing positive services to the social environments of their members and communities.[98] This entrepreneurial model facilitates knowledge sharing and the production of tangible and intangible goods for community development at the local, regional, and even global levels. The primary goal of the Social and Solidarity Economy (SSE) – including cooperative enterprises, cooperative banks, and consumer cooperatives – is to advance a just model of economic activity, ensure the sustainability of wealth-generating resources, and efficiently provide public or common goods.

The cooperative form of production can constitute a formal legal entity under national law, aiming to establish producer communities. Its primary objective is to provide services or produce goods for marketing or free distribution among members. There are countless successful examples of cooperatives. For instance, Rural Electrification Cooperatives provide electricity to over 42 million people in the United States. Inclusive partnerships of producer-commoners across the entire production and distribution chain may engage in producing non-competitive shared products such as Linux software, hardware design (e.g., agricultural tools developed by the French company L'Atelier Paysan), or high-tech sensors, as seen in the case of the Canadian corporation Sensorica. In New Zealand, the company Enspiral has formed a network of professionals and entrepreneurs who produce software and provide related services through open consultation, decision-making, and design and development platforms.[99] Finally, the Associated Press news agency operates as a cooperative, sharing news-related intellectual property while allowing participating journalists to retain their copyrights.[100]

Free, open contributions – mainly knowledge, time, and creativity – are transformed through participatory processes and integration mechanisms into a final product, made available by business networks according to the logic of the commons. Such business alliances comprise professionals

97 Falkner & Buzan 2018.
98 Bauwens & Niaros 2017.
99 Cf. <http://wiki.p2pfoundation.net/Enspiral>. See: Kornilakis 2024: 106.
100 Cf. <https://www.ap.org/about/>.

and legal entities operating in the market, creating added value through the commercialisation of their products. The community of associates produces goods, and profits are distributed among them or reinvested in the network, either directly or through an association of persons. Unlike commercial enterprises seeking maximum profit, enterprises that operate on commons principles reinvest a significant portion of their profits in the network itself, the supporting infrastructure, and the vital fabric of the human environment – what may be termed 'regenerative entrepreneurship'.

Other models of entrepreneurship also seek to mitigate the impact of aggressive capital accumulation while integrating commons-based concerns. Such models embody stewardship principles such as self-governance, purpose-driven profit, and long-term independence guided by shared values and missions. These companies aspire not to be saleable commodities but enduring entities that serve a specific purpose. Profits are therefore not extracted solely for private gain but reinvested to advance the enterprise's constitutive goals.[101]

This business model, based on commons-oriented peer production, focuses on the fair distribution of value. Consequently, it surpasses the state's limited mechanisms of redistribution through taxation and welfare. Such production projects have their roots in the cooperative economy and the commons. While the SSE spans into new sectors, questions of scale and the normative frameworks needed to protect these projects from capitalist encroachment remain paramount.[102] Although this entrepreneurial model is local, international organisations have recognised its efficiency and global social impact. Indeed, there is a worldwide effort to promote the SSE. The International Labour Organization (ILO) adopted the 'Resolution concerning decent work and the social and solidarity economy' on 10 June 2022. After years of advocacy, the UN General Assembly adopted two resolutions: the first, 'Promoting the social and solidarity economy for sustainable development' (A/RES/77/281, 18 Apri 2023), which defines the SSE and acknowledges its potential contribution to achieving the Sustainable Development Goals; and the second (A/RES/79/213, 19 December 2024), which further strengthens global recognition of the SSE and reinforces the need for integrated policy approaches to harness its potential for inclusive and sustainable development.

Within this framework, SSE and public-community collaborations have yielded impressive results and fostered resilience, particularly during economic crises such as the 2008 recession and the 2020–2022 pandemic, as

---

101 van Tuyll 2023.

102 Kotsaka 2026.

shown by studies conducted by the ILO and the Transnational Institute.[103] A transition to a peer-to-peer economy and commons-based peer production requires a shift towards open cooperativism and collaborative, distributed systems that equitably share profits.[104] If this model expands, it can link countless local initiatives through a global network of shared knowledge and resources.

5 An International Law of the Commons?

Entangled with politics and economics, international law constitutes a crucial factor in shifting the paradigm of managing shared goods. According to commons theory, a conceptual distinction is made between 'commons' and 'common resources' when examined at a global level (see Introduction). Within this analytical framework, international law emerges as one of the three foundational components that together form the universal commons (Chapter 2.3). It serves as the regulatory structure that governs the actions and decisions of commoners and those exercising stewardship.

In many cases, the legal and political approaches and practices that dominate the international arena favour the enclosure of global common resources. International law remains indecisive at the intersection of social needs, power-sharing, and decision-making for the commons. It would be unrealistic to claim that states have fully embraced a holistic vision of the universal commons. What, therefore, should be the condition for establishing international rules for the protection of common goods, resources, and spaces, taking into account the rights and interests of commoners, the principle of sustainability, and equitable exploitation?

In 1948, a group of influential figures in the US (the Chicago Committee), promoting the idea of universal federalism and world government, published the *World Constitution*, which provided that 'The four elements of life – earth, water, air, energy – are common property of the human race. The[ir] management and use [...] shall be subordinated in each and all cases to the inherent interest of the common good'.[105] This formulation expressed a romantic idea in response to the horrors of war and the destructive power of the atomic

103 Birchall & Ketilson 2009; Hopman, Kishimoto, Russell & Valentin 2021.
104 For a series of articles on peer-to-peer economy, see <https://primer.commonstransition.org/1-short-articles/>. See also: P2P Foundation, at <https://p2pfoundation.net/>.
105 Preliminary Draft of a World Constitution 1948, at <https://bit.ly/3pnlZlq>.

bomb. However, the notion of legally enshrining the 'commons of life' re-emerged in the post-war era with a meaningful proposal: the formation of an *international law of the universal commons*. Although such terminology is not in use and no distinct discipline of international law is explicitly dedicated to the commons, there is a growing tendency to regulate the relationships among commoners, guarantors, and claimants of relevant rights regarding global common resources.

Norms of international law governing to a certain extend common goods, resources, and spaces at the global scale are sometimes outlined in treaty texts or may evolve as international customary law.[106] In many more cases, rules in the making can be found in soft-law texts[107] – legal instruments without binding force that nonetheless reflect the will of states to create frameworks of understanding and cooperation for the organisation of a universal commonwealth under common stewardship. Sometimes, such texts arise directly or indirectly from the mobilisation of non-governmental organisations, advocacy by social movements, and evidence presented by scientific associations. However, international law in the realm of the commons remains highly ambiguous, at times facilitating enclosures and the appropriation of resources rather than effectively enhancing commoning. The examples discussed in Chapter 4 span tangible and intangible resources, as well as exhaustible and non-exhaustible ones. Oceans, seeds, the internet, science, human genes, and energy are just a few among the many shared resources that fall somewhere between *res communis* and *res nullius*.

The political and normative self-limitation of states favouring coordinated behaviour could be a prerequisite for comprehensively settling relations concerning the universal commons, by prioritising shared interests and concerns. However, the specific content of 'community interests' still needs to be defined through principles and norms essential to conceptualising the commons. One must delineate the boundaries between the legal interests at stake, the means of adopting policies and rules grounded in solidarity, and the responsibilities of those who assume the role of guarantor. Such an approach could help curb market totalitarianism and explore avenues for advancing social justice through the economic security of commoners.

106 Errico & Claeys 2017; Cogolati & Wouters 2018; Cogolati 2020: 248.

107 'Soft law' refers to legal instruments that are not legally binding but recommend conduct. Informal forms of cooperation are based on soft law, which more easily gathers consensus and participation, paving the way for future international legal norms. On soft law and the commons, see: Sinou 2022.

According to Dinah Shelton, the emergence of rules of international law serving the 'common interest' of humanity is already transforming the idea of state sovereignty as we know it. The growing acceptance among states that certain issues are of 'common concern' to humankind heralds the end of the strict exclusivity of national jurisdiction. 'By definition, common concern demands international intervention and new ways of producing law, as well as techniques and ways of enforcing the law'.[108] Moreover, international law should aim to fulfil the public interest and realise the common good of the international community as a whole.[109] Therefore, international cooperation is a *sine qua non* condition for international law-making in relation to the commons. As Alexandre Kiss observes, with reference to environmental protection:

> In principle, a proclamation that safeguarding the global environment or one of its components is a matter of common concern to humanity should mean that such components, due to their global importance and the consequences for all their potential degradation or destruction, cannot be considered as solely under the exclusive and discretionary authority of the state.[110]

For cooperative policies to be effective, they must be implemented *collectively* through internationally coordinated mechanisms. However, cooperation alone is insufficient. A paradigm shift is required in the economy and in our understanding of life, power relations, and sovereignty – and, consequently, in international law itself. This requires universal restrictions on harmful extractive activity not only in areas beyond national jurisdiction but also within state sovereignty.

[*For a New Architecture of International Law*]

The current structure of international law primarily supports resource extraction grounded in capital accumulation. Even when it regulates the appropriation of resources in view to prevent depletion, it does not comprehensively define rights and obligations over those resources. In most cases, the concept of the commons is not explicitly recognised, and no provisions exist for the equal or differentiated treatment of various categories of commoners, such as states, individuals, groups, international organisations, and corporations. The key challenge, therefore, lies in establishing a new human-centric and eco-

108 Shelton 2009: 40.
109 Cançado Trindade 2010: 638.
110 Kiss 2003: 4.

centric framework for international law that transcends the existing state-centric and capital-centric model, introducing new rules and general principles based on the commons.

International legal norms and principles evolve over time before gaining consolidated status.[111] Established principles such as effectiveness, solidarity, preventive action, cooperation, good faith, distributive justice, common heritage, and common concern have already acquired normative weight. Most importantly, *jus cogens* (peremptory norms), *obligations erga omnes* (duties applying to all), and *actio popularis* (the individual right to appeal in the name of a common interest) can play a pivotal role in developing these principles into a *Jus Gentium*[112] – a law of peoples that applies to all, pursuing the common good through the commons. As noted in Chapter 3, the principles of 'common concern' and 'common heritage of mankind' are particularly significant, though often applied inconsistently or contrary to their intended aims.

All of these principles encapsulate community interests, with direct reference to common goods, resources, and spaces, extending into human rights related to environment, biodiversity, culture,[113] and other commons. Their purpose is to avoid legal or factual conflicts and enhance cooperation between states and non-state actors, above all, without being subject to the rule of reciprocity,[114] and constrain states' margin of appreciation towards a 'humanised international law'.[115] These principles still lack an explicit requirement 'to respect and to ensure respect for the norms of protection in all circumstances'.[116] Last, they underscore the interconnectedness of state sovereignties and their shared responsibility[117] – an essential condition for the sustainability of global resources.

The principle of solidarity, for example, is only sporadically enshrined in international law, such as in the law of the sea and environmental protection regimes. It reflects a shared commitment and collective action among states to address global emergencies, particularly pollution, resource management, and equitable distribution of benefits. Often, it entails differentiated responsibilities and support for developing states. The principles of 'common heritage'

111 Verhoeven 2008.
112 See the seminal work of Cançado Trindade (2010), who elaborates on the idea of a new *Jus Gentium*.
113 Francioni 2014: 444.
114 Riddervold & Newsome 2021; Santos 2020.
115 Sicilianos 2024.
116 Cançado Trindade 2010: 313.
117 Wolfrum 2021.

and 'common concern' challenge state sovereignty even when the commons lie within territorial boundaries. It could thus serve as a foundational concept in international law, providing coherent legal content for states' positive obligations[118] to promote the sustainability of the commons through shared, responsible, and transparent sovereignty in an equitable and just manner.

These obligations may be shaped by the proximity principle. The closer commoners are to a resource, the greater their responsibility and the stronger the stewardship regime that applies. In 2025, the ICJ ruled that:

> All States have a common interest in the protection of global environmental commons like the atmosphere and the high seas. Consequently, States' obligations pertaining to the protection of the climate system and other parts of the environment from anthropogenic GHG emissions, in particular the obligation to prevent significant transboundary harm under customary international law, are obligations *erga omnes*. In the treaty context, the Court recalls that the UNFCCC and the Paris Agreement acknowledge that climate change is 'a common concern of humankind' and that it requires 'a global response'. They seek to protect the essential interests of all States in the safeguarding of the climate system, which benefits the international community as a whole. As such, the Court considers that the obligations of States under these treaties are obligations *erga omnes partes*.[119]

In the same year, also in the field of environmental protection, the IACtHR affirmed the force of peremptory norms in relation to the global ecosystem as a commons:

> By virtue of the principle of effectiveness, the peremptory prohibition of anthropogenic conduct that may irreversibly affect the interdependence and vital balance of the common ecosystem that makes life possible for species constitutes a norm of *jus cogens*.[120]

---

118 The positive obligations arising from international responsibility can be divided into three categories: obligations of result, of due diligence, and of progressive implementation (Pisillo Mazzeschi 2014). The obligation to conserve exhaustible commons may likewise be broken down into three separate obligations: protection, restoration, and non-exploitation, in accordance with rules agreed upon by commoners (Armstrong 2017: 221).

119 ICJ, *Obligations of States in Respect of Climate Change*, Advisory Opinion (23.7.2025), para. 440.

120 IACtHR, *Climate Emergency and Human Rights*, Advisory Opinion 32/25 (29.5.2025), para. 8.

Reframing and re-signifying such principles and obligations for consolidating a law of the commons requires departing from current legal considerations to build an 'international law of the commons' genuinely grounded in universality[121] – drawing upon existing, though underused, legal material in both conventional and customary law. As Peri Roberts and Peter Sutch aptly note,

> Highlighting the fairness discourse that is already on the table as at least part of the basis for thinking about distributive justice, both draw on the relative success of the language of Common Heritage of Mankind and capture attention to the moral accessibility of the ideas. There is a good reason to build on relevant norms and values already present in international law as a starting point for discussion – an 'anchor in reality' to offset criticisms of utopianism and irrelevance.[122]

The organisation and consolidation of a universal commons law, spanning national and international legal frameworks, would require the establishment of rights and obligations between commoners and stewards. Such restructuring would inevitably challenge state sovereignty and the foundations of the dominant international economic system, which privileges the concentration of wealth among a few individuals and corporations. A fundamental rewriting of international law would therefore be necessary, reorienting global politics towards the sustainability of the universal commons and the material guarantees of dignity and wellbeing for all.

An international law of the commons presupposes the universal applicability of legal rules and principles both within and beyond state jurisdictions. It would regulate bilateral and multilateral interstate relations in accordance with universal principles and norms, promoting anti-hegemonic globalisation. Such a law would serve the common interests of the international community, as has been repeatedly discussed within UN bodies and related intergovernmental and non-governmental organisations. To understand and strengthen the emergence of community interests, it is essential to move beyond purely legal reasoning and examine the social contexts in which the interests arise.[123] In 1997, Christopher Weeramantry observed:

121 As Chemillier-Gendreau (2011) highlights, in the current state of affairs, international law lacks universality.

122 Roberts & Sutch 2016: 241.

123 Zyberi 2021: 318.

> We have entered an era of international law in which it subserves not only the interests of individual states but also looks beyond them and their parochial concerns to the greater interests of humanity and planetary welfare. In addressing such problems, which transcend the individual rights and obligations of the litigating states, international law will need to look beyond procedural rules fashioned for purely inter partes litigation.[124]

Similarly, Wolfgang Friedmann wrote as early as 1964 that international law 'is becoming a more complex and multifaceted subject. [...] We must overcome the traditional approach that distinguishes public from private law'.[125] This observation is more relevant than ever, especially regarding the universal commons, which require a distinct field beyond public or private law – a law governing collectively shared and stewarded resources, goods, and spaces.

To achieve a coherent, effective, and universal international law, an architecture must be established to regulate relationships formed within the commons – governing through democratic procedures not only the exploitation of globally shared resources but also the universal commons as distinct entities or institutions. Such a law would embed the convergence of individual and collective interests, developing comprehensive patterns of stewardship and collective responsibility for the intricate interrelations between human societies and the ecological, technological, and knowledge systems that compose our shared planetary heritage. Consequently, the prerequisite of individual state consent in reaching consensus would yield to the primacy of shared values. Lastly, the notion of 'subjectivity' warrants reconsideration. The diversity of individuals, local communities, states, civil society organisations, and intergovernmental bodies operating in the global sphere creates complex patterns of agency that international law must recognise and embed within its evolving framework.

[*Human Rights and Rule of Law: International Law as a Commons*]
The principles governing the management of the universal commons are founded upon justice, and the application of the rule of law constitutes a natural extension for the equitable development of the international law of the commons. The rule of law provides the necessary framework for the effective application of the principles of fairness, transparency, and accountability. However, it is crucial to note that as long as private economic interests and

124 ICJ, *Gabcikovo Nagymaros Dam Case* (*Hungary v. Slovakia*), 25.9.1997, Weeramantry, separate opinion, 115.
125 Friedmann 1964: 70.

unregulated laissez-faire economics remain the priority of the international system, achieving uniform justice for all subjects of the universal commons may prove a mission impossible.[126]

To a certain extent, it seems that human rights law is paving the way for the expansion of the scope of international law of the commons, including the incorporation, as noted, of new subjects, the extension of *erga omnes* obligations and *jus cogens* rules, and the evolution of customary law and soft law.

Notably, with regard to the commons, states' enhanced responsibility for matters of common interest requires human rights to be liberated from hegemonic interpretations that, in practice, overlook marginalised groups. In other words, we need rights that effectively serve the emancipation of their subjects – commoners who are meaningful actors in the international arena. Ultimately, these rights should not be interpreted through an essentialist or technocratic lens but rather as open to applications that serve humanity as a whole and all individuals. After all, 'states exist for human beings and not vice versa'.[127]

The international law of the commons is becoming a universal commons, provided that states, as commoners themselves, produce the rules governing their relations, and international bodies act as stewards of law-making procedures and implementation. However, the normative matrix itself is subject to rules that the community of commoners accepts, while ensuring its development. Similarly, the rule of law in its international dimension is a global public good, as it is a prerequisite for the good governance of the universal commons, depending on the contribution of subjects-commoners, especially regarding democratic control and accountability of those who administer the commons.[128]

States, as commoners, contribute to the creation of rules that all members of the international community do not necessarily accept. The same cannot be said of national law, as the authority to produce it lies with a state institution.[129] However, it is crucial to note that managing international law as a commons requires the development of a distinct political culture. Such a political culture involves fostering an understanding that challenges the established legal norms developed over the past few centuries and consolidating a global consciousness of the commons.

---

126 Robinson 2014: 15; Humphreys 2014.

127 Cançado Trindade, Separate Opinion, ICJ, *Declaration of Independence of Kosovo*, Advisory Opinion, 22.7.2010, para. 239.

128 Groff & Karlsson-Vinkhuyzen 2018.

129 On law-making at the national level as a common good, see: Daniels 2012.

A precondition for a new state of affairs is the recognition that law does not exist independently or outside the context of the human condition as an external, objective reality. The conception of international law as a commons is grounded in the idea that, just as any legal order is socially structured, international law is structured not only on the aspirations of states but also in the service of the commons and the just interests of all human commoners. Within this idea lies the capacity of each individual-commoner to claim subversion, since 'law is always a process of commoning',[130] an organic part of social life.

[*A Law on Commoning and Equitable Development*]

The current foundations of international law and the rule of law often embody principles that perpetuate inequality and prioritise private economic interests that shape 'economic development'. Instead of being a vehicle for prosperity based on 'structural sustainability' or 'economic development' allows the uncritical consumption of finite natural resources, offering temporary benefits to those who can acquire them. The reception of 'private property' as a sacred good, primarily through the activity of multinational corporations, normalises the relationship between humans and nature as a 'unifying principle of social exclusion'.[131] Here, international law is called upon to provide solutions for the equitable development of human beings through the commons-based economy. Ugo Mattei argues for subversive regulations that challenge existing structures and promote a more equitable and empathetic approach.[132] The formulation of an obligation to international cooperation and the *right to commoning,* founded on 'common concern' as principles of international law,[133] may well be the normative fuel for the institutionalisation of universal commons, aiming at equitable development.

The establishment of the right to effective participation in social and economic life presupposes the transformation of law from hegemonic to non-hegemonic. At the same time, it requires liberation from the arbitrary and arrogant false belief that humanity is experiencing continuous economic progress through the market. The consequence would be the transformation of the 'common heritage of humankind' from a pretextual principle into a legal-political guide serving human dignity and the creation of a corresponding *jus humanitatis*. Multiple transformations cannot occur without the state involve-

130 Capra & Mattei 2015.

131 Capra & Mattei 2015: 2, 28, and 23.

132 Mattei 2018.

133 Cottier et al. 2014: 25.

ment, as state sovereignty remains the rigid foundation on which international law is built. As Antônio Augusto Cançado Trindade notes, the emergence of new legal strategies facilitates the pursuit of the common good and the abolition of legal positivism, liberal mercantilism, and political realism.[134]

The effective management of the universal commons for the benefit of the global community, based on the right of commoning, requires a governance structure characterised by both centralisation and multi-centrality, or any form of governance with common principles and corresponding rules aligned with the democratic sustainability of resources. At the state level, this involves embracing a democratic paradigm that emphasises broader and more direct participation, along with the rule of law and respect for human rights and commoners' rights. In the universal context, states and individuals, as subjects and rights holders and as bearers of the obligation to ensure the sustainability of the universal commons,[135] participate in this scheme, which remains in its embryonic form. Such a model of governance and law relating to the commons entails regulatory interactions between commoners and the management of the commons within a collaborative system grounded in a pervasive consensus and social regulation.[136]

In the domain of common goods, resources, or spaces, greater communication and convergence of analytical tools are needed to understand the structures, functions, goals, and means. The ecological vision of international law focuses on ensuring the survival of humanity by prioritising the protection of common resources. It also seeks to overturn the paradigm of the opportunistic imposition of state sovereignty, profit, and ownership by multinational corporations in favour of a higher moral value – the highest legitimate good, namely human life – by ensuring intergenerational equity.[137]

When viewed through the lens of holistic inclusion, humans are integral members of the global community and exist as both subjects and commoners, deserving protection within the planet's ecosystem. This legal shift transcends national and international boundaries and conventional temporality, extending to future generations.[138]

From an intergenerational perspective, any resource or good that plays a significant role in ensuring the wellbeing or survival of future generations can

134 Cançado Trindade 2020: 349.
135 Bosselmann 2017.
136 Deleixhe 2018.
137 Bailey, Farrell & Mattei 2013.
138 Santos 2020.

be deemed a commons warranting protection (see Chapter 5.1).[139] Therefore, a coherent body of legal rules, both international and national, is required to regulate how common resources, goods, and spaces – both natural commons and commons of knowledge – are protected in the future, ensuring their sustainability and the position of future commoners.

This vision can be made enforceable through the externalities of the force of commoning. According to a systemic conception of the commons, such externalities would provide guarantees of wellbeing for future generations and protection for non-human life. A radical change is required in the existing legal structure, which currently concentrates power and wealth through mechanisms of exclusion. Ironically, these mechanisms are founded on the basic principles of human rights, namely equality and freedom. These principles and rules offer no alternative and no effective guarantees to vast numbers of people trapped and excluded from the statutory objectives of their rights, with no prospect of a decent living within a global ecosystem constantly plundered, undermining any effort at equitable economic development.

In view to secure a common and sustainable future for humanity, the ICJ invoked the collective wisdom and called for multidisciplinary efforts in the case of emergencies involving environmental resources:

> The latter represent more than a legal problem: they concern an existential problem of planetary proportions that imperils all forms of life and the very health of our planet. International law […] has an important but ultimately limited role in resolving this problem. A complete solution to this daunting, and self-inflicted, problem requires the contribution of all fields of human knowledge, whether law, science, economics or any other. Above all, a lasting and satisfactory solution requires human will and wisdom – at the individual, social, and political levels – to change our habits, comforts, and current way of life in order to secure a future for ourselves and those who are yet to come.[140]

[*Looking to the Future*]

The qualities of the interrelationships developed between individuals and other subjects-commoners, on the one hand, and common resources on the other, vary significantly and are influenced by political and economic dynamics shaped by heterogeneous factors. Just a few decades ago, the idea of pur-

139 See: UN Secretary-General, Report on *Intergenerational Solidarity and the Needs of Future Generations*, 2013, where it is proposed to create a High Commissioner for Future Generations or a Special Envoy for Future Generations. See: Dam-de Jon 1997: 7.

140 ICJ, *Obligations of States in Respect of Climate Change*, Advisory Opinion (23.7.2025), para. 456.

chasing packaged water – traditionally a freely accessible common good – would have been unimaginable. Conversely, the idea of people buying their daily oxygen today seems like a dystopian science-fiction scenario. No one can predict the extent to which enclosures will capture common goods, and the law will regulate further commodification. In any case, law has played, and will continue to play, a crucial role in shaping the future of the rights of the commoners vis-à-vis the commons. The evolving role of international law and the position of individuals in this dynamic and delicate landscape raise intriguing questions about what lies ahead in the coming decades.

Simma noted in 1994, shortly after the end of bipolarism, that international law was finally overcoming the legal and moral deficiencies of bilateralism, maturing into a much more socially conscious legal order that promised to be a law for and of humanity.[141] However, thirty years later, this optimism has not been vindicated, as corporate individualism and aggressive extractionism prevail globally over multilateral cooperation in pursuit of the common interests of people and the planet.

We all 'know that the international society will never be free from violence, poverty, and injustice [...]. We simply intend to suggest in utopian terms new avenues for improving the major deficiencies of the current society of states'.[142] As Antonio Cassese notes in the introduction to his edited volume *Realising Utopia: The Future of International Law*, international law is developing dynamically, and the future lies in the elaboration of *jus cogens* in order to maintain the minimum common normative constants in international law. To what extent, then, can we propose the idea of utopia – navigating the paradoxical blend of the unachievable and the realistic – and actively engage in shaping *eutopic realism*?[143]

International law is not merely the sum of interstate treaties and customary rules regulating *ad hoc* issues. It must be seen as a means of achieving a more advanced stage in which global agendas – such as those concerning the commons – and operating procedures – such as those governing stewardship – are agreed upon. Mireille Delmas-Marty predicts that 'the imaginative forces of law' will lead to organised pluralism through an epistemological revolution of the commons and the design of a shared legal framework that continuously balances countervailing trends while preserving the world's diversity.[144] Similarly, Burns Weston and David Bollier have drafted a proposed international

141 Simma 1994: 234.
142 Cassese 2012: xxi.
143 *Eutopia*: a place of ideal felicity and perfection.
144 Delmas-Marty 2006. Similar conclusion in Cazala 2020: 20.

binding document entitled 'The Universal Covenant Affirming a Human Right to Commons and Rights-Based Governance of Earth's Natural Wealth and Resources', setting out a visionary proposal for future international law. Such visions could be realised through what Prue Taylor calls 'constructive utopianism': a strategy for bridging the growing gap between the destructive impacts of humans on the Earth System and alternative governance grounded in the principle of the 'common heritage'.[145]

Such a perspective presupposes the constitution of an international legal order that creates not only horizontal relations among states but, above all, interactive vertical relations between heterogeneous subjects-commoners (from top to bottom and from bottom to top), focusing on the common interest.[146] Ultimately, it is the universal *demos*, or humanity itself, that is the repository of the values and interests associated with universal commons that transcend states.

The current fragmented management of global common resources relies more on the limitations of state sovereignty than on overcoming them.[147] Moreover, the concept of sovereignty, when coupled with the epistemological notion of global common resources as *res nullius* open to appropriation, undermines the commons. The present ineffective constraints on sovereignty and the extractive policies favouring private profit or state interests give rise to the 'tragedy of the commons' argument, turning it into a self-fulfilling prophecy. Unless and until global common resources are effectively protected from enclosures imposed by states or corporations, they will inevitably be misused.[148]

The universal commons should be understood as an integral part of the general interests of the global community of people and states over common goods, resources, and spaces. Such a shared and profound understanding would provide the legitimate basis for the future emergence of a new universal law of the commons – a complex, multifaceted, and even chaotic process of transition developing amid political and economic rearrangements.

145 Taylor 2016: 105.
146 Bogdandy, Goldmann & Venzke 2017.
147 Schrijver 2016: 1259.
148 Milun 2011: 104.

CHAPTER 7

Conclusions: The Inescapable Utopia of the Possible

Can there be a future without the commons?[1] (George Caffentzis)

Throughout history, common goods, resources, and spaces have functioned as theatres of rivalry, solidarity, and care. Within an apparently asymmetrical global framework, common resources that exist beyond or through state jurisdiction are gradually emerging as both conceptual constructs and tangible entities. It is only through the use of an appropriate methodological approach that the interwoven triadic relationship among resources, communities of commoners, and the legal and political framework can be revealed – thus rendering what has been termed 'universal commons' visible as active systems of production and atypical institutions. A wide range of common resources at a global level follows different paths and acquires diverse, often contradictory, interpretations, understandings, and vocabularies used in international law.

In line with the precepts of commons theory, this study draws a pivotal distinction between 'commons' and 'common resources' at the global scale. Within this framework, international law is viewed as one of the three constitutive elements of the universal commons, providing the normative architecture for commoners and other legal subjects of rights and obligations. The heterogeneity of commoners at the global scale – individuals, communities, states, social movements, non-governmental organisations, and international organisations – renders the interaction schemes particularly complex: cooperative and competitive at once. Yet, the rights and duties related to commoning extend well beyond the traditional scope and content of human rights. The right to commoning, which encompasses and transcends human rights, stands as one of the fundamental pillars of the emerging international law of the commons.

The evolution of the concept of the commons at the global scale is accompanied by an increasing awareness of the need for coordinated and regulated governance. At the same time, new challenges are emerging, to which states and other international actors respond in fragmented and often contradictory ways. The imperative to enhance wellbeing and protect life and the planetary

1 Caffentzis 2010: 23.

 | HTTPS://DOI.ORG/10.1163/9789004764118-008

ecosystem – of which human societies are an integral part – is fostering a collective global consciousness. This awareness is giving rise to influential ideas advocating the sustainability of common resources and the commons as vital entities of international society. The list of global common resources is expanding beyond the natural world to encompass the increasingly complex and critical knowledge commons, potentially accessible to all. Consequently, 'universal commons' of any kind are evolving adaptively within and beyond the territorial sovereignty of states. Frequently, local or regional commons converge to form interconnected networks that evolve into a global phenomenon – the respective commons – organised polycentrically, operating at multiple levels with diverse capacities and functions.

In the realm of global goods, resources, and spaces, states' exclusive competencies are gradually eroding as new actors emerge as commoners or as subjects with rights and responsibilities. Individuals, communities, international organisations, social movements, and various entities with divergent interests – economic or social, profit-oriented or cooperative – are assuming dynamic roles. The growing necessity to manage common resources reinforces the trend towards establishing norms within international law and making formerly insular, state-centred sovereignties more permeable. This permeation is defining the universal commons, their subjects, and their rights and obligations, while shaping the role and responsibilities of states, which remain the primary subjects of international law. In this vibrant environment, the characteristics of the resources, goods, and spaces – especially on the global scale – determine and shape the profiles of the corresponding communities of commoners.

The nature of global common resources also determines the formal and informal laws that govern relations among subjects-commoners, which can be fragmentary and hybrid. It is no coincidence that the developing international law of the commons relates more to nature-based commons and, to a lesser extent, to knowledge commons. The relevant law has a far longer history in relation to natural global common resources than to digital and knowledge-based ones and has advanced much further. Nevertheless, legal norms in both categories seek to regulate similar phenomena concerning extra- or trans-state jurisdiction and the sharing of goods, resources, and spaces.

Legal norms governing global common resources develop through the centripetal tendencies of positive international law, as well as through tendencies towards future law, the form of which remains unpredictable. State sovereignty is thus redefined as a nexus of symbiotic and responsible sovereignties, to the extent that the freedoms and rights of other subjects are guaranteed. In this context, freedom prioritises the wellbeing of all human commoners through equitable access to the commons and their benefits over the unrestricted economic freedom of profit within the market.

The basic premise of property rights traditionally favours individualism and competition over cooperation and solidarity among community members. States often embody this paradox: emphasising individualism in practice while acting collectively and in solidarity in other domains. The effective management of these individualistic tendencies through international cooperation is key to shaping the trajectory of the universal commons. Yet the commons does not negate private property absolutely; rather, a symbiotic model can enhance both common profit and the common good. What is needed is a distinct category of property rights beyond the private-public binary – one capable of accommodating shared global goods, resources, and spaces. A discernible trend in this direction is the attribution of stewardship competencies to international bodies.

To mitigate the enclosures of common resources, it is necessary to transform the hierarchies of power that currently govern the universal commons – hierarchies grounded in extreme individualism and corporate extractivism. This transformation requires the legitimisation of shared obligation and responsibility towards the commons and of the institutions that exercise stewardship, provided these are subject to constant democratic oversight and institutional accountability. Achieving this necessitates new governance structures, economic models, and legal frameworks that foster a dynamic synthesis of duties and rights. Rather than adopting a static, top-down model, such a framework would sustain an ongoing dialogue between functionally engaged commoners and diverse stakeholders within a stable international order of justice and democracy.

Although such a vision may appear utopian given the current planetary condition, it is, in fact, the most rational path forward. A realistic utopia becomes the catalyst for transformation – the creation of a global polity and the prioritisation of the common good. It is irrational to deplete and exploit natural resources to exhaustion or to build ever more enclosures for appropriation. It is rational to advocate an ecological transition grounded in the sustainable use of finite resources for the benefit of the entire human and non-human ecosystem. What is irrational is the continued erosion of social cohesion through exclusion and the perpetuation of deepening inequalities. The universal commons thus play a crucial role in reversing the current trajectory of multiple crises and providing rational guarantees of stability and prosperity.

Entering the second quarter of the twenty-first century, however, the dominant global approach – marked by aggressive neoliberal and nationalist policies (often called 'Trumpism'[2]) – had been adopted by numerous governments targeting global resources. Ideologically and politically, this approach rests on the rejection of multilateral cooperation in favour of private profit and unilateral action. It signifies a broader retreat from shared responsibility for global stewardship policies and law, essential to the sustainability of the commons. These policies reflect a paradigm that reinforces closed territorialities, undermines collective guarantees for a sustainable ecosystem, and advances extractive industries through market-driven logics, often at the expense of collective welfare. Deregulation and market liberalisation have created conditions in which corporate or state interests routinely override community needs and long-term social stability. Market liberalisation translates into the conversion of previously shared resources – common goods, spaces, and even public services – into private property, governed by profit-maximising imperatives.

The global spread of these extractive policies has outpaced the development of adequate regulatory frameworks to manage their consequences. International law and governance institutions struggle to keep pace with the rapid evolution of transnational economic practices, resulting in significant oversight gaps. The disconnect between the speed of extractive capitalism and the regulatory capacity of international institutions is widening.

The transition towards a coherent national and international law of the universal commons requires the redefinition of individuals and local communities as 'global commoners'. This redefinition gives a voice to those rarely heard, enabling their participation in commons governance and elevating them from potential to active contributors. People should thus be recognised as political, social, and legal subjects – participants in the universal *demos*, a vague yet tangible entity that can help redefine economic needs and legal relations around the commons.

The concepts of 'common responsibility', 'common concern', and 'stewardship' must be supported by safeguards that protect common resources, goods, and spaces from appropriation and depletion. Yet, in practice, these very concepts often legitimise the expansion of enclosures and corporate, profit-driven appropriation. These notions must, therefore, be reinterpreted through the lens of commons theory and redistributive democracy, and integrated into international law accordingly. This requires a fundamental re-signification of international law through the prism of the commons – prioritising economic and social objectives that benefit all.

2 Cox & O'Connor 2025.

Nature remains a domain where the logic of *res nullius* too often prevails over that of *res communis humanitatis*. State sovereignty, particularly regarding rights of exploitation and appropriation, continues to expand its reach. The open sea and the seabed exemplify this: Sovereign rights and exclusive exploitation privileges extend continually to the detriment of the common resources. Within state territories, control is absolute; beyond them, the international commons remain inadequately monitored. The principles of the 'common heritage of humankind' and 'common concern' have thus far failed to provide sufficient guarantees against enclosures of the natural commons.

This brings us back to the original questions: Who owns the goods, resources, and spaces – exhaustible and non-exhaustible – the oceans, the air, outer space, the internet, culture, seeds, and the genome? Who has the right to access, use, or appropriate them? The idea that certain rights belong to everyone and to no one at the same time may appear inclusive, yet it conceals an unresolved problem. In the vacuum beyond state jurisdiction, competences are not effectively exercised on behalf of all people for the sake of accessibility, sustainability, and intergenerational equity. International law likewise struggles to respond adequately when global resources fall under state sovereignty but are crucial to the sustainability of humanity and the planet as a whole.

As demands on natural resources, energy, digital data, and knowledge intensify, effective policies and law must recognise the interdependence of the universal commons with the multi-layered communities of commoners who collectively constitute humankind. This recognition calls for a re-evaluation of the dynamics between national and international spheres to develop policies and laws attuned to these realities.

There are many examples of legal regimes, or tendencies towards developing such regimes, that recognise the global concern beyond the narrow confines of state sovereignty, and a growing call for a transboundary mandate to monitor and, in some cases, redistribute profits from common goods, resources, and spaces at a global level, with a focus on the common interest or the common good. Already, treaty-based international law seeks to accomplish goals broader than those pursued by the contracting states.[3]

The international law of the commons would be anchored in a set of principles, legal tools, and concepts that are already embedded. However, when considering concepts such as 'good faith', 'precaution', 'equity', 'justice', or 'solidarity', it is crucial to acknowledge that individuals with rights to the commons inhabit a world characterised by material, economic, and social inequalities.

3 Zyberi 2021; Simma 1994.

Consequently, the content of 'equality' and 'justice' should be analytical, specific, and even asymmetrical, equipped with mechanisms to identify inequalities and with the means to address them effectively. The economic and social imbalances between individuals or states cannot be redressed by normatively blind symmetries, as currently conceptualised in human rights law under the principles of equality and non-discrimination. Therefore, the management of the commons as a right of the people calls for a radical paradigm shift in the normative content of human rights, adopting collective and inclusive interests, far from a short-sighted and individualistic anthropocentrism.

The transition to the universal commons is not a promising paradise. It is a political process grounded in a matrix of principles, with social justice and environmental sustainability at the forefront, governed by a nexus of norms safeguarding these ideas. Under specific international political balances and social conditions, it can become a vehicle for achieving emancipatory effects for commoners-subjects.

As state sovereignty evolves, international law undergoes a fundamental transformation. It is not created by states alone, nor does it bind only states. The domain of the universal commons, especially with respect to transboundary resources, heralds the end of an era of rigid state sovereignty. International cooperation, as a procedural objective, promotes a unified yet uneven regime that encourages international participatory stakeholder oversight.

What is lacking is a universal political vision for reforming international law that goes beyond the axiomatic notion of *terra nullius*. We need a legal framework that supports policies shifting the current paradigm of extractive sovereignty – a paradigm that leads to commodification and appropriation – towards the regeneration of common goods, resources, and spaces. Often, legal imagination appears to have either dried up or lost motivation, as it has failed to develop a comprehensive theory of international law that addresses the broader value of the universal commons for states and other entities. Instead of taking a holistic and proactive approach, it tends to formulate ad hoc regimes in response to problems as they arise.

Of particular importance for the institutionalisation of the universal commons is the exercise of oversight and regulatory policies for the common good. In practice, there is a lack of global normative frameworks to guide subjects in adopting policies and laws in this direction. Such frameworks would mitigate or rationalise tendencies towards the accumulation of individual gain and establish a common denominator that safeguards human life and wellbeing. Establishing such effective mechanisms requires systemic changes in law, politics, and economics. (Re)claiming the commons does not mean a return to a pre-modern era of the commons, but rather the drafting of a new global and just social contract based on the common good and a rethinking of the value of shared resources, distinct from market-driven considerations.

How can the pursuit of the common good be achieved through international law? What are the conditions for a shift in the political and legal paradigm for managing the commons for the benefit of people? How will the resilience of new ideas and trends defending the sustainability of global common resources for the benefit of commoners overcome the tendency towards total appropriation for individual profit? Can the international system strike a balance by actively integrating respect for rights and oversight of obligations into the universal commons? Whatever the answers to these questions, a new law – a *jus humanitatis* – would have to initiate, not terminate, symbiotic social practices within and with the commons; to promote rules and processes defining participation in the commons for the benefit of the global community of human beings; to set aside free-riding and dead-end selfish appropriation; and to establish relations of stewardship for the benefit of human commoners, the universal commons, and the global ecosystem.[4] Such a new normative universe will enable the re-appropriation of global resources by commoners and the establishment of a system of joint or peer management based on democratic principles.

It is not unreasonable to argue that it is ultimately the tragedy of the free market that has led to the crisis of the planet's common resources. It is greedy users and resource exploiters who deplete resources, moving from one to another with little or no concern for sustainability and only for immediate profit. This trend can be reversed if people's commoning rights become a pillar of the political, institutional, and economic organisation of communities, based on a holistic view of the relationship between resources and societies. Such an outcome would depend on people's participation in the design and management of the 'common good' and thus on the consolidation of the rule of law. From this perspective, the right to access and manage global resources is a pillar of a new type of political governance – universal commons governed by a regulatory framework shaped by national and international law. It should be noted that after formulating his theory of the tragedy of the commons, Garrett Hardin himself admitted that he should have spoken of the tragedy of the unmanaged commons rather than of the commons in general.[5]

The universal commons could serve as a safeguard for the protection of life and wellbeing for all communities, shaping the basis for the emancipatory

4 Weston & Bollier 2011: 156; Stern 2011: 213–232.

5 Hardin 1994; Ranganathan 2016: 697–699.

aspect of modernity.[6] Finally, we should speak of the tragedy of the unimagined commons.[7]

Undoubtedly, the international law rules governing the universal commons suffer from compartmentalisation, mirroring the inherent fragmentation and lack of effective sanctioning mechanisms. However, if the commons become a field for the establishment of supranational policies, the boundaries between national and international law will lose their relevance. State sovereignty and national jurisdiction will be transformed in response to the need to regulate access to and use of global goods, resources, and spaces internationally. Perhaps the sporadic provisions of existing international law on the commons will evolve into a comprehensive regulatory framework, provided that this law is both human-centred and eco-centred – or better, transformed into a 'law of the people and the Earth'. This is precisely the core issue: the radical transformation of state law and people's rights towards the democratic management of the commons. In short, it is a non-hegemonic law that aims to secure a shared future for the global human community, free from enclosures and exclusions.

6 Karitzis 2016: 267.
7 Wolcher 2009.

Bibliography

Adede, A.O. (1979). 'The Group of 77 and the Establishment of the International Sea-Bed Authority', *Ocean Development and International Law* 2, 31–64.

Adelman, David (2005). 'A Fallacy of the Commons in Biotech Patent Policy', *Berkeley Tech. Law Journal* 20/2, 989–1032, <https://bit.ly/3UCTLlf>.

Adelman, Sam (2017). 'Tropical Forests, Climate Change and Neoliberal Environmental Governmentality', in *Natural Resources and Sustainable Development*, Celine Tan & Julio Faundez (eds.), Elgar, Cheltenham/Northampton, 186–207.

Adler, David & Pawel Wargan (2021). 'Decarbonisation without Democracy: Tennis-Ball Politics and the Eu Green Deal', *Routledge Handbook on the Green New Deal*, Routledge, Oxon, <https://ssrn.com/abstract=3843125>.

Agamben, Giorgio (1998). *Homo Sacer: Sovereign Power and Bare Life*, Stanford University Press, Stanford.

Akrivoulis, Dimitrios (2018). 'The Irony of the Global Commons: The Common Heritage of Mankind in UNCLOS', in *Retracing the Blue of the Aegean and the Mediterranean: Applications of International Law and International Politics Twenty Years after the Entry into Force of the Law of the Sea Convention*, St. Perrakis & Gr. Tsaltas (eds.), Sideris pub., Athens, 191–202 [in Greek].

Amnesty International (2019). *Surveillance Giants: How the Business Model of Google and Facebook Threatens Human Rights*, Report, <https://bit.ly/4cSqlZ8>.

Anderies, John M., Folke, Carl, Walker, Brian & Ostrom, Elinor, (2013). 'Aligning Key Concepts for Global Change Policy: Robustness, Resilience, and Sustainability', *Ecology and Society* 18, <http://bit.ly/38mJFj9>.

Anderson, Scott R. & Robert B. Allen (2009). 'Envisioning the Archival Commons', *The American Archivist* 72/2, 383–400.

Arvidsson, Adam (2019). *Changemakers: The Industrious Future of the Digital Economy*, Wiley, New Jersey.

Armstrong, Chris (2018). 'Resources Outside of the State: Governing the Ocean and Beyond', *Philosophy Compass* 13/18, <https://doi.org/10.1111/phc3.12545>.

Armstrong, Chris (2017). *Justice and Natural Resources: An Egalitarian Theory*, Oxford University Press, Oxford.

Augé, Marc (2004). *Oblivion*, University of Minnesota Press, Minneapolis.

Baeher, Peter (ed.) (2000). *The Portable Hanna Arendt*, Penguin, London.

Bailey, Saki, Gilda Farrell & Ugo Mattei (eds.) (2013). *Protecting Future Generations through Commons*, Council of Europe Publishing, Strasbourg.

Bance, Philippe (2018). 'Introduction', in: *Providing Public Goods and Commons. Towards Coproduction and New Forms of Governance for a Revival of Public Action*,

CIRIEC & Bance, Philippe (eds.), CIRIEC, Liège, 9–17. <http://doi.org/10.25518/ciriec.css1intro>.

Barnes, Peter (2006). *Capitalism 3.0: A Guide to Reclaiming the Commons*, Berrett-Koehler Pub., San Francisco, <http://www.plancanada.com/capitalism3.pdf>.

Baroncini, Elisa et al. (2018). *Fundamental Values and International Investment Law: The Responses of the New Generation of International Economic Law Agreements and Investment Arbitration Proceedings*, Brill Open Law 1 1–4, <https://bit.ly/3umj8wR>.

Baslar, Kemal (1998). *The Concept of the Common Heritage of Mankind in International Law*, Martinus Nijhoff, Leiden/Boston.

Bavikatte, Kabir Sanjay & Tom Bennett (2015). 'Community Stewardship: The Foundation of Biocultural Rights', *Journal of Human Rights and the Environment*, 6(1), 7–29.

Bauwens, Michel (2010). 'The New Triarchy: The Commons, Enterprise, the State', <https://bit.ly/2GZYFZK>.

Bauwens, Michel, Vasilis Kostakis & Alex Pazaitis (2019). *Peer to Peer: The Commons Manifesto*, University of Westminster Press, London.

Bauwens, Michel & Vasilis Niaros (2017). *Value in the Commons Economy: Developments in Open and Contributory Value Accounting*, <https://bit.ly/32CEDfq>.

Beeching, Jack (1975). *The Chinese Opium Wars*, Hutchinson pub., London.

Beerkens, Maarja (2018). 'Knowledge Commons and Global Governance of Academic Publishing', in *The Commons And A New Global Governance*, S. Cogolati & J. Wouters (eds.), Elgar, Cheltenham, 286–210.

Benkler, Yochai (1998). 'Overcoming Agoraphobia: Building the Commons of the Digitally Networked Environment', *Harvard Journal of Law and Technology* 11/2, 287–400, <https://bit.ly/3qfAy9Q>.

Benkler, Yochai (2003). 'The political economy of the commons', *Upgrade* IV/3, <https://bit.ly/3jplg4O>.

Benkler, Yochai (2006). *The Wealth of Networks How Social Production Transforms Markets and Freedom*, Yale University Press, New Haven/London.

Berman, Mathew (2024). 'A Rising Tide that Lifts All Boats: Long-Term Effects of the Alaska Permanent Fund Dividend on Poverty', *Poverty & Public Policy* 16, 126–145, <https://doi.org/10.1002/pop4.398>.

Berners-Lee, Tim (2024). *Marking the Web's 35th Birthday: An Open Letter*, 12–3–2024, <https://bit.ly/4fvOxDt>.

Besson, Samantha (2018). 'Community Interests in International Law: Whose Interests Are They and How Should Best Identify Them?' in E. Benvenisti & G. Nolte (eds.), *Community Interests Across International Law*, Oxford University Press, 36–49.

Birchall, Johnston & Lou Hammond Ketilson (2009). *Resiliance of the Cooperative Bussiness Model in Times of Crisis*, International Labour Organization, <https://bit.ly/45cenIl>.

Birkbeck, Carolyn (2009). *The Implementation Game: The TRIPS Agreement and the Global Politics of Intellectual Property Reform in Developing Countries*, Oxford University Press, <10.1093/acprof:oso/9780199550616.001.0001>.

Birrell, Kathleen (2023). 'The Anthropocene Archive: Human and Inhuman Subjects and Sediments', in *The Routledge Handbook of Law and the Anthropocene*, P. D. Burdon & J. Martel (eds.), Routledge, Oxon, 51–63.

Birrell, Kathleen & Daniel Matthews (2020). 'Re-strorying Laws for the Anthropocene: Rights, Obligations and an Ethics of Encounter', *Law and Critique* 31, 275–292.

Blomfield, Megan (2021). 'Land as a Global Commons?', *Journal of Applied Philosophy* 40/4, 1–16.

Bodansky Daniel (2012). 'What Is in a Concept? Global Public Goods, International Law and Legitimacy', *European Journal of International Law* 23/3, 651–668.

Bodansky Daniel (2016). 'The Paris Climate Change Agreement: A New Hope?', *American Journal of International Law* 110/2, 288–319.

Boer, Ben (2014). 'Land Degradation as a Common Concern of Humankind', in *International Law for Common Goods. Normative Perspectives on Human Rights, Culture and Nature*, F. Lenzerini & A.F. Vrdoljak (eds.), Hart, Oxford and Portland, 289–307.

Bohoslavsky, Juan Pablo, Liber Martin & Juan Justo (2017). 'BITs State Regulation and Business-Related Human Rights Violations in Water and Sanitation Services', *Natural Resources and Sustainable Development*, C. Tan & J. Faundez (eds.), Elgar, Cheltenham, 75–95.

Bollier, David (2003). *Silent Theft: The Private Plunder of Our Common Wealth*, Routledge, New York.

Bollier, David (2010). 'Academia as a Commons', *Digital Library of the Commons*, Indiana University, <http://hdl.handle.net/10535/5805>.

Bollier, David (2014). *Think Like a Commoner: A Short Introduction to the Life of the Commons*, New Society Publishers, Gabriola Island.

Bollier, David (2015a). *Who May Use the King's Forest? The Meaning of Magna Carta, Commons and Law in Our Time*, <https://bit.ly/2GVexN5>.

Bollier, David (2015b). *Reinventing Law for the Commons*, A Strategy Memo for the Heinrich Böll Foundation, <https://bit.ly/3uP5xx3>.

Bollier, David & Silke Helfrich (2012). 'Introduction', *The Wealth of the Commons: A World beyond Market and State*, D. Bollier & S. Helfrich (eds.), The commons strategies group/Levellers Press, Amherst, p. xi.

Bollier, David & Silke Helfrich (2019). *Free, Fair and Alive: The Insurgent Power of the Commons*, New Society Publishers, *Gabriola Island.*

Boonen, Christiaan, Nicolás Brando, Samuel Cogolati, Rutger Hagen, Nils Vanstappen, Jan Wouters (2019). 'Governing as Commons or as Global Public Goods Two Tales of Power', *International Journal of the Commons* 13/1, 553–577, <https://www.jstor.org/stable/26632732>.

Bourrel, Marie, Torsten Thiele & Duncan Currie (2016). 'The Common of Heritage of Mankind as a Means to Assess and Advance Equity in Deep Sea Mining', *Marine Policy*, <https://bit.ly/3sHpFzi>.

Bosselmann, Klaus (2017). *The Principle of Sustainability. Transforming Law and Governance*, Routledge, Oxon.

Bosselmann, Klaus (2016). 'Shifting the Legal Paradigm: Earth-Centred Law and Governance', in *The Safe Operating Space Treaty: A New Approach to Managing Our Use of the Earth System*, P. Magalhães, W. Steffen, K. Bosselmann, A. Aragão & V. Soromenho-Marques (eds.), Cambridge Scholars pub., Newcastle upon Tyne, 64–82.

Bosselmann, Klaus (2015). *Earth Governance: Trusteeship of the Global Commons*, 2d ed., Elgar, Cheltenham.

Boulton, Geoffrey S. (2021). *Science as a Global Public Good.* Position Paper, International Science Council, Paris, <doi: 10.24948/2021.09>.

Boyce, James K. (2019). *Economics for People and the Planet: Inequality in the Era of Climate Change*, Anthem Press, London.

Boyle, Alan (2012). 'Human Rights and the Environment: Where Next?', *European Journal of International Law* 23/3, 613–642.

Boyle, James (2003). 'The *Second Enclosure Movement* and the Construction of the Public Domain', *Law and Contemporary Problems* 66, 33–74, <https://bit.ly/3Pg8EsA>.

Boyle, James (2008). *The Public Domain: Enclosing the Commons of the Mind*, Yale University Press, New Haven.

Brando, Nicolas, Christian Boonen, Samuel Cogolati, Rutger Hagen, Nils Vanstappen & Jan Wouters (2019). 'Governing as Commons or as Global Public Goods: Two Tales of Power', *International Journal of the Commons* 13/1, 553–577, <https://bit.ly/3WovvVu>.

Bräuninger, Thomas & Thomas König (2000). 'Making Rules for Governing Global Commons: The Case of Deep-Sea Mining', *The Journal of Conflict Resolution* 44/5, 604–629, <https://bit.ly/3sHMog6>.

Bregman, Rutger (2017). *Utopia for Realists: And How We Can Get There*, Little, Brown and Co., Boston.

Brennan, Timothy J. (1998). 'The Spectrum as Commons: Tomorrow's Vision, Not Today's Prescription', *The Journal of Law and Economics* XLI/2, 791–803.

Brousseau, Eric et al. (2012). *Global Environmental Commons: Analytical and Political Challenges in Building Governance Mechanisms*, Oxford University Press, Oxford.

Brown Weiss, Edith (2014). *Nature and the Law: The Global Commons and the Common Concern of Humankind*, Pontifical Academy of Sciences, Extra Series 41, Acta 19, Vatican City, <https://bit.ly/35nkSdjff>.

Brown Weiss, Edith (2007). 'The Evolution of International Water Law', *The Hague Academy of International Law, Collected Courses* 331, 161–404.

Buck-Cox, Suzan (1985). 'No Tragedy of the Commons', *Environmental Ethics* 7/1, 49–61.

Buck, Susan (1998). *The Global Commons: An Introduction*, Island Press, Washington, DC.

Bull, Hedley (1984). *Justice in International Relations, The Hagey Lectures*, University of Waterloo, Waterloo.

Burdon, Peter (2015). *Earth Jurisprudence: Private Property and the Environment*, Routledge, 2014.

Buttigieg, Jean (2018). *The Human Genome as Common Heritage of Mankind*, Ibidem Press, Stuttgart.

Buttigieg, Jean (2012). *The Common Heritage of Mankind: From the Law of the Sea to the Human Genome and Cyberspace, Symposia Melitensia* 8, 81–92.

Buxton, Nick (ed.) (2024). *State of Power. Energy, Power and Transition*, Transnational Institute, <https://www.tni.org/en/publication/energy-power-and-transition>.

Caffentzis, George (2008). *Autonomous Universities and the Making of the Knowledge Commons*, Russell Scholar Lecture IV, <https://bit.ly/3UzrCLP>.

Caffentzis, George (2010). 'The Future of 'the Commons': Neoliberalism's 'Plan B' or the Original Disaccumulation of Capital?', *New Formations* 69/1, 23–41.

Cambou, Dorothée & Stefaan Smis (2013). *'Permanent Sovereignty over Natural Resources from a Human Rights Perspective: Natural Resources Exploitation and Indigenous Peoples' Rights in the Arctic', Michigan State International Law Review* 22, 347–376, <http://bit.ly/3uRcaPi>.

Canadian Council for International Co-operation & Misereor (2010). *Human Rights Impact Assessment for Trade and Investment Agreements* (Berne Declaration), Report of the Expert Seminar, Geneva, <https://bit.ly/3eQmFuR>.

Cantegreil, Julien (2011). 'The Audacity of the Texaco/Calasiatic Award: René-Jean Dupuy and the Internationalisation of Foreign Investment Law', *The European Journal of International Law* 22/2, 441–458.

Cançado Trindade, Antônio Augusto (2010). *International Law for Humankind: Towards a New Jus Gentium* (2d ed.), Brill, Leiden/Boston.

Capra, Fridjof & Hugo Mattei (2015). *The Ecology of Law: Toward a Legal System in Tune with Nature and Community*, Berrett-Kohler Publishers, San Francisco.

Cassese, Antonio (2012). 'Introduction', in *Realising Utopia: The Future of International Law*, A. Cassese (ed.), Oxford University Press, Oxford, 1–11.

Catalano, Claudio (2013). 'Introduction', *Global Commons: Threat or opportunity?*, Cl. Catalano (ed.), FinMeccanica Research Department, 7–12.

Cazala, Julien (2020). 'What International Law can Teach Us about the Commons', *Global Commons: Issues, Concerns and Strategies*, M. Bhaskaran Pillai, & G. Ganapath Doré (eds.), Sage, New Delhi, 12–21.

Chami, Ralf, Thomas Cosimano, Connel Fullenkamp & Sena Oztosun (2019). *A Strategy to Protect Whales Can Limit Greenhouse Gases and Global Warming*, International Monetary Fund, <http://bit.ly/3VjfwYs>.

Chemillier-Gendreau, Monique (2011). 'A quelles conditions l'universalité du droit international est-elle possible?', *The Hague Academy of International Law, Collected Courses* 355, 9–40.

Cocca, Aldo (1981). 'The Advances in International Law through the Law of Outer Space', *Journal of Space Law* 9, 12–28.

Cogolati, Samuel (2020). *International Law to Save the Commons: The International Legal Protection of the Commons in Development*, PhD Dissertation, KU Leuven, Faculty of Law, Leuven, <https://bit.ly/4cb4zD2>.

Cogolati, Samuel & Jan Wouters (2018). 'International Law to Save the Commons', in *The Commons and a New Global Governance*, S. Cogolati & J. Wouters (eds.), Elgar, Cheltenham, 266–290.

Collao, Gabriella (2020). 'Environmental Damages and Armed Conflict', in *Ecological Integrity in Science and Law*, L. Westra, K. Bosselman & M. Fermeglia (eds.), Springer, Cham, 253–264.

Commission on Global Governance (1995). *Our Global Neghbourhood*, Oxford University Press, New York.

Comision Ecumenica de Derechos Humanos & Fédération internationale des ligues des droits de l'Homme (2010). *Exploitation minière à grande échelle en Equateur et violation des droits de l'homme, Dossier Corriente Resources Inc*, <https://bit.ly/35owoXD>.

Connerton, Paul (1989). *How Commoners Remember*, Cambridge University Press, Cambridge.

Contreras, Juan L. (2017). 'Leviathan in the Commons: Biomedical Data and the State', in *Governing Medical Knowledge Commons*, K. Strandburg, B. Frischmann, M. Madison (eds.), Cambridge University Press, Cambridge, 19–45.

Contreras, Juan L. & Bartha M. Knoppers (2018). 'The Genomic Commons', *Annual Review of Genomics and Human Genetics Volume* 19, 1–48.

Contreras, Juan L. (2021). *The Genome Defense: Inside the Epic Legal Battle to Determine Who Owns Your DNA*, Algonquin Books of Chapel Hill, New York.

Coomans, Fons (2003). 'The Ogoni Case before the ACHPR', *International and Comparative Law Quarterly* 52, 749–760.

Cosentino, Gina (2015). 'Governing the Global Commons: How UNSR Anaya's Study of Extractive Industries Can Inform a New Global Human Rights Regulatory Regime for Transnational Conversation NGOs Operating Near Indigenous Territories', *Arizona Journal of International and Comparative Law*, 32/1, 1–20, <https://bit.ly/3d2Lnt7>.

Costalli, Stefano & Alessandro Fasani (2013). 'Cyberspace Securing Critical Infrastructures against Direct Attack and Espionage', *Global Commons: threat or opportunity*? Catalano, Cl. (ed.), FinMeccanica Research Department, 43–51, <https://bit.ly/3pkpoTv>.

Cottier, Thomas et al, (2014). 'The Principle of Common Concern and Climate Change', *Archives of International Law* 52(3), 293–324, <https://bit.ly/2UmKbpC>.

Cotula, Lorenzo (2017). 'Investment Treaties, Natural Resources and Regulatory Space: Technical Issues and Political Choices in International Investment Law', *Natural Resources and Sustainable Development*, C. Tan & J. Faundez (eds.), Elgar, Cheltenham, 8–49.

Council of Europe (2021). *Covid-19 Vaccines: Ethical, Legal and Practical Considerations*, Report, 11.1.2021, PACE, Doc 15212, <https://pace.coe.int/en/files/28925/html>.

Cox, Lloyd & Brendon O'Connor (2025). 'Trumpism, Fascism and Neoliberalism', *Distinktion: Journal of Social Theory*, 1–18.

Craven, Matt (2019). "Other Spaces': Constructing the Legal Architecture of a Cold War Commons and the Scientific-Technical Imaginary of Outer Space', *European Journal of International Law* 30/2, 547–572.

Cullinan, Cormac (2011). *Wild Law: A Manifesto for Earth Justice*, (2d ed.) Chelsea Green.

Dalrymple, William (2015). 'The East India Company: The Original Corporate Raiders', *The Guardian*, <https://bit.ly/2GZWANq>.

Daly, Erin & James May (2016). 'Bridging Constitutional Dignity and Environmental Rights Jurisprudence', *Journal of Human Rights and the Environment* 7(2), 218–242.

Daly, Erin & Dina Lupin (2023). 'Dignity in the Anthropocene', in *The Routledge Handbook of Law and the Anthropocene*, P. D. Burdon & J. Martel (eds.), Routledge, Oxon, 227–243.

Damania, Richard, Ebad Ebadi, Kentaro Mayr, Jason Russ & Esha Zaveri (2025). *Reboot Development: The Economics of a Livable Planet*, World Bank Group, Washington, <https://hdl.handle.net/10986/43522>.

Dam-de Jon, Daniëlla (2015). *International Law and Governance of Natural Resources in Conflict and Post-conflict Situations*, Cambridge University Press.

Daniels, Brigham (2012). *Legispedia*, <https://bit.ly/35toxGV>.

Dardot, Pierre (2018). 'What Democracy for the Global Commons?', in *The Commons and a New Global Governance*, S. Cogolati & J. Wouters (eds.), Elgar, Cheltenham, 20–36.

Dardot, Pierre & Christian Laval (2014). *Commun: Essai sur la révolution au XXIe siècle*, La Découverte, Paris.

Delaere, Simon & Cristina Cullell-March (2014). 'Radio Spectrum Policy in the EU: Concepts, Trends, Issues', in *The Palgrave Handbook of European Media Policy*, K. Donders, C. Pauwels, J. Loisen (eds.), Palgrave Macmillan, London, 360–381.

Deleixhe, Martin. (2018). 'Conclusion: Is the Governance of the Commons a Model for a New Global Governance?', in *The Commons and a New Global Governance*, S. Cogolati & J. Wouters (eds.), Elgar, Cheltenham, 322–334.

Deleuze, Gilles & Felix Guattari (1980). *Mille plateaux: Capitalisme et schizophrénie*, Ed. du Minuit, Paris.

Delmas-Marty, Mireille (2006). *Les forces imaginantes du droit, Le pluralisme ordonné*, vol. II, Le Seuil, Paris.

Dempsey, Jessica et al. (2024). *Exporting Extinction: How the International Financial System Constrains Biodiverse Futures*, The Centre for Climate Justice, Climate and Community Project, and Third World Network, <https://bit.ly/40q9Smj>.

Department of Defense, USA (2012). *Sustaining US Global Leadership: Priorities for 21 Century Defense*, <http://bit.ly/3ADNAGq>.

Deplano, Rossana (2021). 'The Artemis Accords: Evolution or Revolution in International Space Law?', *International Comparative Law Quarterly*, 70(3), 799–819.

De Schutter, Olivier (2011). *Guiding Principles on Human Rights Impact Assessments of Trade and Investment Agreements*, Report of the Special Rapporteur on the right to food, Addendum, Human Rights Council, General Assembly, UN, A/HRC/19/59/Add.5.

de Zayas, Alfred Maurice (2015). *Report on Human Rights and Investment Agreements*, Independent Expert on the promotion of a democratic and equitable international order, Human Rights Council, A/HRC/30/44.

Dinh, Nguyen Quoc, Patric Daillet & Alain Pellet (1999). *Droit international public*, LGDJ, Paris.

Edenhofer, Ottmar, Christian Flachsland & Bernhard Lorentz (2012). 'The Atmosphere as a Global Commons', in *The Wealth of the Commons: A World beyond Market and State*, D. Bollier & S. Helfrich (eds.), The Commons Strategy Group, <https://wealthofthecommons.org/essay/atmosphere-global-commons>.

Edwards, Victoria & Natalie Steins (1998). 'Developing an Analytical Framework for Multiple-Use Commons', *Journal of Theoretical Politics* 10/3, 347–383.

Elliott, Lorraine (2003). 'Imaginative Adaptations: A Possible Environmental Role for the UN Security Council', *Contemporary Security Policy* 24/2, 47–68.

Enerdata (2024). *World Energy and Climate Statistics, Yearbook*, <https://yearbook.enerdata.net>.

Errico, Stefania & Priscilla Claeys (2017). *Human Rights and the Commons: Bridging Gaps and Exploring Complementary Approaches to the Governance of Land and Natural Resources*, <https://bit.ly/2UrtzNr>.

Evans, Barbara (2017). 'Genomic Data Commons', *Governing Medical Knowledge Commons*, K. Strandburg, B. Frischmann, M. Madison (eds.), Cambridge University Press, 74–102.

Fairclough, Graham (2020). 'The Wisdom of the Commons: 'Together' Is Always Better', *Cultural Heritage in the Realm of the Commons: Conversations on the Case of Greece*, S. Lekakis (ed.), v–xi. Ubiquity Press, London, <https://doi.org/10.5334/bcj.a>.

Falk, Richard (1983). 'On the Recent Further Decline of International Law', *Legal change: essays in honour of Julius Stone*, A.R. Blackshield (ed.), N.P., Sydney, 268–291.

Falkner, Robert & Barry Buzan (2018). 'The Emergence of Environmental Stewardship as a Primary Institution of Global International Society', *European Journal of International Relations*, 1–25.

Food and Agriculture Organization (2022). *Global Report on Food Crises*, <https://bit.ly/3W3BE9b>.

Food and Agriculture Organization (2012). *Voluntary Guidelines on the Responsible Governance of Tenure of Land, Fisheries and Forests in the Context of National Food Security*, <http://www.fao.org/3/a-i2801e.pdf>.

Faundez, Julio (2017). 'The Governance of Natural Resources in Latin America: The Commodities Consensus and the Policy Space', *Natural Resources and Sustainable Development*, Celine Tan & Julio Faundez (eds.), Elgar, Cheltenham, 117–138.

Feichtner, Isabel (2019). 'Sharing the Riches of the Sea: The Redistributive and Fiscal Dimension of Deep Seabed Exploitation', *European Journal of International Law* 30/2, 601–633, <https://doi.org/10.1093/ejil/chz022>.

Feichtner, Isabel & Surabhi Ranganathan (2019). 'International Law and Economic Exploitation in the Global Commons: Introduction', *European Journal of International Law*, 30/2, 541–546, <https://doi.org/10.1093/ejil/chz026>.

Fennel, Lee Anne (2011). 'Ostrom's Law: Property Rights in the Commons', *International Journal of the Commons* 5/1, 9–27.

Fia, Tommaso (2021). 'An Alternative to Data Ownership: Managing Access to Non-personal Data through the Commons', *Global Jurist* 21, <https://doi.org/10.1515/gj-2020-0034>.

Fischer, Markus, Mark Rounsevell et al. (eds.) (2018). *Summary for Policymakers of the Regional Assessment Report on Biodiversity and Ecosystem Services for Europe and Central Asia of the Intergovernmental Science-Policy Platform on Biodiversity and Ecosystem Services*, IPBES, Bonn, <https://www.ipbes.net/deliverables/2b-europe-central-asia>.

Fleck, Anna (2024). *A History of Resource Extraction and Acceleration*, statista, <https://bit.ly/46i1ONJ>.

Folke, Carl & Lance Gunderson (2010). 'Resilience and Global Sustainability', *Ecology and Society* 15/4, 43–47, <http://www.ecologyandsociety.org/vol15/iss4/art43/>.

Forsyth, Miranda, Brunilda Pali & Felicity Tepper (2022). 'Environmental Restorative Justice: An Introduction and an Invitation', in *The Palgrave Handbook of Environmental Restorative Justice* B. Pali, M. Forsyth, F. Tepper (eds.), Palgrave Macmillan, Cham, 1–23.

Foster, John B. (2019). 'On Fire This Time', *Monthly Review*, Nov/2019, <https://bit.ly/36wyJof>.

Foucault, Michel (2004). *Sécurité, Territoire, Population, Cours au Collège de France. 1977–1978*, Seuil/Gallimard, Paris.

Frakes, Jennifer (2003). 'The Common Heritage Principle and the Deep Sea Bed, Outer Space and Antarctica: Will Development and Developing Nations Reach a Compromise?', *Wisconsin International Law Journal* 21/2, 409–413.

Franckx, Erik (2010). 'The International Seabed Authority and the Common Heritage of Mankind: The Need for States to Establish the Outer Limits of Their Continental Shelf', *The International Journal of Marine and Coastal Law* 25, 543–567.

Francioni, Francesco (2014). 'International Common Goods: An Epilogue', *International Law for Common Goods: Normative Perspectives on Human Rights, Culture and Nature*, F. Lenzerini & A.F. Vrdoljak (eds.), Hart, Oxford/Portland, 443–448.

Freestone, David (2018). 'An Unfinished Agenda: Governance of Areas beyond National Jurisdiction', *Global Commons and the Law of the Sea*, K. Zou (ed.), Brill, Leiden-Boston, 207–225.

Friedmann, Wolfgang (1964). *The Changing Structure* of *International Law, Columbia University Press, New York.*

Gaja, Giorgio (2012). 'The Protection of General Interests in the International Community' *The Hague Academy of International Law, Collected Courses* 364, 9–186.

Galloway, Alexander & Eugene Thacker (2007). *The Exploit: A Theory of Networks, University of Minnesota Press, Minneapolis/London.*

Gellers, Joshua (2015). 'Explaining the Emergence of Constitutional Environmental Rights: A Global Quantitative Analysis', *Journal of Human Rights and the Environment* 6, 75–97.

Gilbert, Jeremie (2013). 'The Right to Freely Dispose of Natural Resources: Utopia or Forgotten Right?', *Netherlands Quarterly of Human Rights* 31/2, 314–341.

Gilley, Bruce & David Kinsella (2015). 'Coercing Climate Action', *Survival*, 57/2, 7–28.

Giotitsas, Chris, Pedro H.J. Nardelli, Sam Williamson, Andreas Roos, Evangelos Pournaras & Vasilis Kostakis (2022). 'Energy Governance as a Commons: Engineering Alternative Socio-technical Configurations', *Energy Research & Social Science* 84, <https://bit.ly/3gWu01h>.

Giraud, Gaël, Stéphanie Leyronas & Grégoire Rota-Graziosi (eds.) (2016). 'Le Développement au Prisme Des Communs', *Revue d'économie du développement* 24/3, 5–148.

Gjerde, Kristina et. al. (2018). *Conservation and Sustainable Use of Marine Biodiversity in Areas Beyond National Jurisdiction: Options for Underpinning a Strong Global BBNJ Agreement through Regional and Sectoral Governance*, STRONG Open sea Project., <https://bit.ly/3kqyTvl>.

Global Commission on the Economics of Water (2024). *The Economics of Water: Valuing the Hydrological Cycle as a Global Common Good*, Global Commission on the Economics of Water, Paris.

Goldman, Michael (1998). *Privatising Nature: Political Struggles for the Global Commons*, Rutgers University Press, New Jersey.

Grassl Hartmut et al. (2002). *Charging the Use of Global Commons*, Special Report, General Advisory Council on Global Change, <https://bit.ly/2NXSrNd>.

Grear Anna (2014). 'Towards 'Climate Justice'? A Critical Reflection on Legal Subjectivity and Climate Injustice: Warning Signals, Patterned Hierarchies, Directions for Future Law and Policy', *Journal of Human Rights and the Environment* 5, 103–133.

Grgic, Aida, Zvonimir Mataga, Matija Longar & Ana Vilfan (2007). *The Right to Property under the ECHR*, Council of Europe, Strasbourg.

Grimley, Matthew & Kathryn Milun (2017). *Solar Commons: Designing Community Trust Solar Ownership for Social Equity*, University of Minnesota, <http://hdl.handle.net/11299/190208>.

Groff, Maja & Sylvia Karlsson-Vinkhuyzen (2018). 'The Rule of Law and Accountability: Exploring Trajectories for Democratising Governance of Global Public Goods and Global Commons', in *The Commons and a New Global Governance*, S. Cogolati & J. Wouters (eds.), Elgar, Cheltenham, 130–159.

Grotius, Hugo (1916). *The Freedom of the Seas, or the Right Which Belongs to the Dutch to Take Part in the East Indian Trade*, Oxford University Press, New York.

Guattari, Felix (1989). *Les Trois Écologies*, Galilée, Paris.

Gullett, Warwick & Quentin Hanich (2018). 'Rethinking Open Sea Fishing Freedoms', *Global Commons and the Law of the Sea*, K. Zou (ed.), Brill, Boston/Leiden, 112–123.

Gutwirth, Serge & Isabelle Stengers (2016). 'Le droit à l'épreuve de la résurgence des *commons*', *Chronique: Théorie de droit, Revue Juridique de l'Environnement*, 1, 306–343.

Halbachs, Michel (1992). *On Collective Memory* (A. Coser, trans.), Chicago University Press.

Halewood, Michael & Isabel Lopez Noriega & Selim Louafi (eds.) (2013). *Crop Genetic Resources as a Global Commons*, Routledge, Oxon.

Hardin, Garett (1977). 'The Tragedy of the Commons', in *Managing the Commons*, G. Hardin & J. Baden (eds.), W.H. Freeman & Co., San Fransisco, 16–30.

Hardin, Garett (1994). *The Tragedy of the Unmanaged Commons*, <https://bit.ly/3niIbeM>.

Hardt, Michael & Antonio Negri (2004). *Multitude: War and Democracy in the Age of Empire*, Penguin Putnam, N. York.

Hardt, Michael & Antonio Negri (2009). *Commonwealth*, Harvard University Press, Cambridge.

Harrison, Kathryn & Lisa McIntosh Sundstrom (2010). *Global Commons, Domestic Decisions: The Comparative Politics of Climate Change*, MIT Press, Boston.

Harvey, David (1997). *Justice, Nature and the Geography of Difference*, Wiley-Blackwell, New Jersey.

Harvey, David (2011). 'The Future of the Commons', *Radical History Review* 109, 101–107.

Hauser, Oliver Paul (2016). *Challenging Cooperation: Inequality, Global Commons, Future Generations*, Doctoral dissertation, Graduate School of Arts and Sciences, Harvard University, Cambridge.

Hauser, Oliver, Achim Hendriks, David Rand, et al. (2016). 'Think Global, Act Local: Preserving the Global Commons', *Scientific Report* 6, <https://bit.ly/3ETlyI9>.

Heinrich Boell Stiftung (2021). *Plastic Atlas*, <https://www.boell.de/en/plasticatlas>.

Hendlin, Yogi Hale (2014). 'From *Terra Nullius* to *Terra Communis*: Reconsidering Wild Land in an Era of Conservation and Indigenous Rights', *Environmental Philosophy* 11(2), 141–174.

Hess, Charlotte (2008). *Mapping the New Commons*, 12th Biennial Conference of the International Association for the Study of the Commons, University of Gloucestershire, Cheltenham, <https://bit.ly/2IxNnN1>.

Hess, Charlotte & Elinor Ostrom (2007). 'Introduction', *Understanding Knowledge as a Commons: From Theory to Practice*, Ch. Hess & E. Ostrom (eds.), Cambridge, Massachusetts, MIT Press, 5–16, <https://wtf.tw/ref/hess_ostrom_2007.pdf>.

Hewson, Martin & Timothy Sinclair (1999). 'The Emergence of Global Governance Theories', *Approaches to Global Governance Theories*, M. Hewson & T. Sinclair (eds.), State University of New York Press, Albany, 4–19.

Hoel, Alf Hakon (1991). 'Regionalisation of International Whale Management: The North Atlantic Committee for Research on Marine Mammals', Paper presented at the *Common Property Conference, the Second Biennial Conference of the International Association for the Study of Common Property*, Winnipeg, <http://bit.ly/3ijSNwz>.

Hofbauer, Jane A. (2022). 'Community Interests', in *Elgar Encyclopedia of Human Rights*, Ch. Binder, M. Nowak, J.A. Hofbauer, Ph. Janig (eds), Elgar, Cheltenham.

Holman, JoAnne & McGregor, Michael A. (2005). 'The Internet as Commons: The Issue of Access', *Communication Law and Policy*, 10(3), 267–289, <doi:10.1207/s15326926clp1003_1>.

Hopman, Luca, Satoko Kishimoto, Bertie Russell & Louisa Valentin (2021). *Democratic and Collective Ownership of Public Goods and Services: Exploring Public-Community Collaborations*, Transnational Institute, <https://bit.ly/4fabqMV>.

Horvitz, Robert (2008). *Marconi's Legacy: National Sovereignty Claims in Radio*, 1st COMMUNIA Workshop on 'Technology and the Public Domain' NEXA Center for Internet and Society, Politecnico di Torino, <https://bit.ly/32G9mbw>.

Hudson, Blake (ed.) (2024). *Environmental Law and the Public Trust Doctrine*, Cambridge University Press.

Human Genome Organisation [HUGO] (1996). 'Statement on the Principled Conduct of Genetic Research', HUGO, Geneva.

Human Genome Organisation [HUGO] (2003). 'Statement on Human Genomic Database', HUGO, Geneva, <https://bit.ly/2UjGaCD>.

Humphreys, Stephen (2014). 'Climate Justice: The Claim of the Past', *Journal of Human Rights and the Environment* 5, 134–148.

James, Deborah (2020). *Digital Trade Rules. A Disastrous New Constitution for the Global Economy, by and for the Big Tech*, Rosa Luxemburg Foundation, Brussels <https://bit.ly/3HrC4Sm>.

Jasper, Scott (ed.) (2012). *Conflict and Cooperation in the Global Commons: A Comprehensive Approach for International Security*, Georgetown University Press, Washington DC.

Jokilehto, Jukka (2008). *The World Heritage List What Is OUV? Defining the Outstanding Universal Value of Cultural World Heritage Properties*, ICOMOS, <https://bit.ly/2IlYnNz>.

Joseph, Binu & Mohanan Bhaskaran Pillai (2020). 'The Cyberspace as a Distinct Domain of the Global Commons', in *Global Commons*, M. Bhaskaran Pillai & G. Ganapathy-Doré (eds.), Sage, N. Delhi.

Jonas, Hans (1979). *The Imperative of Responsibility: In Search of Ethics for the Technological Age*, University of Chicago Press, Chicago.

Joyner, Christopher (2001). 'Global Commons: The Ocean, Antarctica, the Atmosphere, and Outer Space', in *Managing Common Issues*, PJ Simmons & Chantal de Jonge Outdraat (eds.), Carnegie Foundation, Washington DC, 354–390.

International Law Commission (2022). 'Peremptory Norms of General International Law (*jus cogens*)', UN-ILC, A/CN.4/L.967.

International Law Commission (2001). 'Article 48, Commentary to the Draft Articles on Responsibility of States for Internationally Wrongful Acts', *Yearbook of the ILC*, 126.

International Monsanto Tribunal (2017). Advisory Opinion, The Hague, <https://bit.ly/3CdCs3E>.

International Seabed Authority (2002). *Legislative History of the 'Enterprise' under the United Nations Convention on the Law of the Sea and the Agreement Relating to the Implementation of Part XI of the Convention*, Kingston, <https://bit.ly/38w5vBw>.

International Seabed Authority (2024). *Exploration contracts*, <https://bit.ly/46SgRwg>.

International Task Force on Global Public Goods (2006). *Meeting Global Challenges: International Cooperation in the National Interest*, Report, Stockholm, <https://bit.ly/2IuZsSG>.

International Union for Conservation of Nature and Natural Resources (1980). *World Conservation Strategy*, <https://bit.ly/3pn7OwI>.

Kallis, Giorgos (2017). *In Defence of Degrowth*, Uneven Earth publishers, Brussels.

Kant, Immanuel (1996). *The Metaphysics of Morals*, (tr. M.J. Gregor), Cambridge University Press, Cambridge.

Karitzis, Andreas (2016). 'Postface' in D. Bollier, *Commons: A Short Introduction* [in Greek], angelus novus, Athens, 263–290.

Kaul, Inge (2013). *Global Public Goods A concept for framing the Post-2015 Agenda* – German Development Institute, Discussion Paper 2, Bohn, <https://bit.ly/3kpBTb9>.

Kaul, Ranjana (2024). 'Outer Space: Is It a Global Common?', *Frontiers in Space Technologies* 5, 1–5, <doi:10.3389/frspt.2024.1411610>.

Kelly, Marjorie (2012). *Owning Our Future: The Emerging Ownership Revolution: Journeys to a Generative Economy*, Berrett-Koehler Publishers, Oakland.

Khoshnava, Seyed Meysam et al. (2019). 'Aligning the Criteria of Green Economy (GE) and Sustainable Development Goals (SDGs) to Implement Sustainable Development', *Sustainability* 11, <https://www.mdpi.com/2071-1050/11/17/4615>.

Kim, Rakhyun E. & Louis J. Kotzé (2020). 'Planetary Boundaries at the Intersection of Earth System Law, Science and Governance: A State-of-the-Art Review', *Review of European, Comparative and International Environmental Law* 30(1), 1–13.

Kioupkiolis, Alexandros (2014). *On the Commons of Freedom* [in Greek], Exarheia pub., Athens.

Kioupkiolis, Alexandros (2020). *Heteropolitics: Refiguring the Common and the Political*, AUTH/ERC COG 2016, <http://bit.ly/3gMW4Ej>.

Kiss, Alexandre (1985). 'The Common Heritage of Mankind: Utopia or Reality?', *International Journal* 40, 423–424.

Kiss, Alexandre (2003). 'Globalisations and the Common Concern of Humanity', *Economic Globalisation and Compliance with International Environmental Agreements*, A. Kiss, D. Shelton & K. Ishibashi (eds.), Kluwer Law International, The Hague, 3–16.

Klein, Naomi (2001). 'Reclaiming the Commons', *New Left Review* 9, <http://bit.ly/3FbAeUs>.

Klein, Naomi (2015). *This Changes Everything: Capitalism vs. the Climate*, Allen Lane, London.

Knox, John (2018). *Framework Principles on Human Rights and the Environment: The Main Human Rights Obligations Relating to the Enjoyment of a Safe, Clean, Healthy and Sustainable Environment*, Special Rapporteur, United Nations, <https://bit.ly/3ltmrfx>.

Kolliniati, Maria Aremis (2020). 'Human Rights and Collective Goods: A Non-individualistic Approach', *Ethics. Journal of Philosophy*, (12), 20–28, <https://bit.ly/3Br5wo7>.

Kornilakis, Angelos (2024). *The Contractual Networks of Digital Commons*, Nomos, Baden Baden.

Kostakis, Vasilis (2012). *The Peer-to-Peer Manifesto* [in Greek], Voreiodytikes ekdoseis, Ioannina.

Kostakis, Vasilis, Lucas Lemos & Asimina Kouvara (2024). 'Another Scalability is Possible! From Nonscalability to Cosmolocal Scalability', *tripleC* 22/2, 620–629, <http://www.triple-c.at>.

Kotsaka, Theodora (2016). 'The Greek Water Referendum: The Distinction between Public and Common Goods', in *The Enigma Of Europe. Transform!*, W. Baier, E. Canepa and E. Himmelstoss (eds.), Merlin Press, London, 183–195.

Kotsaka, Theodora (2022). 'The Capitalism of Surveillance and the Political Significance of the Management of the Digital Technology', in *What to Do: Thoughts for the Restart of Radical Policy* [in Greek], K. Galanopoulos & D. Papanikolopoulos (eds.), Themelio, Athens, 235–254.

Kotsaka, Theodora (2026). *Commons 2.0. Institutional interventions, applied policies and production model,* Nisos, Athens [in Greek].

Kotzé, Louis (2014). 'Editorial: Crossing Boundaries: Water and the Rights Paradigm', *Journal of Human Rights and the Environment* 5(1), 1–4.

Lambing, Julio (2012). 'Electricity Commons: Toward a New Industrial Society'. *The Wealth of the Commons. A World beyond Market and State*, The commons strategies group, <https://bit.ly/3yjEgGQ>.

Lekakis, Stelios (2020). 'Cultural Heritage in the Realm of the Commons: Reading a Letter from the Future', *Cultural Heritage in the Realm of the Commons: Conversations on the Case of Greece*, S. Lekakis (ed.) Ubiquity Press, London, 1–14, <https://doi.org/10.5334/bcj.b>.

Lessig, Lawrence (2002a). 'The Architecture of Innovation', *Duke law Journal* 51, 177–191.

Lessig, Lawrence (2002b). *The Future of Ideas: The Fate of the Commons in a Connected World, Random House*, New York, <http://the-future-of-ideas.com>.

Leyronas, Stephanie & Tamatoa Bambridge (2018). 'Lecture croisée de la gouvernance des communs ', *Revue internationale des études du développement* 233 (1), 5–215.

Liaropoulos, Andrew (2017). 'Cyberspace Governance and State Sovereignty', *Democracy and an Open-Economy World Order*, G. Bitros & N. Kyriazis (eds.), Springer, Cham, 25–35.

Linebaugh, Peter (2008). *The Magna Carta Manifesto*, University of California Press, Berkeley.

Locatelli, Rita (2018). 'Education as a Public and Common Good: Reframing the Governance of Education in a Changing Context', Working papers-UNESDOC, Unesco, <https://bit.ly/3sKSx9P>.

Locke, John (1988). *Two Treatises of Government* (Peter Laslett ed.), Cambridge University Press, Cambridge.

Lowenhaupt Tsing, Anna. (2012). 'On Nonscalability'. *Common Knowledge* 18/3, 505–24., <https://doi.org/10.1215/0961754X-1630424>.

Lyster, Rosemary (2019). 'The Idea of (Climate) Justice, neoliberalism and the Talanoa Dialogue', *Journal of Human Rights and the Environment* 10(1), 35–61.

Madison, Michael J., Brett Frischmann & Katherine Strandburg (2010). 'Constructing Commons in the Cultural Environment', *Cornell Law Review* 95, 657–709.

Madison, Michael J., Katherine Strandburg & Brett Frischmann (2016). *Knowledge Commons*, Legal Studies Research Paper Series Working Paper No. 2016–28, Elgar/University of Pittsburgh.

Mann Borgese, Elizabeth (1998). *The Oceanic Circle: Governing the Seas as a Global Resource*, UN University Press, Tokyo, <https://bit.ly/3lpfJaz>.

Marks, Susan (2008). Exploitation as an International Legal Concept, *International Law on the Left*, Susan Marks (ed.), Cambridge University Press, 281–308.

Magalhães, Paulo (2016). 'Earth Condominium: A Legal Model for the Anthropocene', in *The Safe Operating Space Treaty: A New Approach to Managing Our Use of the Earth System*, P. Magalhães, W. Steffen, K. Bosselmann, A. Aragão & V. Soromenho-Marques (eds.), Cambridge Scholars pub., Newcastle upon Tyne, 180–211.

Marmor, Andrei (2001). 'Do We Have a Right to Common Goods?', *Canadian Journal of Law and Jurisprudence*, 7/2001, Cornell Digital Repository.

Mattei, Ugo (2011). *The State, the Market, and Some Preliminary Questions about the Commons*, <http://works.bepress.com/ugo_mattei/40/>.

Mattei, Ugo (2018). 'The Ecology of International Law: Towards an International Legal System in Tune with Nature and Community?', in *The Commons and a New Global Governance*, S. Cogolati & J. Wouters (eds.), Elgar, Cheltenham, 212–230.

Mazar, Haim (2016). *Radio Spectrum Management: Policies, Regulations and Techniques.*, Wiley, New Jersey.

McEldowney, John (2017). 'The Role of Law in the Economy and in Regulating Natural Resources and Environmental Protection in China', *Natural Resources and Sustainable Development*, C. Tan & J. Faundez (eds.), Elgar, Cheltenham, 209–235.

Meredith, Michael P., Jess Melbourne-Thomas, Alberto C. Naveira Garabato, Marilyn Raphael, Jeffrey McGee & Jamie Oliver (2025). 'Introduction' in *Antarctica and the*

Earth System, M.P.Meredith, J. Melbourne-Thomas, A.C. Naveira Garabato & M. Raphael (eds.), Routledge, Oxon.

Mickelson, Karin (2019). 'Common Heritage of Mankind as a Limit to Exploitation of the Global Commons', *European Journal of International Law* 30/2, 635–663, <https://bit.ly/2NVO5Gw>.

Milun, Kathryn (2011). *The Political Uncommons: The Cross-cultural Logic of the Global Commons*, Ashgate, Farnham.

Montini, Massimiliano (2014). 'Revising International Environmental Law through the Paradigm of Ecological Sustainability', in *International Law for Common Goods. Normative Perspectives on Human Rights, Culture and Nature*, F. Lenzerini & A.F. Vrdoljak (eds.), Hart, Oxford/Portland, 271–287.

Mooney, Patrick (2011). 'International Non-governmental Organisations: The Hundred Year (or so) Seed War – Seeds, Sovereignty and Civil Society – a Historical Perspective on the Evolution of 'The Law of the Seed'', in *Plant Genetic Resources and Food Security*, Christine Frison, Francisco López & José T. Esquinas-Alcázar (eds.), FAO, London/New York, 135–147, <https://bit.ly/4vzsun6>.

More, Thomas (1981). *Utopia*, P. Turner (ed.), Penguin Books, London.

Morrow, Karen (2023). 'The Anthropocene and Human Rights: A New Context and the Need to Revisit Collective Human Concerns', in *The Routledge Handbook of Law and the Anthropocene*, P. D. Burdon & J. Martel (eds.), Routledge, Oxon, 211–225.

Moyn, Samuel (2018). *Not Enough: Human Rights in an Unequal World*, The Belknap Press of Harvard University Press, Cambridge/London.

Munier, Manuel et al. (2013). *Legal Issues about Metadata Data Privacy vs Information* <https://bit.ly/38HkatP>.

Nakicenovic, Nebojsa et al. (2016). *Global Commons in the Anthropocene: World Development on a Stable and Resilient Planet*, Working Paper, International Institute for Applied Systems Analysis & Stockholm University, Laxenburg, <https://bit.ly/32AtNXm>.

Khatwani, Naman (2019). 'Common Heritage of Mankind for Outer Space', *Astropolitics* 17(2), pp. 89–103.

Krewer, Jan & Zuzanna Warso (2024). *Digital Commons as Providers of Public Digital Infrastructure*, Open Future, <https://bit.ly/4iggSiE>.

Noam, Eli (1998). 'Spectrum Auctions: Yesterday's Heresy, Today's Orthodoxy, Tomorrow's Anachronism: Taking the Next Step to Open Spectrum Access', *The Journal of Law and Economics* XLI(2), 765–780.

Noga, Aljosa (2014). *The Tragedy of Outer Space as a Global Commons and Public International Law: An Analysis of the Law Governing Outer Space and Its Compatibility with Behavioral Economic Models on Resource Extraction*, MA Thesis, Örebro University, School of Law, Psychology and Social Work.

Okonkwo, Theodore (2017). 'How International Law Can Deal with Lack of Sanctions and Binding Targets in the Paris Agreement', *Journal of Sustainable Development* 10/5, <https://doi.org/10.5539/jsd.v10n5p225>.

Orsini, Amandine, Jean-Frédéric Morin & Oran Young (2013). 'Regime Complexes: A Buzz, a Boom, or a Boost for Global Governance?', *Global Governance* 19, 27–38.

Ostrom, Elinor (1990). *Governing the Commons: The Evolution of Institutions for Collective Action*, Cambridge University Press, Cambridge.

Ostrom, Elinor (2000). 'Private and Common Property Rights', *Encyclopedia of Law and Economics, Vol. II: Civil Law and Economics*, Elgar, Cheltenham, <http://hdl.handle.net/10535/74>.

Ostrom, Elinor (2010). 'Beyond Markets and States: Polycentric Governance of Complex Economic Systems', *American Economic Review* 100/3, 641–72, <10.1257/aer.100.3.641>.

Overland, Indra (2018). 'Norway: Public Debate and the Management of Petroleum Resources and Revenues', *Public Brainpower*, I. Overland (ed.), Palgrave Macmillan, Cham, 217–245, <https://bit.ly/3b8BWXC>.

Owen, John et al. (2022). 'Energy Transition Minerals and Their Intersection with Land-Connected Peoples', *Nature sustainability*, <https://bit.ly/3Gen4Gs>.

Papanikolaou, Giorgos (2017). 'Building Sustainable Alternatives for the Future World' [in Greek], interview, <https://bit.ly/3louZ7m>.

Papanikolaou, Giorgos (2022). 'The Limits of Growth Lead to Planning of an Economy of Common Resources', in *There Is Another Way!* [in Greek], P. Lynardos Rymon, V. Roggas, D. Papanikolopoulos (eds.), Efimerida ton Syntakton pub., 77–86.

Parance, Béatrice & Jacques de Saint Victor (2014). 'Introduction', *Repenser les biens communs*, B. Parance & J. de Saint Victor (eds.) CNRS éditions, Paris, 6–25.

Pardo, Arvid (1967). *Address to the 22nd Session of the General Assembly of the United Nations*, U.N. GAOR, 22nd sess., U.N. Doc. A/6695, <https://bit.ly/47WS8Zu>.

Pardo, Arvid (1993). 'The Origins of the 1976 Malta Initiative', *International Insights* 9/2, 65–69.

Patel, Reema (2017). *Why Economics Has a Democratic Deficit*, Open Democracy, <https://neweconomics.opendemocracy.net/economics-democratic-deficit/>.

Pavoni, Ricardo (2014). 'Public Interest Environmental Litigation and the European Court of Hunan Rights: No Love at First Sight', in *International Law for Common Goods. Normative Perspectives on Human Rights, Culture and Nature*, F. Lenzerini & A.F. Vrdoljak (eds.), Hart, Oxford/Portland, 330–359.

Pazaitis, Alex, Primavera De Filippi, & Vasilis Kostakis (2017). 'Blockchain and Value Systems in the Sharing Economy: The Illustrative Case of Backfeed', *Technological Forecasting and Social Change*, 105–115.

Pazaitis, Alex & Vasilis Kostakis (2021). 'Are the Most Influential Websites Peer-Produced or Price Incentivised? Organising Value in the Digital Economy', *Organization* 29(4), 757–769.

Petersmann, Ernst-Ulrich (2014). 'Why Justice and Human Rights Require Cosmopolitan International Law', *International Law for Common Goods. Normative Perspectives on Human Rights, Culture and Nature*, F. Lenzerini & A.F. Vrdoljak (eds.), Hart, Oxford/Portland, 117–135.

Phillips, Freedom-Kai (2016). 'Intellectual Property Rights in Traditional Knowledge: Enabler of Sustainable Development', *Utrecht Journal of International and European Law* 1/32(83), <http://dx.doi.org/10.5334/ujiel.283>.

Pic, Pauline., Philippe Evoy & Jean-Frédéric Morin (2023). 'Outer Space as a Global Commons: An Empirical Study of Space Arrangements', *International Journal of the Commons* 17(1), 288–301. doi:10.5334/ijc.1271.

Piketty, Thomas (2019). *Capital et idéologie*, Seuil, Paris.

Pinto, Maurice Cranston William (2012). 'The Common Heritage of Mankind: Then and Now', *The Hague Academy of International Law, Collected Courses* 361, 9–130.

Pisillo Mazzeschi, Ricardo (2014). 'Human Rights and the Modernisation of International Law', in *International Law for Common Goods: Normative Perspectives on Human Rights, Culture and Nature*, F. Lenzerini & A.F. Vrdoljak (eds.), Hart, Oxford/Portland, 89–101.

Pörtner, Hans-Otto, Debra Roberts et al. (eds.) (2022). *Climate Change 2022: Impacts, Adaptation and Vulnerability. Contribution of Working Group II to the Sixth Assessment Report of the Intergovernmental Panel on Climate Change*, IPCC, Cambridge University Press, Cambridge/New York, <https://bit.ly/3uetLS6>.

Prieto Manuel (2021). 'Equity vs. Efficiency and the Human Right to Water', *Water* 13/3, <https://doi.org/10.3390/w13030278>.

Purtova, Nadya & Gijs van Maanen (2024). 'Data as an Economic Good, Data as a Commons, and Data Governance', *Law, Innovation and Technology* 16/1, 1–42.

Quillingan, James B. (2012). 'Why Distinguish Common Goods from Public Goods?', *The Wealth of the Commons: A World beyond Market and State*, D. Bollier & S. Helfrich (eds.), The Commons Strategy Group 2012, <https://wealthofthecommons.org/essay/why-distinguish-common-goods-public-goods>.

Raison, Virginie (2010). *2033 Atlas des futures du Monde*, ed. Robert Laffont, Paris.

Ranganathan, Surabhi (2016). 'Global Commons', *European Journal of International Law* 27/3, 693–717, <https://doi.org/10.1093/ejil/chw037>.

Ranganathan, Surabhi (2019). 'Ocean Floor Grab: International Law and the Making of an Extractive Imaginary', *European Journal of International Law* 30/2, 573–600, <https://doi.org/10.1093/ejil/chz027>.

Raymond, Mark (2012). 'The Internet as a Global Commons?' *CIGI Commentary Series on Internet Governance*, <https://bit.ly/2K5ne8R>.

Raz, Joseph (1986). *The Morality of Freedom*, Clarendon Press, Oxford.

Regalado, Antonio (2000). 'The Great Gene Grab', *Technology Review*, MIT, <https://www.technologyreview.com/2000/09/01/236237/the-great-gene-grab/>.

REScoop MECISE (2019). *Mobilising European Citizens to Invest in Sustainable Energy*, Final Results Oriented report, Horizon 2020, Antwerp.

Ritchie, Hannah & Max Roser (2020). 'Co2 Emissions', *OurWorldInData.org*, <https://ourworldindata.org/co2-emissions>.

Riddervold, Marianne & Akasemi Newsome (2021). 'Introduction: Cooperation, Conflict, and Interaction in the Global Commons', *International Relations* 35/3, 365–383, <https://doi.org/10.1177/00471178211036598>.

Rifkin, Jeremy (2015). *The Zero Marginal Cost Society*, St Martin Press, N. York.

Rights and Resource Initiative (2015). *Who Owns the World's Land? A Global Baseline of Formally Recognised Indigenous and Community Land Rights*, RRI, Washington DC.

Ringbeck, Birgitta (2018). 'The World Heritage Convention and Its Management Concept', in *Aspects of Management Planning for Cultural World Heritage Sites*, Simon Makuvaza (eds.), Springer, Cham, 15–24.

Ripple, William J., et al. (2019). *World Scientists' Warning of a Climate Emergency*, BioScience, <https://doi.org/10.1093/biosci/biz088>.

Rizvi, Kazim (2020). *Data Sovereignty: Is It about Empowering the State or the People?*, <https://bit.ly/3eOZ7GG>.

Roeschke, Joseph Elliott (2009). 'Eco-terrorism and Piracy on the Open Sea: Japanese Whaling and the Rights of Private Groups to Enforce International Conservation Law in Neutral Waters', *Villanova Environmental Law Journal* 20/ 99, <https://bit.ly/3B4RA2O>.

Roberts, Peri & Peter Sutch (2016). 'The Global Commons and International Distributive Justice', *Distributive Justice Debates in Social and Political Thought*, Camilla Boisen and Matthew Murray (eds.), Routledge, New York, 230–250.

Robinson, Mary (2014). 'Social and Legal Aspects on Climate Change', *Journal of Human Rights and the Environment* 5, 15–17.

Rockström, Johan et al. (2009). 'Planetary Boundaries: Exploring the Safe Operating Space for Humanity', *Ecology and Society* 14/2, 32–55, <https://bit.ly/3P9EUox>.

Rose, Carol M. (2011). 'Ostrom and the Lawyers: The Impact of Governing the Commons on the American Legal Academy', *International Journal of the Commons*, 5/1, 28–49.

Ruggie, John (2008). *Protect, Respect and Remedy: A Framework for Business and Human Rights*, Report of the Special Representative of the Secretary-General on Human Rights and Transnational Corporations and Other Business Enterprises, United Nations, Economic and Social Council, A/HRC/8/5, <http://bit.ly/37DjIfd>.

Rawls, John (1971). *A Theory of Justice*, Harvard University Press, Cambridge.

Sala, Enric, Juan Mayorga, Darcy Bradley et al. (2021). 'Protecting the Global Ocean for Biodiversity, Food and Climate, *Nature* 592, 397–402, <https://bit.ly/4gP1w37>.

Sand, Peter H. (2005). 'The Right to Know: Environmental Information Disclosure by Government and Industry', in *Making Law Work: Environmental Compliance and*

Sustainable Development, vol. 2, D. Zaelke, D. Kaniaru, & E. Kruziková (eds.), Cameron May.

Santos, Boaventura de Sousa (2020). *Towards a New Legal Common Sense: Law, Globalisation, and Emancipation* (3d ed.), Cambridge University Press, Cambridge.

Santos, Boaventura de Sousa (2015). *If God Were a Human Rights activist*, Stanford University Press, Stanford.

Sauvêtre, Pierre (2018). 'Forget Ostrom: From the Development Commons to the Common as Social Sovereignty', in *The Commons and a New Global Governance*, S. Cogolati & J. Wouters (eds.), Elgar, Cheltenham, 82–94.

Scherhorn, Gerhard (2012). 'Transforming Global Resources into Commons', in *The Wealth of the Commons: A World beyond Market and State*, D. Bollier & S. Helfrich (eds.), The Commons Strategy Group, <https://bit.ly/3IGPZXK>.

Schlosberg, David (2013). 'Theorising Environmental Justice: The Expanding Sphere of a Discourse', *Environmental Politics*, 2013 22/1, 37–55.

Schmitt, Carl (2006). *The Nomos of the Earth*, Telos Press, New York.

Schrijver, Nico (1997). *Sovereignty over Natural Resources: Balancing Rights and Duties*, Cambridge University Press, Cambridge.

Schrijver, Nico (2016). 'Managing the Global Commons: Common Good or Common Sink?', *Third World Quarterly* 37/7, 1252–1267, <https://bit.ly/305AOoH>.

Scholten, Andrew & Julien Bresson (2016). *International Environmental Law: A Human Rights Oriented Approach*, <http://hdl.handle.net/10535/10104>.

Schreuer, Christoph, Loretta Malintoppi, August Reinisch & Anthony Sinclair (2009). *The ICSID Convention: A Commentary* (2nd ed.), Cambridge University Press, Cambridge.

Shaffer, Gregory (2012). 'International Law and Global Public Goods in a Legal Pluralist World', *European Journal of International Law* 23/3, 669–693 <doi:10.1093/ejil/chs036>.

Sharable (eds.) (2017). *Sharing Cities. Activating the Urban Commons*, <https://bit.ly/36teUHt>.

Sharma, Aaditya Vikram (2025). 'Starlink and International Law: The Challenge of Corporate Sovereignty in Outer Space', *Blog of the European Journal of International Law*, <https://bit.ly/4pzUMe9>.

Shaw, Malcolm (1997). *International Law*, Cambridge University Press, Cambridge.

Shelton, Dinah (2009). 'Common Concern of Humanity', *Iustum Aequum Salutare* 1, 33–40, <http://ias.jak.ppke.hu/hir/ias/20091sz/05.pdf>.

Shiva, Vandana (2013). 'Foreword. The Commons: The Ground of Democracy and Sustenance', in *Nature for Sale*: *The Commons versus Commodities*, Giovanna Ricoveri, Pluto Press, London.

Sen, Amartya (1999). *Development as Freedom*, Oxford University Press, Oxford.

Sen, Amartya (2009). *The Idea of Justice*, Penguin Books, New York.

Snider, J. H. (2002). 'Who Owns the Airwaves? Four Theories of Spectrum Property Rights', New *America Foundation,* Spectrum Series 3, Public Assets Pr., Washington D.C.

Sicilianos, Linos-Alexandre (2024). *La Dimension Humaine Du Droit International,* Collected Courses, Recueil des cours, vol. 440, The Hague Academy of International Law.

Simma, Bruno (1994). 'From Bilaterism to Community Interests in International Law', *Collected Courses of the Hague Academy of International Law* 250, 229–255.

Sinou, Despina (2022). « La *Soft Law* Et Les "Communs" En Droit International », in *Droit souple et nouvelle(s) normativité(s) / Soft law e nuova(e) normatività,* P. Duret, G. Guiglia, J.-J. Menuret, D. Sinou (eds.), Edizioni Scientifiche Italiane, Naples, 59–68.

Soh, Changrok, Daniel Connolly & Seunghyun Nam (2018). 'Time for a Fourth Generation of Human Rights?', *From Disruption to Transformation; Linking Technology and Human Rights for Sustainable Development,* UNRISD Think Piece Series, <http://bit.ly/308DL0g>.

Soroos, Marvin (1997). *The Changing Atmosphere: The Quest for Global Environmental Security,* University of South Carolina Press, Columbia SC.

Soroos, Marvin (2001). *The Evolution of Global Commons, Global Environmental Policies: Institutions and Procedures,* Palgrave, New York.

Soroos, Marvin (2005). 'Garrett Hardin and Tragedies of Global Commons', *Handbook of Global Environmental Politics,* P. Dauvergne (ed.), Elgar, Northampton, 36–50.

Soscolne, Colin, Martin Bunch, Colin Butler & Margot Parkes (2018). 'Navigating Complexity, Promoting Health: Insights from the Emergence of "Ecohealth" and "One Health"', in *Ecological Integrity, Law and Governance,* L. Westra, K. Bosselmann, J. Gray & K. Gwiazdon (eds.), Routledge, London/N. York, 79–89.

Stamatopoulou, Elsa (2024). *Indigenous Peoples in the International Arena. The Global Movement for Self-Determination,* Routlege, London/N. York.

Standing Guy (2022). *Plunder of the Commons: A Manifesto for Sharing Public Wealth,* Pelican Books, London.

Stephenson, Andrea (2010). 'Germany's Ban of Monsanto's Modified Maize (MON810): A Violation of International Law', *Trade, Law and Development* II/2, <https://bit.ly/32CJiOa>.

Stern, Paul (2011). 'Design Principles for Global Commons: Natural Resources and Emerging Technologies', *International Journal of the Commons* 5, 213–232.

Sturges, Melissa (1999). 'Who Should Hold Property Rights to the Human Genome? An Application of the Common Heritage of Humankind', *American University International Law Review* 13/1, 219–261.

Supiot, Alain 2010. *L'esprit de Philadelphie. La justice sociale face au marché total,* Le Seuil, Paris.

Takle, Marianne (2021). 'The Norwegian Petroleum Fund: Savings for Future Generations?', *Environmental Values* 30/2, 147–167.

Tanzi, Attila (2019). 'The Global Water Treaties and Their Relationship', in *Research Handbook on International Water Law*, S. McCaffrey, Ch. Leb, & R. Denoon (eds.), Elgar, Cheltenham, 11–25.

Taylor, Prue (2011). 'Common Heritage of Mankind Principle', in *The Encyclopedia of Sustainability, Vol. 3: The Law and Politics of Sustainability*, K. Bosselmann, D. Fogel, & J.B. Ruhl (eds.), Great Barrington, MA. Berkshire Pub., 64–69, <https://bit.ly/38COsxE>.

Taylor, Prue (2016). 'The Common Heritage: Constructive Utopianism', in *The Safe Operating Space Treaty: A New Approach to Managing Our Use of the Earth System*, P. Magalhães, W. Steffen, K. Bosselmann, A. Aragão & V. Soromenho-Marques (eds.), Cambridge Scholars pub., Newcastle upon Tyne, 104–129.

Taylor, Prue (2023). 'Ocean Acidification and the Anthropocene: An Emergency Response', in *The Routledge Handbook of Law and the Anthropocene*, P. D. Burdon & J. Martel (eds.), Routledge, Oxon/New York, 130–146.

Thara Srinivasan, U., Reg Watson & U. Rashid Sumaila (2012). 'Global Fisheries Losses at the Exclusive Economic Zone Level, 1950 to Present', *Marine Policy* 36, 544–549.

't Hoen, Elen (2021). 'The Pandemic Treaty and Intellectual Property Sharing: Making Vaccine Knowledge a Public Good', Petrie-Flom Centre, Harvard University, <https://bit.ly/48q8BGd>.

Tladi, Dire (2015). 'The Common Heritage of Mankind and the Proposed Treaty on Biodiversity in Areas beyond National Jurisdiction: The Choice between Pragmatism and Sustainability', *Yearbook of international Environmental Law*. 25/1, 113–132.

van Aaken, Anne (2018). 'Behavioral Aspects of the International Law of Global Public Goods and Common Pool Resources', *American Journal of International Law*, <http://dx.doi.org/10.2139/ssrn.3118104>.

van den Hurk, Anke (2011). 'The Seed Industry: Plant Breeding and the International Treaty on Plant Genetic Resources for Food and Agriculture', in *Plant Genetic Resources and Food Security*, Ch. Frison, F. López & J.T. Esquinas-Alcázar (eds.), FAO, London/N. York, 163–174, <http://www.fao.org/3/a-bb143e.pdf>.

van Tuyll, Bryony Jansen (2023). *Steward-Ownership: Join the 'Economic Avant-Garde' and Make a Real Impact*, <https://bit.ly/42cf6cv>.

Verhoeven, Joe (2008). 'Considérations sur ce qui est commun', *The Hague Academy of International Law, Collected Courses* 331, 9–434.

Vivero-Pol, Jose Luis, Tomaso Ferrando, Olivier De Schutter & Ugo Mattei (2019). 'Introduction. The Food Commons Are Coming…', *Routledge Handbook of Food as a Commons*, J.L.Vivero-Pol, T. Ferrando, O. De Schutter & U. Mattei (eds.), Routledge, London.

Vogel, Jefim & Jason Hickel (2023). 'Is Green Growth Happening? An Empirical Analysis of Achieved versus Paris-Compliant CO_2–GDP Decoupling in High-Income Countries', *Lancet Planet Health* 7, 757–759.

Vogler, John (2000). *The Global Commons*, 2d ed., Wiley, New Jersey.

Vogler, John (2012). 'Global Commons Revisited', *Global Policy* 3/1, 61–67.

Vogler, John (2016). *Climate Change in World Politics*, Palgrave-McMillan, London.

von Bogdandy, Armin, Matthias Goldmann & Ingo Venzke (2017). 'From Public International to International Public Law: Translating World Public Opinion into International Public Authority', *The European Journal of International Law* 28/1, 115–145.

Voss, Joel (2020). 'Contesting Human Rights and Climate Change at the UN Human Rights Council', *Journal of Human Rights and the Environment* 11/1, 6–29.

UN Office of the High Commissioner for Human Rights (2010). *The Right to Water*, Fact Sheet 35, <https://bit.ly/3G77bQX>.

UN Environment, (2016). *Annual Report and Programme Performance Report for 2016*, <https://bit.ly/3puHjWn>.

UN System Task Team on the UN post 2015 UN development agenda (2013). *Global Governance and Governance of the Global Commons in the Global Partnership for Development beyond 2015*, <https://bit.ly/3lpC9bn>.

UNESCO (2019). *Leaving No One Behind*, The United Nations World Water Development Report, World Water Assessment Programme, Paris.

Walt, Stephen (2019). 'Who (and How) Will Save the Amazon?', *Foreign Affairs*, <https://bit.ly/36vqtoM>.

Waters, Nathan (2017). 'Blockchain Commons: The End of All Corporate Business Models, How to Create Value in the Coming Era of Decentralization', <https://bit.ly/3kqhvqy>.

Webersik, Christian & Marc Levy (2016). 'Reducing the Risk of Conflict Recurrence: The Relevance of Nature Resource Management', in *Governance, Natural Resources, and Post-conflict Peacebuilding*, C. Buch, C. Muffet & S. Nichols (eds.), Routledge, New York.

Weiser, Philip & Dale Hatfield (2005). 'Policing the Spectrum Commons', *Fordham Law Review* 74/2, 663–694.

Wehrbach, Kevin (2004). 'Supercommons: Toward a Unified Theory of Wireless Communication', *Texas Law Review* 82(4), 863–973.

Weston, Burns & David Bollier (2011). *Regenerating the Human Right to a Clean and Healthy Environment in the Commons Renaissance*, <https://bit.ly/3IJfrvP>.

Weston, Burns & David Bollier (2013). 'Universal Covenant Affirming a Human Right to Commons and Rights-Based Governance of Earth's Natural Wealth and Resources', *Journal of Human Rights and the Environment* 2/2, 215–225, <https://bit.ly/3OFQaQD>.

Westra, Laura (2016). *Ecological Integrity and Global Governance: Science, Ethics and Law*, Routledge, New York.

Westra, Laura (2011). *Human Rights: The 'Commons' and the Collective*, University of British Columbia Press Vancouver.

White, Stuart (2022). *Citizens' Assemblies and Democratic Renewal*, ENA Institute for Alternative Policies, Athens, <https://bit.ly/4lRBwqC>.

Wolcher, Louis (2009). *The Meaning of the Commons*, <https://bit.ly/3VFa5mJ>.

Wolfrum, Rüdiger (2021). 'Solidarity and Community Interests: Driving Forces for the Interpretation and Development of International Law', *The Hague Academy of International Law, Collected Courses* 416, 9–479.

World Economic Forum (2024). *Space: The $1.8 Trillion Opportunity for Global Economic Growth*, <https://bit.ly/3YDglhW>.

World Meteorological Organisation (2022). *WMO Provisional State of the Global Climate 2022*, Report, <https://library.wmo.int/doc_num.php?explnum_id=11359>.

World Meteorogical Organisation (2026). *State of the Global Climate 2025*, Report, <https://bit.ly/4cic4Z1>.

Wu, Tim (2003). 'Network Neutrality, Broadband Discrimination', *Journal on Telecommunication and High Technology Law* 2, 141–175. <https://bit.ly/3eU7HnG>.

Young, Oran (1997). 'Rights, Rules and Resources in International Affairs', in *Global Governance: Drawing Insights from the Environmental Experience*, O. Young (ed.), MIT Press, Cambridge, 3–17.

Zacharie, Arnauld (2012). 'Reclaiming Finance and the Economy: Economic Commons', in *The Commons (Co)managing Commonly Owned Resources*, G. Errembault (ed.), e-topia, Oikos, Green Foundation, Brussels, 40–46.

Zalasiewicz, Jan et al. (2008). 'Are We Now Living at the Anthropocene?', *GSA Today*, 18/2, <https://bit.ly/35lrUzn>.

Zenz, Anna and Julia Powles (2024). 'Resisting Technological Inevitability: Google Wing's Delivery Drones and the Fight for Our Skies', *Philosophical Transactions of the Royal Society A.*, <https://ssrn.com/abstract=4866385>.

Zyberi, Gentian (2021). 'The Protection of Community Interests in International Law: Some Reflections on Potential Research Agendas', in *Protecting Community Interests through International Law*, Gentian Zyberi (ed.), Intersentia, Cambridge, 307–334, <http://dx.doi.org/10.2139/ssrn.4299071>.

Ziegler, Jean (2008). *Report of the Special Rapporteur on the Right to Food*, Human Rights Council, A/HRC/7/5, <https://bit.ly/3pm5AgW>.

Zou, Kenyan (2022). 'Climate Change and Fisheries Regulation: What We Should Consider for the Future?', in *Preserving Community Interests in Ocean Governance towards Sustainability*, K. Zou & Y.-Ch. Chang (eds.), MDPI, Basel, 1–11.

Zuboff, Shoshana (2019). *The Age of Surveillance Capitalism: The Fight for a Human Future at the New Frontier of Power*, Public Affairs, New York.

Zuboff, Shoshana (2020). 'You Are Now Remotely Controlled', *New York Times*, 24 May 2020, <https://www.nytimes.com/2020/01/24/opinion/sunday/surveillance-capitalism.html>.

Zulfiqar, Khadija & M. Jahanzeb Butt (2022). 'Preserving Community's Environmental Interests in a Meta-Ocean Governance Framework towards Sustainable Development Goal 14', in *Preserving Community Interests in Ocean Governance towards Sustainability*, K. Zou & Y.-Ch. Chang (eds.), MDPI, Basel, 83–107.

Index

www.ingramcontent.com/pod-product-compliance
Ingram Content Group UK Ltd.
Pitfield, Milton Keynes, MK11 3LW, UK
UKHW022219051026
15624UKWH00001B/240